THE AUTHOR

ROBERT T. GOLEMBIEWSKI received his A.B. from Princeton University and his M.A. and Ph.D. from Yale University. He is presently Associate Professor of Political Science and Management at The University of Georgia and has also taught at Princeton University, the University of Illinois, and Yale University (as a visiting lecturer).

In addition to **Men, Management, and Morality**, Professor Golembiewski has written **The Small Group: An Analysis of Research Concepts and Operations; Behavior and Organization;** and **Organizing Men and Power: Patterns of Behavior and Line-Staff Models.**

His articles have appeared in several contributed volumes and in the scholarly journals. The author has served as a consultant to both business and governmental organizations and has participated extensively in executive development programs.

MEN, MANAGEMENT, AND MORALITY:

Toward a New Organizational Ethic

MEN, MANAGEMENT, and MORALITY
Toward a New Organizational Ethic

ROBERT T. GOLEMBIEWSKI

**Associate Professor of Political Science
and Management**

The University of Georgia

McGRAW-HILL BOOK COMPANY

New York • St. Louis • San Francisco
Toronto • London • Sydney

McGRAW-HILL SERIES IN MANAGEMENT

KEITH DAVIS, Consulting Editor

ALLEN Management and Organization
ALLEN The Management Profession
BERGEN AND HANEY Organizational Relations and Management Action
BOWMAN Management: Organization and Planning
DAVIS Human Relations at Work
DAVIS AND SCOTT Readings in Human Relations
FLIPPO Principles of Personnel Management
GOLEMBIEWSKI Men, Management, and Morality
GRIMSHAW AND HENNESSEY Organizational Behavior
HARBISON AND MYERS Management in the Industrial World
JOHNSON, KAST, AND ROSENZWEIG The Theory and Management of Systems
KEITH AND GUBELLINI Business Management
KOONTZ Toward a Unified Theory of Management
KOONTZ AND O'DONNELL Principles of Management
KOONTZ AND O'DONNELL Readings in Management
MAIER Problem-solving Discussions and Conferences
MAYER Production Management
McDONOUGH Information Economics and Management Systems
McNICHOLS Policy Making and Executive Action
MINER The Management of Ineffective Performance
PIGORS AND PIGORS Case Method in Human Relations
SALTONSTALL Human Relations in Administration
SARTAIN AND BAKER The Supervisor and His Job
SCHRIEBER, JOHNSON, MEIER, FISCHER, AND NEWELL Cases in Manufacturing Management
STEINER Managerial Long-range Planning
SUTERMEISTER People and Productivity
TANNENBAUM, WESCHLER, AND MASSARIK Leadership and Organization
VANCE Industrial Administration
VANCE Management Decision Simulation

MEN, MANAGEMENT, and MORALITY:
Toward a New Organizational Ethic

Library of Congress Catalog Card Number 65-22106

5 6 7 8 9 – MP – 9 8

TO GREGORY,
 whose salvation was our sorrow and our joy.

TO PEGGY,
 whose sorrow and joy are mine.

PREFACE

Ours is an age of almost desperate questioning that commonly counts for little. The tragedy is not so much that our seeking often becomes mired in the superficial and our inquisitiveness is deceived by the manufactured image. These, after all, are some of the dangers of the game; moreover, the truth still has a chance of emerging, whatever the opinion of the moment; and playing that game may be *the* human thing after all. The tragedy is rather that our passions so often dead-end in the contraceptive of our inability or our unwillingness to act upon the fruits of our inquiry.

The present concern with ethics in organizations illustrates the general case. Thus we have been told recently that a large majority of businessmen think themselves ethical, but that fully four-fifths of them are not at all certain that others measure up.[1] Ethical change—even if specifics could be agreed upon and ways of implementing them were developed—will hardly be aided by such opinional cross-pressures. The product of the search is likely to count for little against the massive opinion that it is the other guy, not us.

A literal flood of work in the same general area comes from a similar mold: a kind of energetic beating of the body organizational, which exercise must remain an end in itself and which with few exceptions[2] also tends toward a moderate critical pessimism, if not worse. Most authors typically (and accurately) avow that they have not arrived at any answers to the ethical problems facing organizations, but rather that they have raised some of the proper questions to which answers must be sought.[3] A few authors go further. There are no answers to the proper questions they raise or to the fears they express.[4] In their view we are en route to an organizational hell, irrevocably, whether we know it or not.

Such efforts cannot be condemned in general with wisdom or justice. They do raise a serious problem nonetheless. And that is the danger of losing the interest of the activist publics who hear numerous alarms—all of them urgent—that go unanswered because of our lack of knowledge, the enormity of the problem, or what have you. Men of affairs may agree that all would be for the better in some perfect world, but this is no great help in getting the job done.

The present study proposes to treat problems of ethical consequence in organizations, problems that are restricted enough to permit remedial action based upon relatively firm findings from the developing behavioral sciences. The specific focus is upon organizing work, and the aim is dual: to use what we know about behavior in organizations to approach a set of moral values accepted in the Western tradition; and to approach those values without sacrificing either efficiency or economy. Skepticism has been expressed about the ability of the behavioral sciences to do the job,[5] but the record will speak for itself.

This effort is past and prologue in the development of the behavioral science approach to organizational phenomena. The main theme to be developed no doubt will be modified over time in its specifics. However, radical change does not seem likely.

In any case, I trust the book-as-constituted yields some return on the investments of many helpful people, and even of a few who helped while they contrived to hinder. My particular indebtedness is to the Committee for the Study of Individual Freedom, an offspring of the Lilly Endowment Foundation. Chairman Donald L. Kemmerer and other committee members—including Profs. Edgar L. Erickson, Robert W. Mayer, and Francis Wilson, all of the University of Illinois—have proved resourceful and understanding and helpful. I trust that in supporting my individual freedom they have also sponsored a contribution to the individual freedom of Everyman who spends his life in large-scale enterprises.

The book was completed while I served as visiting lecturer, department of industrial administration, Yale University. My debts to Chris Argyris during this period were many and varied, and if these debts are beyond repayment in kind, they may at least be publicly acknowledged. The numerous kindnesses of Donald Taylor which facilitated this work also are acknowledged.

The present argument was sketched originally in an article which appeared in the *Public Administration Review,* with whose permission certain sections of this book are reproduced.

Robert T. Golembiewski

Footnotes: PREFACE

1. Reverend Raymond Baumhart, S.J., "Business Ethics," mimeographed report available from the Clergy-Industry Relations Department, National Association of Manufacturers, New York.
2. For such exceptions, see Leonard R. Sayles, *Individualism and Big Business* (New York: McGraw-Hill Book Company, 1963); and Harlan Cleveland and Harold D. Lasswell (eds.), *Ethics and Bigness* (New York: Conference on Science, Philosophy and Religion in their Relation to the Democratic Way of Life, Inc., 1962).
3. See, for example, Reverend Thomas M. Garrett, S.J., *Ethics in Business* (New York: Sheed & Ward, Inc., 1963); Herbert Johnston, *Business Ethics* (New York: Pitman Publishing Corporation, 1961); Reverend Henry J. Wirtenberger, S.J., *Morality and Business* (Chicago: Loyola University Press, 1962); William A. Spurrier, *Ethics and Business* (New York: Charles Scribner's Sons, 1962); and Luther M. Hodges, *The Business Conscience* (Englewood Cliffs, N.J.: Prentice-Hall, Inc., 1963).
4. Roderick Seidenberg, *Post-Historic Man* (Boston: Beacon Press, 1957).
5. Lyndall F. Urwick, *The Pattern of Management* (Minneapolis: The University of Minnesota Press, 1956), p. 37.

CONTENTS

Introduction

This book is directed at aiding a class of men in grappling with their awesome responsibilities. These men are the managers of today's larger enterprises; they are the managers of the future in this country's many schools of business and of public administration; and they are the teachers of both apprentice and long-time practitioner.

Certainly the human targets of this book require aid. Their responsibility is onerous: to produce an unparalleled volume of goods and services, of unprecedented variety and complexity, while taking into account an array of factors that leave them yearning for the comfort of those days (if they ever existed) when making a profit was test enough of the mettle of a manager. No wonder, then, that the targets of this book are in turn overwhelmed, belligerent, eager to learn, and stimulated to outstanding effort.

How this book will do its job may be outlined, first in terms of what is deliberately neglected and then in terms of what is stressed. Why multitudinous demands were made of, and accepted by, managers is an intricate and significant historical question. Let us beg this question, as well as whether these demands should have been made in the first place. More than enough attention has been spent determining whether things had to happen as they did or, alternatively, whether they should have happened as they did. But how the manager can meet these various demands as he pursues his traditional objectives is a question this study helps answer.

The managerial challenge often has been perceived, but seldom has it been faced with success and moderation. Attempts to meet the manager's awesome responsibilities tend toward extremism, particularly in organizational applications of behavioral knowledge. Countless students have directed great talents and enthusiasm toward understanding man's behavior in cooperative effort, and they have often been motivated by dicta such as that of the psychologist G. Stanley Hall: "Our task is nothing less than to rehumanize industry." [1] Many critics have not accepted such professions unreservedly. They stress the inadequacies of existing research, they make merry of its humbuggeries in practice, and they deplore the fact that humanistic values are neglected by slick managerial techniques designed to manipulate organization members all the more subtly and all the more effectively. C. Wright Mills spoke for the opposition with characteristic sweep and definiteness: "Many whips are inside men, who do not know how they got there, or indeed that they are there." As material standards rose, Mills explained, exploitation became more psychological and less material. The effect has been to emphasize manipulation as opposed to naked power, the anonymous as opposed to the known. [2]

Neither advocate nor critic contributed to a fruitful synthesis; rather, they tended to goad one another to extremism. Critics note with varying degrees of acute concern the coming of a relentless and thoroughgoing exploitation beyond man's most grim experiences. Commonly, unlike the biblical prophets of old, the critics are content to warn of the impending tragedy. This compounds the pessimism of their message, for it implies that there is no way out short of cataclysm. Still protagonists of behavioral research in organizations plunge on, even if they sometimes become "servants of power" [3] who rush incomplete research findings into use without due attention to values.

The recourse to extremes is studiously avoided here. *Men, Management, and Morality* is a moderate approach to a set of problems that must rank among the major ones facing man. The study is moderate in two senses. It recognizes man's deep commitment to expanding his knowledge about all nature; and it also recognizes the triumphs and tragedies that have been born of this distinctly human passion. To make the most of triumph and the least of tragedy in the application of behavioral knowledge in organizations is the present goal.

The task is not a trifling one, and this for many reasons. First, and make no mistake about it, if behavioral knowledge is not disciplined by values about which considerable consensus has developed, somebody will use that knowledge to discipline all men in organizations without their knowledge. In this the critics of the application of behavioral research in organizations are undoubtedly correct, even though decision-makers in our several bureaucracies respond to motives other than profit and power. The analysis also will demonstrate that a sensitivity to questions of value in organizing does not imply enormous costs. The demonstration cannot be avoided. No organization can exist on lofty thoughts alone, and the death of an organization is not a matter of moral indifference.

Second, the "employee society" (in Drucker's suggestive terms) increasingly "determines and sets the ethos of American society." [4] That people increasingly work for a "boss," but not for an "employer" or "owner," has enormous implications for life. Here note only that the "employee society" describes a condition under which behavior is at once more difficult to control—the boss is himself an employee, and thus cannot command the authority of the owner—while close cooperation is increasingly necessary in ever more complex organizations.

Hence the common resort to "science." The motivation is not only to permit greater control but also to provide a replacement for the mystique of the "natural rights" of ownership that had provided such a firm ethical base for earlier managerial action.

Science is not up to the tasks of telling us what is the case and of prescribing for us what ought to be the case, however. Far too many intellectual hernias have been caused by strenuous efforts to prove that science in fact has such dual faculties. There also has been much looking the other way in the hope that the problem will disappear. Neither tactic helps much. Values must discipline the use of the results of scientific inquiry. Our only choice lies between determining precisely which values will do the job or resigning ourselves to the values chosen by influential others.

Third, like it or not, larger organizations increasingly are becoming the "qualitatively, socially, and morally decisive realm." [5] It is in organizations, if anywhere, therefore, that our values will be achieved, that individual freedom will be attained. This datum invites pessimism, for the assumptions upon which our organizations of today are based do not promise tender cultivation of individual freedom. Thus one industrialist demands that we face the plain fact that free enterprise as practiced in the United States is authoritarian in principle. "One man decides," he explains. "At each step in the process of production and distribution, the will of one man is the activating force when a decision has to be taken. He speaks and others obey." [6] How matters might be otherwise—defined in terms of specific structural arrangements and managerial techniques—has a great and growing significance. Without such specific ways and means individual freedom at work will become increasingly forfeit.

The emphasis upon organization and work still may seem anachronistic, given our present preoccupation with "technological unemployment" and particularly with automation. It is, however, far too early to conjure up dreams of enormous unattended factories bringing forth incredible volumes of goods that an unemployed population cannot buy or goods that a newly contrived leisure society can consume to satiation. Some commentators note that even if automatic controls were introduced wherever they are applicable, and even if costs were disregarded, only 8 per cent of the labor force would be affected directly. [7] And two big "ifs" are required to inflate the figure to even 8 per cent. We have to live with our organizational problems at work a good deal longer, that is, even if the appropriate figure is much higher than 8 per cent.

Fourth, indirect solutions of the problems of work seem ineffective, if they are not actually mischievous. Thus Elton Mayo complained that the "extensive maladjustment of our time" was due to the failure to call a spade just that, to the marked tendency to attempt to make the demands of work tolerable by remedies that left the pattern of work undisturbed. Mayo complained that "in the process of continuously raising the standard of living American civilization has unwittingly destroyed all *standards* of living." [8]

To be sure, there is no evil per se in raising the standard of living. But if that standard of living is increased chiefly to induce the employee to accept some inhuman burdens of work, difficulties arise. The utilitarian habit of mind—leading to the calculus of exact incentives alleged to yield just the correct amount of effort—is a dangerous one, for it runs the risk of just that destruction of standards which Mayo notes. Merely increase the incentives enough, that utilitarian calculus prescribes, and the desired behavior will result, whatever it is and however unacceptable it is. More's the pity, just this will often happen as standards are abandoned temporarily (or perhaps, permanently) by individuals serving their own convenience or succumbing to that which only heroic efforts could overcome.

All this is neat enough, but only an incurable optimist can neglect the vicious dynamics set in motion. A question nags the mind. After the basic notion of standards has been destroyed, then what? There is ample reason to expect the worst. Note only that the most thoroughgoing of utilitarians—Jeremy Bentham—spent some twenty years of his life developing in characteristically precise detail his factory-prison, the *panopticon*. The panopticon was to be a star-shaped building, so designed "that every convict would pass his life in perpetual solitude, while remaining perpetually under the surveillance of a warder posted at the center." [9] And indeed, why not, given the utilitarian point of view.

For these reasons and others as well, the questions of the application of behavioral knowledge in organizations cannot be treated at the extremes of support and opposition. The victory of either extreme would be pyrrhic, while the continued tension between both evades many major issues. Leaving matters to the extremes, that is to say, must be as perpetually frustrating as the life of the scientist who has two ambitions: to develop a universal solvent and to develop a universal container. The purpose here is to pose the issues of behavioral applications in organizations in a less awkward way than our hypothetical scientist and to describe specific structural innovations and managerial techniques that promise effective and moral resolutions of major organizational problems.

Footnotes: INTRODUCTION

1. G. Stanley Hall, address to the Vocational Association of the Middle West, Jan. 17, 1919, as reported in Lionel D. Edie (ed.), *Practical Psychology for Business Executives* (New York: The H. W. Wilson Company, 1922), p. 36.
2. C. Wright Mills, *White Collar* (Fair Lawn, N.J.: Oxford University Press, 1956), p. 110.
3. Loren Baritz, *The Servants of Power: A History of the Use of Social Science in American Industry* (Middletown, Conn.: Wesleyan University Press, 1960).
4. Peter F. Drucker, "The Employee Society," *American Journal of Sociology,* vol. 59 (January, 1953), pp. 358–363.
5. *Ibid.,* p. 358.
6. Clarence B. Randall, "The Myth of the Management Committee," *Dun's Review and Modern Industry,* vol. 76, no. 1 (1960), p. 37.
7. Daniel Bell, *Work and Its Discontents: The Cult of Efficiency in America* (Boston: Beacon Press, 1956), p. 49.
8. Quoted in Baritz, *op. cit.,* p. 110.
9. Quoted in Bell, *op. cit.,* p. 1.

1

Organization as a Major Locus for Preserving Individual Freedom

Men can be free within wide limits in organizations, but almost everywhere they are in unnecessary and ineffective bondage. This is a revolutionary tocsin, but it is more restrained than ringing pronouncements that men have only to break the chains of bondage. A great deal more, in point of fact, requires doing; and the doing requires a moral discipline and technical awareness beyond that of a simple call for unshackling man in organizations.

This study details how men can be more free in organizations, but it has no vision of the end of the particularly human condition, the tension between the self and the social order. Freedom is not viewed as "free and easy," then. Rather, the emphasis is upon freedom as "free, responsible, and responsive."

The scope of the study is ambitious in three major senses. First, the effort rests upon the belief that society and its several institutions exist for man, rather than that man exists for them. This is a burden heavy enough. For even in Western societies the belief hardly receives unqualified support in *au courant* opinion, and practice often is more gross in its denial. Justice Oliver Wendell Holmes thus was forced to conclude that "the sacredness of human life is purely a municipal ideal of no validity outside the jurisdiction. I believe that force . . . is the *ultima ratio*." [1] And most states deny the prior claims of the individual in theory and are true to their pronouncements in practice. Worse still, the developing behavioral sciences have sharply increased the temptation to use men for purposes other than their own through the application of such knowledge.

The task here, then, is to put this knowledge about men to work for us in directions that have the sanction of tradition before we are set irrevocably to work by this knowledge in directions we reject or of which we may even be unaware.

Second, although great and many have been the crimes committed in behalf of humanity, this analysis does not suffer for lack of disciplining guidance. Indeed, the approach here patently demands some tethers on the self (and on the author), some outline of the boundaries within which man can be free. A limited set of values derived from the Judaeo-Christian tradition will provide those boundaries.

Acknowledging the place of values in organizational life rejects two dominant strains of contemporary thought. Thus this analysis stands apart in that it is a revolutionary notice and one which also relies upon moral boundaries. The combination is uncommon. Marxism, for example, blandly promised a oneness of the self and social order at some point in time that was at once unspecified and yet thought to be near at hand, if only workers would unite to break their shackles. This simplified matters for Marx, but left his analysis embarrassingly dependent upon the unlikely condition that men would be angels and would live in a society from which nonmaterialistic values were excluded. Matters can be improved upon only by acknowledging the crucial place of values in organizing work.

More clearly, this study also must do battle with the powerful folk myth that Christian ethics and the ethics of the marketplace and productive enterprise simply are and must be independent, if not antagonistic. This analysis will labor long to demonstrate the sharp limits of this folk myth, even though it cannot presume to announce that henceforth organizations can and will become cities of God on earth.

Third, this analysis must face the significant fact that most students view the contemporary growth of large organizations with foreboding. Their pessimistic consensus patently must be understood. Hence attention will be devoted immediately to outlining the enormous problems that derive from attempts to organize more and more of man's activities. The titles of three significant recent books will help develop the dimensions of the problem, its implications for broader social life, and its effects on men as members of organizations.

THE ORGANIZATIONAL REVOLUTION

Some Dimensions

Our modern lives increasingly will be spun out in an organization context, whether business or government or philanthropic-religious. Kenneth Boulding freezes for the mind's eye this prominent contemporary fact of life in his book *The Organizational Revolution*. His picture is a striking, if familiar, one. The scene is a monolith, whether the focus is upon organized labor or industry or government, upon the church or charitable institutions or (we might add) crime, upon the home with the built-to-order community or upon the school, or upon work or leisure. Organization is king, exponents of "rationalization" are its legions, and massive scale its model.

There is no need to document heavily the all-too-obvious, but some fragmentary data can usefully suggest the proportions of this organizational revolution. As in industry the demands of technology in agriculture have worked themselves out so as to substantially increase the size of viable units of production. A few data make the point. The number of farms at first kept pace with population growth, that number rising from 5.7 million in 1900 to 6.8 million in 1935. The effects of technological advance then took over to such a degree that by 1950 some 2 million fewer farms were producing far more than had been produced in 1935.[2] These stark data imply greater mechanization, greater scale of operations, and greater capital investment. The data also reflect greater organization among farmers, their suppliers, their unions and trade associations, and supporting or regulating agencies of government. Both the pattern and the timing in agriculture are generally typical of contemporary trends.

The individual must be affected by these massive organizational forces generated in the process of living the contemporary life. Consider only the fact that each of our lives is influenced in myriad ways by countless "voluntary organizations," as well as by multitudinous economic and government units, often without our knowledge and usually with but minimal participation on our parts.[3] Certainly there is no lack of peak organizations to represent the American publics in an incredible range of activities. Some 4,000 national associations of this kind were listed in a 1949 publication of the Department of Commerce, including

    1,500 trade associations
      300 national associations of businessmen
      500 professional associations
      200 labor unions
      100 women's associations
       60 veteran's and patriotic societies
       55 farmers' associations
       50 Negro associations
       50 associations of public officials
       25 fraternal associations
      100 recreational associations
    1,000 other types

One can like the state of affairs adumbrated above, or one can loathe it. However strong "American individualism" was in days past, the environment never could have been less congenial to that quality which is often praised, is seldom found, and is almost never consciously nurtured in any society. The land of the free and the home of the brave might be represented by the bald eagle, that is, but its people have the habits of more organized animals than those awesome birds of prey. And all this to the end that there are increasingly fewer crags on which Americans—and bald eagles—can be their solitary selves if they so choose.

THE ORGANIZATIONAL SOCIETY

Pessimistic Prognoses

The convenient has a way of becoming the desired, or at least the acceptable. The dictum "if you can't beat 'em, join 'em" suggests the human capacity for such comfortable accommodations. And the advice is apt, in general. Mental health, for most people, implies coming to some agreement with their environment. Common man tends to act so as to reduce the tension he feels, whatever concessions to sanity, or good taste, or trust of his faculties are necessary. The matter forms the basis of a useful general law of behavior, and experiments aplenty testify elaborately to man's capacity for making do within his social and physical environment. Examples of the point are everywhere. Consider how few can act sane in an insane society. Herman Goering perceived only one aspect of the incomparably insane slaughter of Jews, for example, and this long after the evil deed. He noted during his trial that the Jews could have been handled quite differently. The Communists among them could have been liquidated as Communists, and the Jews might have been cultivated as friends of the regime. "I bet there were plenty [of Jews] who were just as fanatically nationalistic Germans as anybody," Goering concluded, "and that they could have helped the cause.—It was this nonsense of calling Jews Communists and enemies of the state.—God Almighty!" [4] God Almighty indeed.

This rule of thumb seems to fit the most common adaptation to our contemporary organizational society. Roderick Seidenberg, for example, gives close attention to attempts to "bind, coordinate, define, and control . . . duties and activities [of man], his purposes and behavior, in relation to those of his fellow men." [5] Seidenberg finds an unmistakable and overwhelming trend toward such increasingly explicit and consciously drawn relations everywhere: "in our systems of production, distribution, and consumption; in the operations of labor, capital, and finance; in the spheres of communication and transportation; in art, in sport, in education; in the fields of commerce, industry, and agriculture —in the recent totalitarian functioning of Nazi Germany . . . no less than in mechanized America or socialized Russia." This trend toward "organized totality or unification," enormously accelerated of late, is the child of intelligence seeking some coherent arrangement of parts oriented toward some desired ends. The contemporary trend contrasts sharply with "organic wholeness or unity," that is, long-accepted forms of social cohesion that are the products of innate growth and of man's instincts. Organic wholeness is said to characterize primitive societies.

Seidenberg's judgment of the common reaction to all this is flatly made: "Modern man has learned to accommodate himself to a world increasingly organized." Seidenberg's feelings are clearly with organic wholeness or unity, he sees tragedy implied in the dependence on intelligence alone, and he recoils at the opportunities implicit in organization for manipulating man against his own interests. But Seidenberg also notes that few consider any alternative to the trend he fears. Even "occasional and incidental rumblings" do not challenge the basic notion of organizing. They merely criticize the effectiveness of a particular pattern of organizing or imply that its administration ought to be in other hands.

If Seidenberg is correct, prophets once again are strangers to their own people. Most articulate opinion has not made its peace with the organizational society. Robert V. Presthus well represents the unreconciled in a book whose title heads this section. He notes approvingly the "dominant theme in the antiorganizational refrain" has been that bureaucracy smothers the flickering candles of individual self-realization and independence. But this theme is taken to be too limited. The "dysfunctions" of big organizations, Presthus insists, also raise "grave questions about our competitive ability in the international arena." Indeed, they "touch upon the very capacity of our society to survive." [6]

One must be impressed with the variegated assortment of observers who come to similar conclusions, or worse. Christian and atheist, Capitalist and Communist, libertarian and collectivist, careful social thinker and the most obstinately opinionated hack—all these observers point with alarm to the growth of organizations and note its consequences with grave concern.

Explanations of the proliferation in Western societies of business and government bureaucracies illustrate this dark consensus. "Liberal economists" explain bureaucratization in terms of the forces generated by capitalism, with its powerful business organizations creating irresistible pressures for the growth of large-scale public bureaucracies to support the business organizations and to regulate them. There are many subtle variations on this theme of a fecund capitalism devouring its own young, but their press is the same. "Libertarian economists," in contrast, explain the same phenomenon in terms of the political decision to interfere with the workings of a freely competitive system. Business bureaucratization, then, came largely as a necessary protection against political tinkering with the market mechanism.

If they disagree diametrically on the cause, however, such camps agree basically at critical points. Thus they are as one about the evil fruits of large-scale bureaucratization. As Peter Blau concluded: "Strangely enough [the] authors who advance these conflicting theses about the historical origins of large-scale bureaucracy, however, are in agreement concerning its consequences. Bureaucratization concentrates power in the hands of a few men and curtails the freedom of individuals that is essential for democracy." [7]

Most observers also agree—whatever other issues separate them—that we must eat of this evil fruit, like it or not. Indeed, a kind of atavistic technological determinism raises this necessity to the dignity of an all-but-universal law of nature. Thus Talcott Parsons—a high priest of the most influential wing of social scientists of the last decade or two—put matters plainly: "technological advance almost always leads to increasingly elaborate division of labor and the concomitant requirement of increasingly elaborate organization." Nor are the reasons for this inexorable relation obscure to Parsons. He explained that[8]

With elaborate differentiation of functions the need for minute coordination of the different functions develops. . . . There must be a complex organization of supervision to make quite sure that exactly the right thing is done. . . . Feeding the various parts into the process, in such a way that a modern assembly line can operate smoothly, requires very complex organization to see that they are available in just the right quantities at the right times and places. . . .

This is not a loaded example. Indeed, if the descriptions above can be considered merely realistic, many other observers are compelled to more blatantly pessimistic conclusions. Consider Boulding, a well-known economist, who approaches organization from the vantage point of a Christian pondering why "human progress [is] so slow, and so self-defeating?" The villain is a familiar one, and Boulding reads as if he were embarrassed to bring so obvious a point to the reader's attention. "The trouble lies, of course, in the 'flesh'," he explains, "that is, in organization." This is no careless metaphor for Boulding. "All bodies are corruptible," he continues, "whether the body of literal flesh or the body of the state, the corporation, the trade union, the philanthropic organization, or the church." [9]

Marx reached a similar conclusion, if from a radically different point of view and if indirectly. Marx was so touchy about the specialization of work that he promised a return in his utopia to a harmonious state of nature in which everyone performs every economic function whenever he gets the urge. Thus would the injustice born of specialization be eliminated. Other Marxists were at once more realistic and more incredible. They realized that Marx's harking back was effective propaganda, at best. Yet they also realized the significant advantage that Marx's state of nature provided so cheaply. Consequently, Marx's evasion became so exaggerated that some conceived the job of administering the Communist state as requiring no talents greater than those of the ordinary clerk, which any comrade could provide as he willed.

Marx was astute while disingenuous. His simplicism did have the effect of blunting the embarrassing questions of a James Burnham. Burnham stressed that control of the means of production required very skilled hands—whoever the owners—and that this managerial elite stood firmly in the way of the freedom and equality that allegedly would flow as an inevitable consequence of the public ownership of the means of production. Burnham noted perceptively, if too broadly, that "the managers will exploit the rest of society . . . , their rights belonging to them not as individuals but through their position of actual directing responsibility which they occupy." Moreover, Burnham argued that the managers also can determine within limits who will become the new managerial recruits. The managerial circle will grow increasingly tighter as a consequence. [10]

Marx nipped such notices in the bud by his vision of a return to a nonspecialized economy. In so doing, Marx, no less than Burnham, despaired of the traditional pattern of organizing work, and at the same time both implied that there were no reasonable alternatives to it. The two observers differ in that the one is largely content to describe the state of affairs while the other is desperate to change the overall organization of society to overcome the problems of organizing work at the level of the plant or the firm. Such are the most common alternatives in the pessimistic approach to the growth of large-scale organizations. But more of this in the concluding two sections of this chapter.

Such a catalog might be extended interminably, but the effort is not necessary. The few examples already presented permit a fair characterization of the pessimistic literature of the organizational society. Three characteristics are particularly prominent. First, the overwhelming preponderance of informed opinion stresses the problems of the traditional approach to organizing. Such stress is often deserved, of course, but it has tended to abort in common carping. For, second, the literature commonly assumes that there is no alternative to the traditional approach, that there is *a* pattern of organizing. Or, alternatively, different patterns of organizing (as for Seidenberg) all may be conceived as similarly heir to the difficulties inherent in the very act of organizing. Third, the traditional approach to organizing also is compared unfavorably to some allegedly earlier idyllic state, a return to which is sometimes advocated but which is most often merely held out as a tease. These characteristics constitute a pessimistic dead end.

THE ORGANIZATION MAN

A Case Study in Pessimism

An age is known in significant measure by the books it keeps. Great significance therefore must be accorded the formidable sales record of William H. Whyte's *The Organization Man,* that unflattering portrait of the human products of the organizational society. This significance motivates a close look at Whyte's argument.

The Organization Man does not tarry with details, and perhaps wisely so. For the sweep of the argument takes in not only the work environment, but also, and in particular, suburbia, the church, education, and social life. Whyte's focus is consistent throughout, on the "organization man" and his kind. And in spite of a certain fuzziness in describing his quarry, the species is found everywhere by Whyte: in the corporation, the church hierarchy, government laboratories, research teams, "law factories," and so on. His targets do not include all those who work for the Organization but only those who belong to it as well. "They are the ones of our middle class who have left home, spiritually as well as physically, to take the vows of organization life," Whyte notes, "and it is they who are the mind and soul of our great self-perpetuating institutions." [11]

How the organization man got that way is Whyte's major concern. And get that way he certainly did, for there once was a breed of real men in organizations and the Protestant Ethic was their code. But this particular paradise has been lost at least temporarily, Whyte argues, and he stresses three contemporary forces that perpetuate this sad state of affairs as they shape men in their organizations. These forces are the belief in the group as the prime source of creativity; the belief in "belongingness" as the ultimate need of the organization member; and the belief that "scientism," that is, pseudoscience, can lead to this achievement of belongingness and viable group relations. Whyte does a craftsman's job of sketching some of the limits of these three beliefs, of developing their contradictions and consequences, and of dwelling upon their derivative inanities in practice.

All of this adds up to a pessimistic viewpoint, despite the fact that Whyte states with optimism that "individualism is as possible in our times as in others." For Whyte's optimism dissolves into the prescription that such a happy state of affairs will eventuate if only we can learn "how to resist . . . [how] to fight . . . the organization." Not that Whyte advocates antagonism as opposed to cooperation. As he notes of his remedy: "Out of context this would be . . . irresponsible. . . ." But the context is such as to void such a charge. Whyte explains that: "philosophical individualism can venerate conflict too much and cooperation too little. But what is the context today? The tide has receded far enough the other way, I submit, that we need not worry that a counteremphasis will stimulate people to an excess of individualism." [12]

His careful statement notwithstanding, one must entertain great reservations about the ability of Whyte's argument to support optimism. Given the array of hostile forces he marshals, the advice to fight the organization seems puny and ineffectual. Whyte moreover speaks of the possibility of "individualism *within* organization life," but that possibility seems a delicate blossom indeed. The developments he surveys were not inevitabilities, of course. But how are they to be undone? "It is organization man who has brought them to pass," Whyte notes of such "constrictions on the individual" as personality tests, "and it is he who can stop them."

Finally, Whyte does hold that the "organization society can be as compatible for the individual as any previous society." This may be the case, and certainly any substantial optimism would depend on its being the case. But *The Organization Man* fails the acid test. It is largely innocent of those structural innovations and managerial techniques that permit serving the needs of individualism within organization. Certainly such changes are required, for we know that responses must be repeatedly reinforced as a rule if they are to persist. Reasonably, then, some significant part of the behaviors that Whyte notes with concern must derive from the specific structural arrangements within which men work and which provide such an important influence over men's behavior in organizations. Nevertheless, Whyte counsels refuge in blatant resistance to the organization.

But enough of this. Such matters are not settled on a priori grounds. The following chapters will present considerable evidence that structural innovations in organizations can support a real optimism in the matter of setting men free within wide limits in organizations.

PESSIMISM AND THE HIGH ROAD

Capitalism, Communism, and Socialism

Take as given, then, the pessimism of most informed opinion concerning the organizational revolution. The point was worth establishing in some detail, for the pessimistic spirit has had profound consequences for the direction of much (although hardly all) socioeconomic thought.

Just one of these significant directions of thought will engage our attention here. By way of preview, pessimism concerning the contemporary growth of organizations encouraged the search for salvation in patterns of massive socioeconomic organization. This circumvention proved abortive. Indeed, the dominant pessimism was only deepened as a result, for time has made increasingly apparent the failures of these gross gods to provide viable answers to the problems of man's life in organizations.

The present argument is not commonly made. Let the previewed point, therefore, be restated in slightly different terms. Pessimism about the traditional pattern of organizing relatively small units—such as individual factories or multiplant firms—encouraged commentators to take to the High Road. Consequently, attention has long been fixated upon these alternative macroscopic patterns for organizing such massive units as nation-states: capitalism, or socialism, or communism. Evidences of the exclusiveness of this bias are everywhere. Emphasis upon other levels of organization was looked upon as an evasion of *the* important issues.

There was ample reason for strong emphasis upon the High Road, but there is no doubt that neglect of the Low Road—patterns of organization appropriate for smaller units—was in significant degree the result of naïveté and convenience. These are a compelling combination. As for naïveté, most pessimistic observers of the organizational revolution have thought that the Low Road is irrevocably preempted. There is *a* "one-best way" to organize, there is *an* "organization theory": these typify the common position.

Convenience also pointed to the High Road. For example, the armchair speculations of a Marx concerning the meaning of history would have been more complicated had he tempered his analysis of "class" with some rudimentary empirical observations. Instead Marx argued tightly that consciousness was determined by economic factors, and that class therefore was also based upon them. How, then, did a bourgeois product such as Marx become the tribune of the revolutionary proletariat? Marx's analysis, that is, did not cover even his own case. The High Road did not encourage such sensitivity to empirical data and, in many cases, the very neglect was raised to the dignity of a method. This does have a kind of intriguing convenience, but it pays a high price.

This analysis rejects both assumptions of the pessimistic tradition. It denies that there is *an* organization theory. Moreover, the existing research literature now permits taking the Low Road to organizing, and with profit. That research permits the articulation of an alternative pattern of organization that is congenial to values generally held in the Western world and that encourages the high satisfaction and the high productivity of organization members.

Let us get to the main point of this section, then, before the introduction swallows the analysis. Taking the High Road was thought to provide relief from the problems posed by the organizational revolution. This capsule history of much socioeconomic thought of the past century may be carried still further. To simplify only a little, capitalism had a bad press. Patently, early capitalistic ventures did see practices within its factories and mills that we would not care to re-experience today, although the general lot of the workers was a glorious improvement upon preindustrial life. But there is no accounting for tastes. The periodic preindustrial famines and pestilences, and the consequent Brobdignagian death rates, somehow took on an attractive patina. Many students, therefore, sought for an alternative pattern of macroscopic organization in socialism or communism, always with the expectation that significant improvements would follow as a matter of course for the worker at his job site.

Marx framed his studies in just such terms. He traced many of the evils about which he read to the common pattern of organizing work, and he tied this pattern irrevocably to capitalism. Marx then concluded that a change in the form of ownership (a macroscopic pattern of organization) would inexorably result in changes in the hated pattern of organizing individual factories or firms. These are large assumptions, but they were necessary for the Marxian analysis. Consider Marx's treatment of the specialization and routinization of work. They were an important feature of the traditional Low Road to organizing, and they were bugbears for Marx. To him they were the source of all evil: they deprived the worker of his control over his environment; they put the overspecialized worker at the mercy of the capitalist; and they expelled man from a paradisiacal state. To illustrate, Marx complained that the division of labor forces individuals into increasingly narrow spheres of activity from which they cannot escape, lest they lose their means of subsistence. The derivative rigidity—which Marx called a "consolidation of our own product into an objective power over us"—shackles man. Marx concluded that this social rigidity "outgrows our own control, thwarts our expectations, brings our calculations to nothing, [and] is one of the principal distinguishing points in historic evolution up to this day. . . ." [13] Although it is not clear how it was to come about, Marx consistently "solved" these problems of the traditional Low Road to organizing. Somehow, in the Communist society, "each one does not have a circumscribed sphere of activity but can train himself in any branch he chooses, society by regulating the common production makes it possible for me to do this today and that tomorrow, to hunt in the morning, to fish in the afternoon, to carry on cattle-breeding in the evening, also to criticize the food—just as I please—without becoming either hunter, fisherman, shepherd or critic."

Others in the pessimistic tradition have done as Marx did, more or less, when they did not merely despair of the organizational society. Some were drawn to socialism or communism. Others sought salvation in other gross gods—unionization, big government, industrial paternalism, "welfare capitalism," or anti-bigness. The variety was wide, but their goal was similar.

Whatever the other merits of these several approaches along the High Road, macroscopic patterns of organization have no necessary connection with patterns of organizing work within an individual plant or firm. This macroscopic pattern can be equally oppressive under capitalism, socialism, communism, or any other *ism*. Thus early communism hardly improves upon early capitalism in the short run in enlarging individual freedom in organizations, and certainly the former has done far more poorly in the long run. All three macroscopic systems face similar organizational pressures. Professor Joseph Schumpeter, for example, has drawn telling attention to the fact that socalism can exist in modern society in no "form other than that of a huge and all-embracing bureaucratic apparatus." [14] Similar comments could apply with equal force to other approaches along the High Road.

Other students came to a conclusion similar to Schumpeter's and in doing so reflected the logical contradiction blundered into by many who eagerly took to the High Road. If there were indeed no alternatives to the traditional pattern of organizing work, it was pointless to trouble over capitalism or socialism or communism. Max Weber was more thoroughgoing than most, in this case as in others. He accepted the traditional pattern for organizing work as unavoidable, whatever the overall economic system. He also was unique among prominent thinkers in that he acknowledged the consequences of that acceptance. Alvin Gouldner incisively characterized the position Weber took: "If Marx said that the workers of the world had nothing to lose but their chains by revolting, Weber contended that they really had nothing to gain." [15]

In sum, all alternative gross patterns of organizing stumble ungraciously over the problems of organizing work at lower levels they (in part) propose to solve, if they do not in fact enormously exaggerate these problems. Certainly the most extreme efforts along the High Road have not induced any spontaneous and marked reformation at lower levels of organization. Even Communist China's Mao admitted that "certain contradictions do exist between the Government and the masses." The contradictions included those "arising from the bureaucratic practices of certain state functionaries in their relations with the masses." The Yugoslav Milovan Djilas put the matter even more directly. In discussing the Russian Revolution, he pungently observed that the destruction of the "capitalist and other classes of ancient origin" had only seen "a new class, previously unknown to history" arise from the ashes. This new class is "the bureaucracy which formally uses, administers, and controls . . . property as well as the entire life of society." The bureaucracy's "state machine" is used both as "a cover and as an instrument" to gain privilege.[16]

These comments—clearly enough pessimistic reactions to the organizational society—permit a conclusion generally applicable to seekers along the High Road. Let us focus on Marx, conveniently. Marx's simplistic treatment of specialization was motivated by a real problem correctly perceived, the threat to individual freedom posed by organizations. But his solution was irrelevant to the problem, if it did not facilitate the more abject enslavement of the individual. In such ways have many of the pessimists concerning organizational growth played a cruel trick upon themselves and others. They looked for answers in the wrong places. Their gross gods having failed, their despair has only deepened.

OPTIMISM AND THE LOW ROAD

The Judaeo-Christian Ethic, Structural Properties, and Managerial Techniques

This study acts upon the conviction that the pessimists have not seen enough to justify optimism because they have looked in the wrong places, or have not gone beyond merely perceiving the problem. The latter approach is incomplete. The former misplaces faith either in a return to some allegedly idyllic state or in some macroscopic pattern for organizing.

This may seem precious, this patronizing reference to looking in the wrong places. It is, however, accurate. Recall Talcott Parsons' conclusion about bureaucratization as organizations grow in size. He also noted: "Though with many individual exceptions, technological advance almost always leads to increasingly elaborate division of labor and the concomitant requirement of increasingly elaborate organization." [17] Parsons chose to neglect these "many individual exceptions," for what reasons we do not know, and went on to drive home the point that modern technology had to be paid for in terms of substantial restrictions on individual freedom in organizations. Others have done pretty much as Parsons did.

In sharpest contrast, this study focuses on the many individual exceptions that do not require so easy a forfeit of individual freedom in organizations. The approach here takes the Low Road, stressing specific managerial techniques and structural properties that ameliorate many of the problems raised well enough by pessimistic analyses, but despaired of or ingenuously solved by the pessimists. The heading of the present section—Optimism and the Low Road—seems apt, therefore. For these specific techniques and structural properties will be consistent with values derived from the Judaeo-Christian Ethic and they will free man from organizational restraints that have reduced his effectiveness over the long haul.

Optimism and the Low Road will pay their own way. This well suits the temper of an age which presumes that the question is not what ought to be done but what business enterprise can do. Discretion, we are preached at, rests not with moralists but with businessmen who "cannot allow themselves to play fast-and-loose with business principles" in response to mere humanitarian motives.[18] This "realism" seems too simple. In any case, this analysis is not just a pious testimonial for a set of values which could free man but which we cannot afford. Rather, approaching the J-C Ethic in organizations will tend to yield high output and high satisfaction of members. This should provide reassurance enough even for the most realistic.

With Theodore Houser, then, this analysis agrees that it "is possible to pursue the ends of business without destroying human values in the process." Furthermore, the effort "is not only compatible with success but can be the source of increasing success." These are not utopian hopes, as later analysis will amply document. To illustrate only the general point, the large organization has a great stake in developing its people, and thus in serving human values and organizational ends. The success of any organization must be written in large part in terms of its performance in that dual effort. The task is a difficult one in today's economy, for the individual usually goes to work for someone else, and commonly for a large corporation. As Houser explained, from his vantage point at the heights of Sears, Roebuck:[19]

There is still a premium on native capacity, skilled effort and initiative, but these must be exercised within the framework of an organization. What actually happens to the individual is ultimately determined not by the free play of a market, but by the administrative processes of an organization.

It can no longer be taken for granted that ability will find its own level. In this age of the corporation, management must take specific steps to make sure that people have an opportunity to grow and develop; otherwise too many of them are likely to be lost in the labyrinthine recesses of the organization.

The challenge need not intimidate us, although its scope must leave us content with even tentative steps toward a working solution. A large and recently developed research literature permits taking such steps. This literature provides directions aplenty for effective optimism that both practical and moral demands can be met within an organization context, with mutual benefits to effective performance and to individual freedom.

That this research literature exists bears patent testimony that not all observers have taken a pessimistic approach to the challenge of the organizational society. Many students have generated additions to our knowledge that are overturning traditional thought about organizing. The research is often piecemeal, however, although over the last decade significant efforts have been made to systematize research into comprehensive guides for organizing. The present debts to existing work will be manifest throughout this book. This study, then, will fit within and extend the tradition of synthesis. The study's more distinctly novel contribution is the framing of the synthesis within a set of values consistent with the Judaeo-Christian Ethic.

Footnotes: CHAPTER 1

1. Oliver Wendell Holmes, *Holmes-Pollock Letters,* edited by Mark De-Wolfe Howe (Cambridge, Mass.: Harvard University Press, 1941), vol. II, p. 36.
2. Robert V. Presthus, *The Organizational Society* (New York: Alfred A. Knopf, Inc., 1962), p. 80.
3. John K. Galbraith, *American Capitalism: The Concept of Countervailing Powers* (Boston: Houghton Mifflin Company, 1952).
4. Quoted in G. M. Gilbert, *The Psychology of Dictatorship* (New York: The Ronald Press Company, 1950), p. 260.
5. Roderick Seidenberg, *Post-historic Man* (Boston: Beacon Press, 1957), pp. 1–2. Copyright by University of North Carolina Press.
6. Presthus, *op. cit.,* p. 288.
7. Peter M. Blau, *Bureaucracy in Modern Society* (New York: Random House, Inc., 1956), pp. 114–115.
8. Talcott Parsons, *The Social System* (New York: The Free Press of Glencoe, 1951), pp. 507–508.
9. Kenneth Boulding, *The Organizational Revolution* (New York: Harper & Row, Publishers, Incorporated, 1953), p. 67.
10. James Burnham, *The Managerial Revolution* (New York: The John Day Company, Inc., 1941), p. 126.
11. William H. Whyte, Jr., *The Organization Man* (Garden City, N.Y.: Anchor Books, Doubleday & Company, Inc., 1956), p. 3.
12. *Ibid.,* pp. 13–14.
13. Max Eastman (ed.), *Capital and Other Writings by Karl Marx* (New York: Modern Library, Inc., 1932), p. 1.
14. Joseph A. Schumpeter, *Capitalism, Socialism, and Democracy* (New York: Harper Torchbooks, Harper & Row, Publishers, Incorporated, 1962), p. 206.
15. Alvin Gouldner (ed.), *Studies in Leadership* (New York: Harper & Row, Publishers, Incorporated, 1950), p. 58.
16. Milovan Djilas, *The New Class* (New York: Frederick A. Praeger, Inc., 1957), pp. 35, 37–38.
17. Parsons, *op. cit.*

18. Thorstein Veblen, from *The Theory of Business Enterprise,* quoted in Loren Baritz, *The Servants of Power: A History of the Use of Social Science in American Industry* (Middletown, Conn.: Wesleyan University Press, 1960), p. 1.
19. Theodore V. Houser, *Big Business and Human Values* (New York: McGraw-Hill Book Company, 1957), p. 4.

2

The Complex Problems
of Organization:
Technical and Moral
Approaches

The prominence of pessimistic analyses of the organizational revolution requires explanation, and that explanation must support a corrective approach. Prophecies of doom do find a ready audience, and pointing with alarm does not make as great demands as developing ways and means of avoiding calamity. More to the point, most pessimistic analysts have assumed that there is a one-best pattern of organization. This clears the board of alternatives, but nothing else; and it forces the pessimist into the role of a common scold or a utopian reformer. Tersely, one can praise the one-best pattern, or revile it. That is all.

Why this "one-best" assumption has been made so commonly is a complex problem. Many forces encouraged making what is a very convenient assumption. A brief sketch of some of these forces will prove useful, and particularly so because convenience has been an intolerable straitjacket for the analysis of organizations. Understanding the point, then, is indispensable to finding a way out of its analytical bind. The last few sections of this chapter will attempt to capitalize on the lesson of the wages of convenience by outlining the more complex approach required for a full-fledged analysis of organization phenomena.

THE LEGACY OF THE ENCYCLOPAEDISTS

Positivism as a Dominant Idea of Our Time

Man often is tethered by the leash of dominant ideas anchored in the history of centuries long past. This is the case with the study of organization. Indeed, one dominant theme connects the work of the French Encyclopaedists of the eighteenth century, the seminal work in "scientific management" around the turn of the present century, and such popular contemporary efforts as the *Administrative Behavior* of Herbert A. Simon.

Let this section briefly sketch the nature of these relevant leading ideas as they were developed long ago by students devoted to a scientific approach to man and society. A following section will demonstrate how these leading ideas captivate contemporary efforts specifically concerned with productive organizations.

Any brief summary of any major body of ideas must inadequately reflect their richness and complexity, but the main drift of major ideas is less fugitive. While realizing that we may be sinning boldly thereby, the main ideas compelling the Encyclopaedists will be set down starkly. Friedrich Hayek has given the matter close attention. He saw the work of the Encyclopaedists as setting in motion a massive change in outlook on social problems that has all but captured contemporary thought and analysis, as in "positivism." The sense of this change in outlook rested upon the uncritical application of thought patterns of the natural scientist and the engineer to social problems. This application was accompanied by a predisposition "to discredit the results of the past study of society which did not conform to their prejudices and to impose ideals of organization on a sphere to which they are not appropriate." [1]

The Encyclopaedists, in sum, made too much of a good thing. Thus Hayek saw their work as but another proof of this adage: "Never will man penetrate deeper into error than when he is continuing on a road that has led him to great success." The methodological insights derived from the string of brilliant successes of the eighteenth century in unlocking the secrets of the physical world and developing the rational power of man via the several mathematics, that is, first were applied too broadly to the study of man and his social relations. Soon these insights were inflated into an exclusive philosophy, if not a bloated and compelling passion.

The fairness of this thumbnail characterization may be demonstrated at some length. Thus Jean d'Alembert in the "Discours preliminaire" to the *Encyclopédie,* stressed that as in the physical sciences the appropriate method in the social sciences was a preoccupation with "positive truths." This corollary has guided an age: "All occupations with purely speculative subjects should be excluded . . . as profitless pursuits." The common development of this approach sharply distinguished between matters of fact and matters of value, between the "is" and the "ought." And just as commonly, the approach was interpreted as deprecating the importance of the role of the "ought." The "ought" often went unrecognized, consequently, and atrophied as an object of interest.

Common developments of D'Alembert's basic insight reflect much of the curious, if not of the tragic. For example, the suppression of liberties by Napoleon probably encouraged extreme extensions of the approach. Four other senses in which the present characterization also applies must be considered at more length.

First, the extreme separation of the "ought" and the "is" and the preoccupation with the latter—both of which have pervaded much thinking about organization phenomena—went far beyond the boundaries of the early calls for emphasis on the "positive truths." D'Alembert, for example, considered the "moral sciences" to be as likely sources of positive truths as the physical or social sciences, the former being a priori sciences comparable to mathematics.[2] By implication, the positive truths of the moral sciences would provide overall direction for the applications of knowledge derived from physical or social research. But this implication usually was lost sight of.

Second, the extreme development of the positivistic position could not support its own weight. Indeed, early in the game, values had to be admitted to positivistic analyses by the back door, as it were. For example, early positivistic thinkers legitimately could rail at the "vague and metaphysical idea of liberty," although they improved matters not at all by complaining that liberty "impedes the action of the masses on the individual." [3] For liberty after all was a nonpositivistic notion and, given their point of view, positivists in good conscience could attack it. But where to go when liberty is done with? This was a real enough question for the positivists, and cannot be dismissed by the flip note that they aimed at perfecting society by destroying it.

Some value constraints were necessary to provide direction even for the programs of the positivists, that is to say, if exaggerations of that approach permitted no straightforward admission of the point. Subterfuge therefore became the order of the positivist day. Almost predictably, positivistic thinkers soon plunged into a kind of quasi-religious mysticism, one of whose curious fruits was the "discovery" of a "spiritual power" that would "choose the direction to which the national forces are to be applied. . . ." [4] This spiritual power, conjured up in despair and required by the philosophical poverty of the positivist exaggeration, was somehow capable of choosing values itself. It thereby saved positivistic thinkers from admitting that such choices must be made. Note also that what began as a legitimate struggle to free the minds of men from the prejudices of the past became—when extended too far—an enslavement of the minds of men to the burdensome tyranny of a spiritual power guiding the nation-state.

Third, the positivist rejection of the possibility (or the significance) of introspective moral insights encouraged a kind of "methodological collectivism." Hence the resort to a spiritual power to guide the nation-state. Hayek described this orientation as the tendency to treat such concepts of society as "wholes," as "definitely given objects about which we can discover laws by observing their behavior as wholes." [5] How else, indeed, to know the required direction for the "action of the masses on the individual"? No doubt with great care this methodological collectivism could have been kept under tight rein as a major hypothesis-to-be-investigated. Quite often, however, the hypothesis subtly became a bench mark from which derivations were made and against which positivistic truth was to be measured. But this was no signal that positivists had relinquished anything to forces beyond their control. For my methodological collectivism can have just that direction I give it, there being no way to verify whether "national forces" exist in anything more than careless metaphor.

The positivist world was the best of all possible worlds, then. One was free from the restraints of the past; one could design restraints for others in the future; and one could attribute it all to the inexorable dictates of science.

Fourth, the extreme development of the positivistic approach neglected a crucial difference between the physical sciences and the social sciences. The physical sciences—dealing with questions of the relation of things to things—depend only upon the discovery of the laws that more or less govern the fixed relations of matter under specified conditions. This describes a relatively simple state of affairs. In contrast, the relations between man and men and man and things may be studied just as objectively as in the physical sciences. Yet these relations in the social sciences are fixed only for a specific set of values or for the goals of specific actors at some specific point in time. These values or goals also may be evaluated and changed, with consequent changes in the relations observed.

The difference is not niggling. Atoms cannot will to practice genocide, to put the matter over-simply. But people may will to use atoms for that purpose, or any other. This makes life simpler for atoms and students of atoms.

The extreme development of the positivistic approach neglected this crucial difference, with considerable mischief. Thus not even positivists could be content with their philosophical position. By and large, the positivists lusted after change. Their approach left no room for the explicit admission of values to guide change, however, and this fact motivated the hanky-panky with spiritual power discussed above. Moreover, in their commendable zeal to guarantee that observations of the "is" remain uncontaminated by the fancies of the student, positivists often went so far as to deny the importance of "oughts" under any circumstances. In this sense, the positivists' zeal commonly got out of hand. The reasonable advice given long before by Aristotle, Plato, Machiavelli, and others—to avoid seeing only what one wants to see —was exaggerated into condoning a neglect of what one wants to do about what one really sees.

THE LEGACY OF WORK ANALYSIS

A Positivistic Application

Innocent of the subtleties and philosophical niceties of the efforts of the Encyclopaedists, the detailed analyses of work by students such as

Frederick W. Taylor fit neatly within the positivist tradition. This work has had an enormous vogue, as in scientific management. It exercised great influence, not merely through specific applications at work sites, but also in conditioning major habits of thought about work.

Scientific management was a carrier of the positivistic pattern of thought by inadvertence, as it were. Frederick W. Taylor was no toiler over words. He was a doer in the grand style, and is easy enough to fault as a careless thinker and an artless writer. Without evaluating Taylor by standards other than his own, however, one finds that at least four features of his work reflect a positivistic theme.

First, as with the Encyclopaedists, Taylor and his followers assumed that Science (with a capital S) provided solutions for all problems facing man. Or, to put the same matter differently, no problems facing man really can be solved until the methods of Science are applied. Problems of pay and work pace, for example, were to be solved once and forevermore by his techniques. "As reasonably might we insist upon bargaining about the time and place of the rising and setting sun," he once noted,[6] as in disputing how hard one should work or how much he should be paid after the System had been applied. This was music to the ears of the manager, then eagerly seeking some new rationale for managerial action to replace the wilting notions about the absolute rights of property, which grew increasingly inappropriate with industrialization and urbanization. The new science of management, then, was to replace the moral authority of beliefs about unlimited rights of property. And good riddance. Such beliefs were arbitrary conventions and subject to change. But in Science one had an unchanging standard.

Second, scientific management and its several variations on a common theme proposed to replace metaphysics with measurement. This seems a broad enough statement, but it is nonetheless accurate. Dwight Waldo's careful analysis, for example, led him to this straightforward paraphrase of the relevant body of opinion:[7]

Measurement is in fact the criterion of genuinely scientific research. When measurement is possible, science at last has arrived; until measurement is possible research is of dubious merit and even of questionable legitimacy. Facts, research, and measurement are assumed to answer questions not only of "What is the case?" but of "What should be done?"

In the spirit of the scientific maxim, "When we can measure, then we know," the assumption is made that measurement "solves problems."

The refrain should be a familiar one.

Third, scientific management reflected a positivistic bias in two related senses: it proved a jealous master; and it induced its own version of "methodological collectivism." That is, the insights of scientific management were applied successively to metals and materials, men, societies, and then the world. The convenient assumptions were that these several levels all posed exactly the same problems and required the same approach. This patently reflects a cavalier attitude toward the place of values in matters social, but there was no real alternative to this jerry-built inclusiveness. Orders concerning the handling of materials often would conflict with the desires of men, for example, which desires might be traced to man's social experiences. Taylor did not shrink from the implied job. He dutifully went about designing that state of affairs under which the tail of work would wag the dog of society and the world. Thus he and others gave attention to designing that convenient "whole" receptive to the "fundamental philosophy" of scientific management, a utopian society which was called (without a touch of humor and with grotesque, but accurate, description) "The New Machine." And, of course, the design of a congenial world came next.

Solving problems at one level of organization by creating some congenial higher level can be troublesome. At best, it provides a convenient excuse against any charge of failure. As Taylor noted: "The substitution of this new outlook—this new viewpoint—is of the very essence of scientific management, and scientific management exists nowhere until after this has become the central idea of both [labor and management.]" [8] At its worst, this methodological collectivism excused very significant limitations on the freedom of individuals who were obstreperous enough to set their wills against the several utopian wholes. These wholes, after all, can take on a compelling quality as being somehow universally necessary, and restrictions of freedom may seem justifiable in the light of longer-run payoffs. No doubt of it, the vision of tomorrow under scientific management was compelling enough to encourage massive restrictions on individual freedom. One eminent spokesman for the movement put the matter with that lack of restraint so characteristic of the true believers: "We shall never fully realize either the visions of Christianity or the dreams of democracy until the principles of scientific management have permeated every nook and cranny of the working world." [9]

This is heady stuff and can overpower man. One is reminded of the eschatological morality of the Marxists. It justifies actions only in terms of whether or not they lead to some idyllic state somewhere off in the future, no matter what those actions are. There are hidden dangers aplenty in the positivistic approach to work, then.

Fourth, these dangers were exaggerated gravely by the positivistic disregard in scientific management of values other than by-and-by visionary promises of its "fundamental philosophy": the end of class conflict as a consequence of, and a condition for, the general submission to the System. As Taylor put it, time and time again: "In the past man has been first; in the future the system must be first." This System was presumed applicable to any work problem. A solution was considered "immanent in" any collection of data from which it would leap obligingly for the trained analyst, and that solution was the one-best way. This concept avoids many difficulties, but only by eliminating both sets of troublesome actors, men and values. As Waldo notes perceptively of the "correct" application of scientific management: "When this is done it is not man, nor caprice, nor will, that rules; it is the System." [10]

These are the vigorous main ideas that at once form the foundations for the early study of productive organizations and tie our age to one now past. Subsequent analysis must both respect these data and strive to build toward a theory of organization more sensitive to values. To this end, three topics will be of immediate concern. The complex problems of organization will be shown to overload the positivistic approach. Two approaches to the complex problems of organization lately much in the public eye also will be analyzed. They are the Individualistic Ethic and the Social Ethic. Finally, the neglected role of the social scientist as a moralist will be outlined.

THE COMPLEX PROBLEMS OF ORGANIZATION

Dual Demands on Theory

The positivistic heritage has had a profound effect on the study of organization, whether that heritage is applied full-strength or whether it is diluted in the filmy ethos that surrounds most applications of scientific management. The purpose here is to sketch the limits of this heritage in coming to grips with the complex problems of organization. The implied challenge will be accepted. Attention will be given to developing more useful guidelines for the analysis to follow, therefore.

This may put a straightforward, if messy, chain of argument too mysteriously. The burden of this section may be previewed in somewhat more detail, then. In the round, the positivistic approach has encouraged an over-simple approach to organization phenomena. And this approach has been influential enough to color the thought even of those students who are dimly aware of its positivistic roots and, indeed, of those students and practitioners who hold contrary beliefs. Such is the power of the approach against which this study is directed. Its power motivates the somewhat tedious (but necessary) isolation of the two major kinds of tasks facing the student of organization, one of which the positivistic approach neglects.

A. ORGANIZATION AS SIMPLEX

The act of organizing often has been considered a technical problem, and a low-level technical problem at that. Hence the uncomplicated, Tinker Toy terms in which the study of organization commonly is formulated. To Albert Lepawsky, for example, organization is to administration as skeletology is to medicine. "An organization," he noted, "can be sketched and charted just as the human body can be physically depicted." The graphics are not of overpowering difficulty. Indeed, organization is "mainly a matter of structure" and, Lepawsky concluded, organization is the "most elementary aspect of administration." [11]

Narrow technical concepts paralyze thought about organization. The analogy of the healthy body, or the well-oiled machine, is not far below the surface of much of the work on organization. The mirage of *a* "healthy" organization, of *an* optimum and invariant arrangement of parts, has guided many students and practitioners. The early work in scientific management illustrates the point. This early work assumed that "the system emerges from and is immanent in the 'facts' of existence and emerges from them when they are recorded and manipulated" in much the same way as observation reveals the proper relation of the bones of a body or the parts of a machine. Time has not eliminated this bias. Recent observers still stress the search for *the* organization theory.[12]

The narrowly technical view of organization may be challenged from many points of approach. The approach taken here is that the emphasis upon a single theory of organization forecloses a moral evaluation of that theory.

B.   ORGANIZATION AS COMPLEX

The neglect of organization as a moral problem cannot be condoned. For the man-to-man relations implied in patterns of organization have more than a technical aspect. Organization, in this sense, is more akin to psychiatry than to skeletology. The concept of healthy in skeletology can be determined (for general purposes) by observing many specimens. Observing individuals or organizations, in contrast, merely describes. Observation does not determine "moral health."

Organization theorists have tended to neglect an important distinction between types of theories. The complex problem of organization derives from the two types of questions which must be treated: What is related to what in organizations? and, What relations are desirable and how are they to be achieved in organizations?

The first question requires an *empirical theory*. Considerable progress has been made of late toward developing such a theory applicable to organizations. For example, we know that high cohesiveness of work units will be associated with a high degree of control of the behavior of its members, a datum of great interest and significance. The injunctions of the early positivists apply with but minor qualifications to empirical theory. It simply would not do in developing such a theory to let our prejudices or desires pervert the observation of what exists, and insistence upon "positive truths" provides a useful reminder of the point.

Empirical theory does not impose the sole burden on the administrative analyst. Handling the second question above requires a moral, or value, orientation as well as a firm understanding of the empirical world. That is, the analyst is concerned both with *what* desired states are to be achieved and with *how* these desired states may be achieved, given a knowledge of the important relations which exist under the full range of conditions encountered in organizations.

These prescriptions, or guides for action, may be called *goal-based empirical theories.* Their usefulness is as great as their designation is awkward. For example, one such theory-fragment might prescribe the ways and means of inducing low cohesiveness in work units, the better to meet an administrator's value of inducing highly competitive behavior among the members of any unit. The development of such goal-based empirical theories has been conspicuously lacking, however, a result to which the positivistic bias in thinking about organizations has contributed very significantly. In sum, that tradition did not encourage the analyst to put explicitly to the service of our values that knowledge achieved by observation relatively free of unscientific prejudices.

The development of goal-based empirical theories complicates the study of organization substantially. This is the case in a number of senses. First, patently, there can be many goal-based empirical theories of organization. Gone, therefore, is the solace of *an* organization theory. In contrast, there will be *one* general empirical theory of organization. Of course, this theory will change substantially over time as it is extended to more and more phenomena. Empirical theory in the physical sciences, for example, has followed this course while working toward a single network of propositions which uniquely and convincingly describe reality.

Moreover, second, not every goal-based empirical theory is right in a moral sense. For example, such a theory could be developed around the goal of increasingly friendly social contact on the job. Similarly, a goal-based empirical theory could be developed—relying heavily on the experience with SS officers during World War II—to guide selection and training consistent with the goal of a smoothly run extermination program. These theories are generically similar. But they should be evaluated as more and less desirable, respectively.

These considerations suggest the burden of the following analysis, although this study has not yet developed enough to equip us fully to meet the challenge. First, a set of values which should guide the act of organizing will be hazarded. These values—J-C, for convenience—derive from the Judaeo-Christian tradition discussed in Chapter 3. Second, some behavioral findings relevant to organization will be reviewed with the purpose of determining whether they support the values implied in traditional organization theory or the J-C values.

These findings support this important point: it is realistic to approach the Judaeo-Christian values in organizing.

C.   MAN IN ORGANIZATION

Men-in-relation, our prime focus, serve to compound the complications introduced into organizational analysis by acknowledging goal-based empirical theories. The point may be made by contrast. If organizations were a complex of gears and driveshafts, the development of suitable theories of organization would not be onerous. It would be enough to deal with relatively uncomplicated empirical properties in achieving desired states. That is, if a design were decided upon (a value choice), only factors like gear speed, the nature of materials, and so on, would require attention. Such part-to-part relations are relatively uncomplicated.

But man is a prime component of organizations. These man-to-man relations add important dimensions to the difficulty of developing goal-based empirical theories of organization. Thus, it is necessary to know that such and such a leadership style will have such and such consequences for behavior which will accomplish the required job. In addition, however, the moral desirability of those behavioral consequences must be determined.

There is an even more confusing aspect of the problem, finally. The choice of a leadership style, for example, might be based upon a value-preference for authoritarian supervision. The use of this style, in turn, might have the effect of causing employees to act as if such a style were necessary to restrain them. That is, employees might express their dissatisfaction with the style of leadership by various forms of behavior management considers undesirable (which the research literature tells us often happens). Such behavior could be interpreted as proof that an authoritarian style is not only desirable but is necessary as well. This visible reinforcement of a value by an apparent necessity often makes it difficult to raise the question of values, for it can be argued that realistically no choice exists. The problem of values can have subtle, self-fulfilling features.

But enough of what must rank with the proverbial complaint about the weather. The analyst of organizations has no alternative but to accept this burden of complexity. That is how things are, whether we like it or not.

MEETING THE COMPLEX PROBLEMS OF ORGANIZATION

Individualistic Ethic and Social Ethic

That the positivist approach is not up to the task of guiding attempts at organizing may be demonstrated usefully from a less tedious point of view. In fact, two major bodies of thought have been relied upon (if often implicitly) to give moral support to the dominant positivistic approach to organization phenomena. The clash of these two bodies of thought—the Individualistic Ethic and the Social Ethic—has been brought vividly to public attention in Whyte's *The Organization Man*. These ethics deserve description and analysis here, the better both to understand them and to build upon them.

The Individualistic Ethic is not well designed for the tenderhearted or squeamish. It sanctions competition by individuals for individual gain, and unbridled competition at that. Suffice it here to note that social misinterpretations of the Darwinian "survival of the fittest" in the biological world—all the vogue near the turn of the present century—must be counted among the major dogma of the Individualistic Ethic.[13] Advocates of this persuasion often bluntly made the case for competition and its beneficial consequences: "Under nature's laws all alike are put on trial. If they are sufficiently complete to live, they *do* live, and it is well they should live. If they are not sufficiently complete to live, they die, and it is best they should die."[14] John D. Rockefeller only put the matter a little more delicately—for his audience, after all, was a Sunday school class—when he explained that his Standard Oil Trust was[15]

. . . merely a survival of the fittest. . . . The American beauty rose can be produced in the splendor and fragrance which bring cheer to its beholder only by sacrificing the early buds which grow up around it. This is not an evil tendency in business. It is merely the working-out of a law of nature and a law of God.

Such philosophizing had its subtler features as well. Thus if the image of the atomistic individual pervaded such naturalistic explanations, man's social obligations were not neglected. Indeed, they were alleged to be served automatically as each individual sought his own interests. Archbishop Whately gave the point clerical sanction in these words: "It is curious to observe, how through a wise and beneficent arrangement of Providence, men thus do the greatest service to the public when they are thinking of nothing but their own gains." [16]

This quasi-religious spirit was at the heart of the Individualistic Ethic, and not incidental to it. Lest the matter be misunderstood, men like Rev. Russell Conwell made even more explicit that the fittest were not only the richest, but also the morally best. "That is why they are rich," Conwell explained. Hence only a few of the poor deserved sympathy or help. "To sympathize with a man whom God has punished for his sins, thus to help him when God would still continue punishment," Conwell concluded definitely, "is to do wrong, no doubt about it. . . ." [17] In this and similar ways was established the validity of the several virtues deriving from Protestantism: thrift, hard work, sober living, and the like. So prominent were these features in early economic thought, in point of fact, that a famous interpretation of history argues that capitalism had to wait on religious changes that resulted in the "Protestant Ethic." [18]

These views—considered as morally absolute and immutable—all but monopolized an earlier age. Positivistic pseudoscience added convenient support in the improbable extensions of Darwin's work with animals. William Graham Sumner put the import of this highly popular theme in no-nonsense terms: "The truth is that the social order is fixed by laws of nature precisely analogous to those of the physical order. The most that man can do . . . by his ignorance and conceit [is] to mar the operation of the social laws." [19]

"Conservative Darwinism" was a formidable and stable guide for behavior, indeed. "Progress" might be the goal of this cash-nexus society, but it is to be made only in terms of those immutable social laws of which Sumner wrote. To do otherwise is to court disaster, if not damnation. These laws promised no imminent change, in addition, that was clear to a friend of Henry George. "What do you propose to do about it?" George asked in response to his friend's concern over the poverty and corruption in New York City. "Nothing!" the friend replied. "You and I can do nothing at all. . . . We can only wait for evolution. Perhaps in four or five thousand years evolution may have carried men beyond this stage of things." [20] The shorter-run translations of this doctrine also were equally clear. Thus one executive noted that he could do nothing about the 75-cent daily wage of employees in his plant. "I don't think anything could be done," he concluded. "The law of the 'survival of the fittest' governs that." [21]

One need not grope for hidden meaning. The Individualistic Ethic proposed both a morality and a science of individual selfishness.

The Social Ethic seems to provide a starkly opposed alternative. Whyte's *The Organization Man* characterized the Social Ethic in terms of three major and related emphases: the assumption that the group and not the individual is the prime locus of creativity; the derivative assumption that belongingness is the ultimate need of members of an organization, or is a need usefully cultivated in members of an organization; and a dependence on a positivistic scientism to achieve and to guide this belongingness.

The factors underlying the development of these two ethics are many and diverse. From a revealing angle, however, the Individualistic Ethic drew adherents because it facilitated the gradual transformation of a rigidly organized, hierarchic society (as the England of preindustrial days) into an environment in which men could at least attempt to shape their own lives. Competition was the common result, as men strived to gain their livelihoods and pursue wealth as they would. Our "open frontier," for example, provided strong support for such a point of view, reinforcing the doctrine of natural liberty and the Protestant Ethic which had been nurtured in Europe. Figure 1 depicts other predisposing factors. Together they let in fresh air to societies long stagnant, unchaining the individual and at once testing him severely. Consider, to make the point, the vistas held open to the individual. Henry Clews painted a typical portrait in 1908. He argued that any individual may choose his own trade or profession or change it; any individual is free to apply himself or curb his efforts at work; and he is free to acquire property or renounce it. And any man's neighbor is free to emulate either success or failure. "If anyone has a genius for making and managing money," Clews concluded, "he is free to exercise his genius, just as another is free to handle his tools." [22]

Many influential modern commentators have been wont to dwell

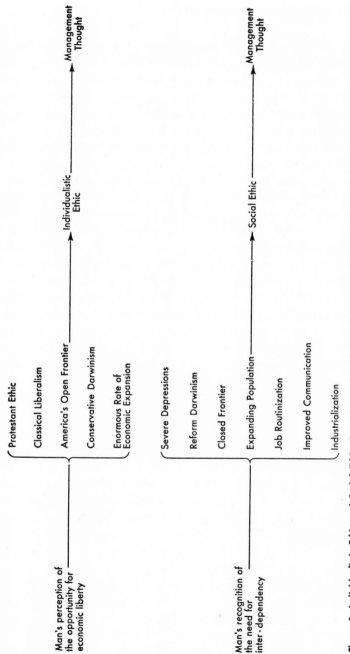

Figure 1. **Individualistic Ethic and Social Ethic: Some Supporting Factors. Based upon William G. Scott, *Human Relations in Management*** (Homewood, Ill.: Richard D. Irwin, Inc., 1962), p. 19.

favorably on the age of giants developed in the environment induced by the Individualistic Ethic. But it had its significant costs, and these costs buoyed the Social Ethic to prominence. The rise of the Social Ethic, indeed, was implied by the bias of the Individualistic Ethic. For that ethic was the product of massive changes in institutions and beliefs that had lived too long and were therefore discarded hurriedly and unreservedly. The reason is clear enough. Only the emancipation of the individual from the prevailing cultural bondage could have supported such pervasive changes, and this enlarges the freedom of the individual. Understandably, then, the insistence on individual rights "irrespective (in Tawney's words) of any social purpose to which their exercise contributed" was *the* dominant theme in the new industrial societies like England and the United States that produced the Individualistic Ethic.[23]

The very idea of social purpose became a casualty, therefore, and the derivative excesses perpetrated in the name of the Individualistic Ethic contributed significantly to the emergence of the Social Ethic. As Richard Hofstadter expressed the point: "In time the American middle class shrank from the principle it had glorified, turned in flight from the hideous image of rampant competitive brutality, and repudiated the once heroic entrepreneur as a despoiler of the nation's wealth and a monopolist of its opportunities."[24]

The Social Ethic also derived support from the very successes of the Individualistic Ethic and the enormous forces toward change caused by these successes. Figure 1 depicts a number of these forces, and suggests the ways in which the Individualistic Ethic "could not win for losing."

Although the Individualistic Ethic brought many benefits, the Social Ethic attempted to answer new social and economic problems. Consider Whyte's application of the point to modern organizations. Roughly, the Individualistic Ethic might have been necessary to *develop* a large business, but it had very significant limits in *running* one.

With some justification the organization man argues that the old-style individualist was often far more of a bar to individualism in other people and that in the modern organization the desk-pounding type of leader drastically inhibits the flow of ideas, not to mention making life unpleasant for everybody. As organization men see it, through an extension of the group spirit, through educating people to sublimate their egos, organizations can rid themselves of their tyrants and create a *harmonious* atmosphere in which the group will bring out the best in everyone.[25]

This brief characterization of the Social Ethic implies an ethical revolution. Adaptation and equilibrium and solidarity, in short, become the watchwords; competition is no longer exalted. And if the individual is not neglected entirely, his satisfactions are seen as largely deriving from his participation in harmonious and closely knit group relations. Thus, for F. K. Berrien, individual self-realization results basically from "the development of close relationships which anchor the individual securely in some stable, continuing group." [26]

Even if the problems faced were novel, however, the Social Ethic did not escape the past entirely. In many significant respects, indeed, the Individualistic Ethic called the tune. For example, the Individualistic Ethic admitted of evolution, if an ever-so-slow evolution, and the Reform Darwinians seized the opportunity provided. Thus Henry George observed that Conservative Darwinism was an unvarnished argument for the protection of economic interests, a theory which "parries change [and charges poverty,] want, and starvation . . . to individual greed." But there was an easy way out for the Reform Darwinians. Since an idea was at fault, that idea must be changed. Reform Darwinians, then, emphasized a new but related theme: "the injustice of society, not the niggardliness of nature, is the cause of . . . want and misery." [27] Change society by changing its leading ideas, and poverty, want, and starvation will diminish or disappear. This redirecting and speeding up of evolution was the heart of Reform Darwinism, and is an important support of the Social Ethic.

Management thought, as Figure 1 illustrates, has leaned heavily on the two ethics. Indeed, the two ethics emphasize two strains of thought that are commonly found together in the approaches of the same organization analysts, if they are not always emphasized equally. Frederick W. Taylor, for example, reflected many of the virtues associated with the Individualistic Ethic: thrift, scrupulous honesty, and hard work among them. And the style of supervision deriving from Taylor's approach well suits the authoritarianism consistent with that ethic. However, Taylor also placed premium (if only implicit) stress on social solidarity. This strain of Taylor's thought has not received due attention, but it is consistent with the Social Ethic.

This picture of ideological tension holds as well for the broader history of the two ethics in management thought. Not uncommonly, for example, separate camps will develop within colleges of commerce that emphasize each of the two ethics. If seldom framed in the terms used here, the resulting conflict can yet be sharp. More generally, Scott noted the uneasy coexistence of the two ethics might be tearing management apart, since "lip service is given to the symbols of individualism while collectivism is the practical and acceptable form of management practice." [28]

MEETING THE COMPLEX PROBLEMS OF ORGANIZATION

Toward the Judaeo-Christian Ethic

The two ethics trigger reactions that are strangers to moderation. The Social Ethic does not lack fervent support, of course. Nor is opposition lacking. Thus Whyte's enormously influential *The Organization Man* makes much of the conflict between the Individualistic Ethic and the Social Ethic and of the positive dangers of the fact that the latter ethic has largely replaced the former in setting the tone of behavior in organizations. Others also have been champions of the Individualistic Ethic, marshaling both subtle and heavy-handed arguments, the latter under such striking banners as "To Hell with Human Relations." And the twain seldom meet, although they often clash.

This section takes an unorthodox position on this tension. Neither ethic by itself is adequate to the task; both are morally unspecific; and neither the Individualistic Ethic nor the Social Ethic can muster evidence to show it is necessary and sufficient for inducing effective performance under existing conditions. This is a substantial bill of particulars. Each item will be considered in turn.

First, both ethics are clearly inadequate. For example, Whyte complains that the fetish of equilibrium or stability in the Social Ethic acts to complicate change or to restrict innovation, with the long-run possibility that organizations of some size will wallow in a chronic going-nowhereness of their own making. The Individualistic Ethic, in contrast, may be useful in getting a change formulated as a policy, but it is less useful in developing consensus about that policy among those upon whom the implementation of the policy depends, for good or ill. Upton Sinclair suggests the point in his description of a plant owner bent on making as much money as he can, and not caring a whit as to how he does it. In his novel *The Jungle,* Sinclair trenchantly observes that "from top to bottom the place was simply a seething caldron of jealousies and hatreds; there was no loyalty or decency anywhere about; there was no place where a man counted for anything against a dollar." [29]

Even such fragmentary considerations demonstrate that man is neither purely individualistic nor purely collectivistic. He is both, and sometimes volatilely so, although a wide variety of forces can induce him to emphasize starkly one side of his nature or the other. V. A. Demant is of one mind with the present view. "The community and individualist propensities," he observed, "are part of man's *nature* in dialectical interplay. . . ." [30] Neither emphasis is complete unto itself.

Second, both the Individualistic Ethic and the Social Ethic are morally unspecific, at best. True, both ethics have been paraded as the expression of morality. The Individualistic Ethic usually was clothed in the garb of unalterable moral law; and the Social Ethic reflects an attempt to provide a moral sanction against, for example, authoritarianism in organizations. But both frank egoism and frank adaptation suffer from the same lack of standards.

The required argument will be made for each ethic in turn. Thus if the Individualistic Ethic sanctions the unrestricted behavior of individuals short of the point of adversely affecting other individuals, the significant question still is the precise point at which one's behavior affects others adversely enough. The Individualistic Ethic shrinks from this question. Consider only one common formulation of this ethic. If labor and capital are truly free, as in the "order of nature undisturbed" that is the "law of competition," then the "flow of each . . . toward an equilibrium, is as natural as that of waters of the ocean under gravitation." No doubt of it, moreover, that this equilibrium is "God's method," which "God has ordained, and which, though man may temporarily disturb it, he can never overthrow." [31] The morality, then, is in allowing equilibrium to be reached, not in how this is done or what "level" is reached. That may explain the strong stomach of many true believers for even the worst perversions of a basically reasonable and necessary emphasis on individualism.

Seeking guidance from man's works may be reasonable enough from a positivistic point of view, but it stands ethical problems on their head. The Conservative Darwinians sought natural roots for ethical feelings, and thereby enlisted an age and its institutions in the search for support of the existing or the convenient. Henry F. May concluded that matters had gone so far that "in 1876 Protestantism presented a massive, almost unbroken front in its defense of the social status quo." [32] Moreover, the pervasive emphasis in American thought on pragmatism and instrumentalism gives ample evidence of the preoccupation with developing a philosophy of the convenient.

The Social Ethic has similar foundations and begs similar questions. The Social Ethic received support from many who were dissatisfied with the Individualistic Ethic, but they sought satisfaction in existential processes considered as moral or desirable per se. Thus the Social Ethic sanctions adaptation to others and equilibrium. But adaptation to what? And equilibrium at which point and for which purposes? Such questions are neglected, and the significance of the neglect is great. Note only that local units of the Mafia are groups, as were the Twelve Apostles. The group processes of adaptation and equilibrium that characterize both are morally neutral as such; the divergent directions of these processes, in contrast, are of some consequence morally. The Social Ethic fudged the distinction, and group forces were raised to the unseemly level of an unqualified moral principle.

Emphasis upon these ethical limitations of the Social Ethic is not philosophical nitpicking. Witness the concern among many tough-minded observers and practitioners of the organizational life. They are troubled by the amorality of both managerial ethics. James Worthy sketches some of the reasons for his concern in these terms: "While modern business enterprise has evolved within a matrix of Judaeo-Christian ethics and its values have been profoundly shaped thereby, . . . these ethical principles are generally expressed in secular rather than religious terms. . . ." This fact implies a serious weakness. For business policy and personal conduct have but a "tentative, unstable, and an unsure guide" in a nonreligious ideology.[33] Others, if anything, are more definite. Edwin Canham, for example, has no reservations about the consequences of positivistic patterns of thought: "Unless we discern and restore a more accurate sense of values, our system is in gravest danger of decline and fall." Definite, stable, and certain guides for behavior were required. To Canham, then, the "only valid social goal is improvement of the lot of men and the better relationship of men to one another and to God, to fundamental truth." [34]

Third, both the Individualistic Ethic and the Social Ethic lack empirical support of their ability to induce and sustain effective performance under existing conditions. The Social Ethic's major premise that preoccupation with individuals misses much of relevance in organizations helps make the point. The premise disposes of any claims that the Individualistic Ethic alone can guide effective performance in organizations, for the power of group influence has been acknowledged at least since the famous Hawthorne experiments of the 1920s and the 1930s. In some of these experiments, for example, newly developed group relations proved capable of raising levels of output far above the levels its members attained before the experiment. Not even these early experiments, however, permit placing unlimited faith in group processes. For these very experiments also show that group influence might be used to restrict output. And subsequent research has demonstrated that the directions in which a group's influence will be exerted are many and varied.

Encouraged by their often-unacknowledged, major value premises, many analysts of organization life let their enthusiasm get the better of them by imputing too much to the research literature. The organizational world of groups was given a simplistic rosy hue. That this is so has had profound effects on organizational practice. Whyte provides apt demonstration of the point in considering those "abstractions" underlying the Social Ethic that are "so taken for granted as good," such as participation and consensus. He observed:[35]

Held up as a goal without any reference to ends, they are meaningless. Why participate, for example? Like similar abstractions, participation is an empty goal unless it is gauged in relation to the job to be done. It is a means, not an end, and when treated as an end, it can become more repressive than the unadorned authoritarianism it is supposed to replace.
And why should there be a consensus? . . . All creative advances are

essentially a departure from agreed-upon ways of looking at things, and to over-emphasize the agreed-upon is to further legitimatize the hostility to that creativity upon which we all ultimately depend.

Over and above the overt praise for the pressures of the group, the very ease, the democratic atmosphere in which organization life is now conducted makes it all the harder for the individual to justify *to himself* a departure from its norm. . . . The hunch that wasn't followed up. The controversial point that didn't get debated. The idea that was suppressed. Were these acts of group co-operation or individual surrender? We are taking away from the individual the ability even to ask the question.

These are weighty considerations, for they dramatically underscore the poverty of blatant adaptation. Whyte's argument highlights the lack of value boundaries in the Social Ethic within which group influence may be tolerated, and beyond which it must be resisted. The surrender to the group therefore can be as threatening to freedom as the individualism preached by the Conservative Darwinians.

The common characteristics of the Individualistic Ethic and the Social Ethic, then, challenge any attempt to replace them in three senses. Any new ethic must apply to a wider range of organizational problems than did those two ethics. That new ethic also must be morally specific, and it must provide ready guides for behavior relevant in organizations. Finally, the new ethic must be supported by proof of its contributions to effective performance in organizations under conditions commonly encountered today.

No easier road can be taken. Our lives must be lived by the values in terms of which we make countless decisions, and organizations are not somehow above that requirement. Our operative ethical systems will more or less approximate the truth, they will be more or less realizable under the conditions that must be dealt with, and we may be more or less aware of them. Ethical systems there must be in any case. All societies are cemented together, James Burnham noted, "by accepted ways of feeling and thinking and talking and looking at the world, by ideologies." [36] Ideologies supplement the use of force, reinforce established patterns of behavior, and support long-standing institutions.

Following chapters will accept the challenge of offering and analyzing such a new ethic applicable in organizations, the Judaeo-Christian Ethic. In a certain sense, the J-C Ethic builds upon the two earlier ethics that have guided management thought. The Individualistic Ethic was the dominant guide for behavior in organization; the Social Ethic presently plays the more important role; and the Judaeo-Christian Ethic refers to a set of values that can generate useful structural arrangements and managerial techniques.

If the Judaeo-Christian Ethic is developmental and built upon the two earlier managerial ethics, it also stands apart from them in significant ways. These differences will be outlined in detail. Here note only that the J-C Ethic violates all of the "rules" for an ideology which Thurman Arnold proposed—if perhaps with his fingers crossed ever so slightly—in his seminal *The Folklore of Capitalism.* The ideal creed, he noted

1. Must be based upon very simple notions that may be personified, thereby gaining wide acceptance
2. Must be inspirational, that is to say, cannot be an accurate description
3. Must set impossible standards, thereby giving great advantage to the unprincipled
4. Must be unrealistic[37]

Both the Individualistic Ethic and the Social Ethic fit these standards rather closely, of course. This, in a nutshell, says it all.

MEETING THE COMPLEX PROBLEMS OF ORGANIZATION

The Social Scientist as a Moralist

One major point of this analysis has been to retailor the scope of the activities of the social scientist to include an emphasis upon values, as well as upon empirical theory. This may occasion surprise, for the social scientist often cuts the cloth of his professional garb to fit only the development of empirical theory. His preoccupation with the "Facts" involves building models to express the relations capable of accounting for existing observations and of predicting outcomes not yet observed. Values do not cover the facts, in contrast. They express the desirable, or reflect our existing knowledge of absolute truth, rather than capture empirical reality.

There are several senses—particularly in the analysis of organizations—in which the melding of empirical and value approaches is both useful and necessary. Consider these facets of the usefulness and necessity of developing what were called goal-based empirical theories. First, the empirically possible and the normatively desirable must both be kept in sight, and particularly so when technological breakthroughs permit a closer approach to our values than had been possible. This happens to be the case at present in organization theory, a fact which motivates and shapes this study. Moreover, gaining the acceptance of men of affairs cannot be avoided. Consequently, there exists no real alternative to attempting to marry the desirable and the attainable. The point has been neglected. Thus one observer expressed confidence that "religion may have something to do with the world and its problems, and in fact with the problems of business administration." But he and other seasoned observers of life in organizations had difficulty beyond this point. "Yet so far as I could tell," he concluded, "no one knew what to do about it in a practical sort of way." [38]

Second, the growth of organizations poses a particular challenge to our traditional moral prescriptions. For example, the first four of the Ten Commandments are intensely personal, while the last six encompass no organization greater than the immediate family. None of the ten applied directly to structural arrangements or managerial techniques applicable in organizations, therefore. That this is so does not provoke great wonder, yet the point has a great significance. Derivative problems are long-standing, and they grow increasingly acute. Tawney saw some of these problems raised by the breakdown of ecclesiastical authority in the sixteenth century, for example. As international trade and finance expanded, the Church faced some new versions of old questions. Certainly one should love his neighbor as himself. But appropriate action required answers to these new questions, as Tawney noted: "Who precisely *is* my neighbor? and How exactly am I to make my love for him effective in practice?" [39]

The contemporary challenge requires careful treatment of both ethical and empirical factors, then, lest our moral tradition be violated in organizations. Indeed one need not be so tentative. Such careful treatment has been largely absent in such influential approaches to organization phenomena as scientific management (as was demonstrated above). Not surprisingly, our moral traditions have been violated (as subsequent analysis will show). Making the point is not a locking of barn doors after the ethical horses have been stolen. This analysis will improve upon matters by designing structure and techniques that are more sensitive to our moral traditions as well as more effective than those generated by more careless treatments of value and empirical elements.

Third, the clergy has not been adequate to the task of prescribing organization structure and practices consistent with our moral tradition. Evidence for the point is compelling. Many may agree with Thomas A. Campbell that there is no necessary conflict between religious values and the day-to-day problems of a business or a government agency, but typically these same individuals also note they can find no specific guides for organizational life in the doctrines of the several churches representing the Judaeo-Christian faiths.[40] Moreover, we are informed constantly that "religion plays little part, or at least at the conscious level, in the decisions" made by individuals in organizations.[41] Even more broadly, four careful analysts of the "American business creed" conclude that "the creed bows to the importance of religion, admits seeking religious guidance, but continues to be a predominantly secular ideology." [42]

Why the clergy should have failed in this way defies easy explanation. A few contributing factors seem significant enough, however. The clergy seldom commands the technical skills for organizational analysis, although their number includes many experienced and capable administrators. Moreover, the clergy has tended to take what has been called the High Road to matters organizational. The net of this level of approach, simply, is too coarse for much that is significant in organizations. The so-called "Social Creed of the Churches" reflected the Protestant version of such an approach via the High Road, while a number of papal encyclicals sketch the Catholic viewpoint. The value of such notices at their appropriate level is enormous, of course, but they seldom convey clear directions for the practicing administrator.

The clergy need not bear the sole burden. Indeed, there is a nasty circularity implicit in both the Individualistic Ethic and the Social Ethic that discourages any deep concern with the values to be pursued in organizations or with ways and means of achieving them. Since the Individualistic Ethic leaves so much to individual decision, ethical restrictions are more or less beside the point. In the Social Ethic, similarly, the group and adaptation to it are emphasized. Consequently, appropriate restrictions will be sought in internal group processes, rather than in a moral order external to the group.

The implied lesson requires stating. There are close links between the Judaeo-Christian Ethic and organizational life, but those links must be forged along the Low Road. Sir Josiah Stamp's advice of the level at which to seek this close link, then, directs this effort: "There are clear and definite injunctions for the Christian life in the individual, and precepts for personal habit and attitude towards others and towards the values of life which follow upon allegiance to Christ, and faith in Him." [43]

Fourth, and finally, close attention to the empirically possible and to the ethically desirable in matters organizational also is motivated by the crucial problems of encouraging identification with work and setting standards in terms of which work and its fruits may be judged. Common approaches tend to be self-defeating or tautological, as via ever-higher wages or a rising standard of living. Such emphases have their merits, but surrender to them panders to materialism, begs the significant question of "satisfactory levels," and consequently must attempt to fill the maw of continually expanding desires while it leaves at least business organizations in an indefensible position, should the economy falter substantially. Nor does it suffice to preach self-interest, enlightened or not. For in naïve formulations self-interest may be reduced to meaning "acting as you are motivated to act," which hardly amounts to a unique insight or a useful guide for behavior in organizations. Refinements of the concept do not avoid similar difficulties. [44]

A more useful approach to encouraging identification with work, in contrast, seems to lie in large part in making the organizational experience meaningful and satisfying in itself. Oppositely, of course, the meaning and satisfaction of work are subordinated to the products or the leisure to which it leads. This is a cul-de-sac. As O. A. Ohmann concluded: [45]

I am convinced that the central problem is not the division of the spoils as organized labor would have us believe. Raising the price of prostitution does not make it the equivalent of love. Is our industrial discontent not in fact the expression of a hunger for a work life that has meaning in terms of higher and more enduring spiritual values? How can we preserve the wholeness of the personality if we are expected to worship God on Sundays and holydays and Mammon on Mondays through Fridays?

The issue is joined, then. This analysis tries its hand at a workable solution of the central problem of encouraging commitment to work. Do not misunderstand. Goods or leisure deriving from work are not irrelevant; indeed, they may be desirable. But there are organizational ways of achieving high productivity, and then there are ways. Focusing upon products or leisure forecloses a moral judgment of these alternative ways. Work in this sense is something one suffers to get other things. If one does not accept the one-best way of organizing work, then these other things are forfeit. This is heavy-handed intimidation and is often without a real basis in the bargain. Hence subsequent analysis will demonstrate that moral sensitivity can be associated with satisfactory output and employee satisfaction. Indeed, structure and techniques derived from the traditional theory of organization often will run a very poor second in meeting organizational and individual needs. Sheltering this theory from moral scrutiny, then, has practical as well as ethical costs.

Footnotes: CHAPTER 2

1. Friedrich A. Hayek, *The Road to Serfdom* (Chicago: University of Chicago Press, 1944), p. 20.
2. Friedrich A. Hayek, "The Counter-revolution of Science," *Economica,* vol. 8, new series (February, 1941), pp. 9–11.
3. Friedrich A. Hayek, "The Counter-revolution of Science, II," *Economica,* vol. 8, new series (May, 1941), p. 127.
4. *Ibid.,* pp. 146–147.
5. Friedrich A. Hayek, "Scientism and the Study of Society, II," *Economica,* vol. 10, new series (February, 1943), p. 41.
6. Daniel Bell, *Work and Its Discontents: The Cult of Efficiency in America* (Boston: Beacon Press, 1956), pp. 7–8.
7. Dwight Waldo, *The Administrative State* (New York: The Ronald Press Company, 1948), p. 58. Copyright 1948, The Ronald Press Company.
8. H. S. Person, "Origin and Nature of Scientific Management," in H. S.

Person (ed.), *Scientific Management in American Industry* (New York: Harper & Row, Publishers, Incorporated, 1926), p. 10.

9. M. L. Cooke, "The Spirit and Social Significance of Scientific Management," *Journal of Political Economy,* vol. 21 (June, 1913), p. 493.

10. Waldo, *op. cit.,* pp. 50–51. Copyright 1948, The Ronald Press Company.

11. Albert Lepawsky (ed.), *Administration: The Art and Science of Organization and Management* (New York: Alfred A. Knopf, Inc., 1952), p. 219.

12. William G. Scott, "Organization Theory: An Overview and an Appraisal," *Journal of the Academy of Management,* vol. 4 (April, 1961), pp. 22–26.

13. Richard Hofstadter, *Social Darwinism in American Thought, 1860–1915* (Philadelphia: University of Pennsylvania Press, 1944).

14. Herbert Spencer, quoted in *ibid.,* p. 27.

15. Quoted in William J. Ghent, *Our Benevolent Feudalism* (New York: The Macmillan Company, 1902), p. 29.

16. V. A. Demant, *Religion and the Decline of Capitalism* (London: Faber & Faber, Ltd., n.d.), p. 43.

17. Quoted in Marquis W. Childs and Douglass Cater, *Ethics in a Business Society* (New York: Mentor Books, New American Library of World Literature, Inc., 1954), p. 137.

18. Max Weber, *The Protestant Ethic and the Spirit of Capitalism,* trans. by Talcott Parsons (New York: Charles Scribner's Sons, 1930).

19. Quoted in Merle Curti, *The Growth of American Thought* (New York: Harper & Row, Publishers, Incorporated, 1951), p. 638.

20. Henry George, *A Perplexed Philosopher* (New York: Charles L. Webster, 1892), pp. 163–164 n.

21. Testimony of Thomas M. Miller before the Senate Committee on Education and Labor, *Report . . . upon the Relations between Labor and Capital* (48th Cong., 2d Sess., 1885), vol. II, p. 28.

22. Quoted in William H. Whyte, Jr., *The Organization Man* (Garden City, N.Y.: Anchor Books, Doubleday & Company, Inc., 1956), p. 17. Rights held and permission granted by Simon & Schuster, Inc.

23. R. H. Tawney, *The Acquisitive Society* (New York: Harcourt, Brace, and Company, Inc., 1920), p. 9.

24. Hofstadter, *op. cit.,* p. 174.

25. Whyte, *op. cit.,* p. 54.

26. F. K. Berrien, *Comments and Cases on Human Relations* (New York: Harper & Row, Publishers, Incorporated, 1951), p. 236.

27. Henry George, *Progress and Poverty* (New York: Modern Library, Inc., 1929), pp. 550–552.
28. William G. Scott, *Human Relations in Management* (Homewood, Ill.: Richard D. Irwin, Inc., 1962), p. 12.
29. Upton Sinclair, *The Jungle* (New York: The Viking Press, Inc., 1946), pp. 59–60.
30. V. A. Demant, *Religion and the Decline of Capitalism* (New York: Charles Scribner's Sons, 1952), p. 139.
31. Quoted in Thurman W. Arnold, *The Folklore of Capitalism* (New Haven, Conn.: Yale University Press, 1937), p. 187.
32. Henry F. May, *Protestant Churches and Industrial America* (New York: Harper & Row, Publishers, Incorporated, 1949), p. 91.
33. James C. Worthy, "Religion and Its Role in the World of Business," *Journal of Business,* vol. 31 (October, 1958), p. 293.
34. Edwin A. Canham, "For a Revised Set of Values," in Dan H. Fenn, Jr., *Management's Mission in a New Society* (New York: McGraw-Hill Book Company, 1959), p. 82.
35. Whyte, *op. cit.,* p. 65.
36. James Burnham, *The Managerial Revolution* (New York: The John Day Company, Inc., 1941), p. 185.
37. Arnold, *op. cit.,* pp. 139–140.
38. James W. Culliton, "Business and Religion," in Edward C. Bursk (ed.), *Business and Religion: A New Depth Dimension in Management* (New York: Harper & Row, Publishers, Incorporated, 1959), p. 4.
39. Quoted in Childs and Cater, *op. cit.,* p. 101.
40. Harold L. Johnson, "Can the Businessman Apply Christianity?," in Bursk, *op. cit.,* p. 147.
41. Childs and Cater, *op. cit.,* pp. 173–174.
42. Francis X. Sutton, et al., *The American Business Creed* (Cambridge, Mass.: Harvard University Press, 1956), p. 269.
43. Sir Josiah Stamp, *Christianity and Economics* (New York: The Macmillan Company, 1938), p. 30.
44. Sutton, et al., *op. cit.,* pp. 303–304.
45. O. A. Ohmann, " 'Skyhooks' (With Special Implications for Monday through Friday)," in Bursk, *op. cit.,* p. 71.

3

Man in Organization: the Judaeo-Christian Ethic and the Organizational Revolution

Moving toward a new ethic is not a lonely journey through a moral wilderness of gigantic organizational *Sequoia sempervirens*. There are numerous signs of many levels of interest in the tough problems that provoke this analysis. Edward C. Bursk, for example, clearly saw a ground swell of just such management thought from his advantageous position as editor of the *Harvard Business Review*. He noted that "individuals in business are becoming increasingly concerned about problems of ethics, morals, and religion. And they are increasingly willing to say so for all to hear, and to discuss their deep worries and their high hopes with all who feel the same. . . ." [1]

ETHICAL QUESTIONS AND TODAY'S ORGANIZATIONS

The Need for Guidelines

The interest in ethical guides for behavior derives from, and is motivated by, such base-problems of the organizational revolution that face the managers of any enterprise: husbanding power in organizations and inducing identification with the organization. Both problems raise acute ethical questions, and practical ones as well, and typify those quandaries which are induced in large organizations.

The problems of husbanding power in organizations increase at least in proportion to the size of organizations. Indeed, perhaps the classical competitive model of the economists describes the only set of conditions under which problems of power in organizations can be disregarded safely, and we are forevermore removed from that uncomplicated state. The Selekmans appropriately concluded that administrators cannot realistically and morally discharge their responsibilities until they recognize that they monitor power systems. "In this day and age," they said, "social and moral imperatives carry with them not the giving up of material things but the giving up of absolute, unilateral power." [2]

This puts in a low key a problem of enormous importance. The manager is on the spot. Power, in the sense of control over the environment, is required to induce and maintain cooperative effort. Yet on every side the manager must face more or less insistent demands for dibs on what were once relatively unchallenged "managerial prerogatives," these challenges coming from corporate headquarters as well as from labor unions, government agencies, et al. The manager must somehow contrive to share power while preserving or enhancing the effectiveness of his organization. The days are gone when a manager could claim a kind of divine right to monopolize power, and feel morally justified in doing so.

How is this sharing of power to be accomplished? The very question discomforts the manager, if it does not trigger a sense of sin or guilt or futility. Certainly a technical approach to organization does not promise to alleviate these pangs. For the husbanding of power must raise value questions, at least one point at issue being the question of the desirable allocation of power among the several competing interests. Any such allocations must be grounded deeply in our moral tradition, if they are not to become mere booty of war. Lacking such ethical standards, the advantage also goes to those in organizations who feel few or no qualms about the misuse of power and who are irresponsible in the deepest sense of the word, and who therefore have an enormous advantage over their more morally restrained colleagues.

Without ethical guides that are both applicable and accepted, then, the husbanding of power in organizations must be a tense matter indeed.

The problems of integrating an organization as a social system, of inducing the identification of its members with common or interlocking purposes, also raise serious ethical questions. Consider but three related problem areas.[3] First, an employee's attachment to an organization is largely voluntary. This implies significant practical difficulties, and sets formidable boundaries on the techniques that may be employed to encourage identification, particularly under conditions of relatively full employment and of various hedges against insecurity such as unemployment compensation. The voluntary nature of the employee's attachment also places a premium on identification so as (for example) to cut rates of turnover and to avoid their great costs.

These forces-in-opposition imply difficult problems of choice. But what guidelines define the morally acceptable that is also practicable under present conditions? Let no one mistake the associated and painful ethical problems, such as those raised by the catalogs surreptitiously sent to the wives of salesmen so that the wives might encourage their providers on to more extreme efforts, the *quid pro quo* being a prize for the wife.

Second, as with any social system, any organization implies the development of unifying emotional symbols that can engage the loyalties of members. The nature of these emotional symbols and of the techniques employed to induce or sustain them both raise grave ethical issues, and they grow more acute as organizations increase in size. In this category are conscious attempts to encourage an extravagant style of living—or a deep involvement in community activities—among an organization's executives, all the better to reduce the mobility of the breadwinner.

Third, the hope of advancement might be used to induce loyalty to the organization. Commonly, the concomitants are a heavy reliance on person-to-person discipline and the development of a "tall" hierarchic structure, with levels aplenty, so as to extend these upward strivings all the longer by rewarding the employee periodically. The operative theory seems to be that even extreme and perhaps arbitrary discipline will be tolerated if the individual has a tall hierarchy to climb, the goal of climbing being at once the rationale for the treatment and the reason for tolerating it. Or as Carl Dreyfuss put the matter, relatively little of the complex division of labor can be explained in terms of technical requirements alone. Rather, its motivation is to provide "psychic income" and to enhance control over the employee.[4]

This theory of increasing the number of motivational carrots along the way, as it were, has its limits. For it is not at all clear that the people who rise to the bait are therefore more desirable managers for the experience. And, in any case, all but a few organization members will protect themselves from such pressures by curbing their aspirations for promotion. They retire from the game, thereby cheating the system designed to elicit their allegiance. The self-defeating consequence may be a resort to still more punitive techniques. There is no easy way out of this circularity. As Francis Sutton and his colleagues observed:[5]

The business organization must therefore rely heavily on discipline. . . . This discipline does not always inspire unquestioning compliance or keen competition for approval and promotion among employees. After all, employees are free of both hierarchy and discipline off the job, and they naturally bring to their working-hours society some of the standards of their other personal relationships.

The third approach to encouraging organizational identification reeks of value problems, then. Hence the relevance of an accepted ethical set that may be approached under present conditions without sacrificing effectiveness. Such an ethic could provide the guides and the emotional symbols for unifying behavior in organizations, thereby reducing the need for extreme reliance on hierarchy and discipline.

TOWARD THE JUDAEO-CHRISTIAN ETHIC

An Analytical Preview

Goaded by the interest of managers and the significance of the issues at stake, this study moves through four emphases before tackling the research literature on organizational behavior. Several distinctions will aid the analysis. A limited set of values relevant in organizations—the Judaeo-Christian Ethic—then will be presented. Following this, the three ethics applicable in organizations will be evaluated in terms of the traditional theory of organization, which has tended to monopolize the choice of structural arrangements and managerial techniques. The Individualistic Ethic and the Social Ethic are consistent with the traditional theory of organization; the Judaeo-Christian Ethic violates it in all significant respects. The contrast dictates a final emphasis: upon specific organizational arrangements and techniques that violate the traditional theory of organization and also respect the Judaeo-Christian Ethic, while they contribute to high levels of output and high employee satisfaction.

All of this will help demonstrate that optimism is not out of place in the question of handling the challenge of the organizational revolution. Contrary to pessimistic analysts such as Kenneth Boulding, the organizational body can be relatively good or relatively evil. It is neither intrinsically, and it certainly is not the always-evil flesh contending against the spirit. There is no immovable roadblock in the path of men seeking the good life in our organizational society.

CONDUCT, ETHICS, AND MORALS

Some Useful Distinctions

This study does not intend to get lost in the backwaters of fine differentiations of matters of value. Present purposes permit begging off this subtle enterprise, which has been conducted in rewarding style in other investigations of the role of values in organizations. Abram Collier, for example, usefully has distinguished five types of values and presented interesting case studies that highlight their omnipresence in matters organizational.[6]

Being heavy-handed has its penalties, however. Consequently, the compromise here is to spend some time on some distinctions that need to be made in a study of this kind. But not much time will be spent, and certainly not on all possible useful distinctions. Let the focus be upon conduct, ethics, and morals, then.

Relying upon Crane Brinton but perhaps modifying his approach in the process,[7] simple distinctions will suffice. Thus "conduct" refers simply to the observed behavior of individuals or groups of individuals. "Ethics," in turn, refers to the contemporary standards at any point in time in terms of which men evaluate their conduct and that of men about them. "Morals," finally, refers to absolute standards that exist beyond time, standards of the good and the true. The *existence* of these transcendant standards is the key belief of the Christian tradition; but *knowledge* of these standards is possessed by man only in part, and that part through great effort and considerable dabbling with error over the centuries. This is not precious. There are more or less powerful objections to the position here,[8] but it is generally accepted by commentators who consider themselves in the Judaeo-Christian tradition.

These simple distinctions help dispose of the pseudo-issue of "ethical relativism." We all know that some Eskimo peoples would take it as an affront, if not a serious breach of honor, were a guest to refuse an invitation to enjoy bodily the wife or daughter of a host. Some are less generous in such matters. The ethics sanctioning both kinds of behavior also are a reflection of the total environment. Thus the problems of transportation and weather being what they are (or were) among the Eskimo, the ethical norms developed seem a reasonable adaptation to difficult circumstances, people being people. The moral order, however, is above all of this, unchanging and unchanged. In a nutshell, the human drama involves adjusting our ethical sets so as to approach more closely our knowledge of the moral order as it becomes increasingly possible to do so and as our moral insights become increasingly precise.

Certainly this constant adjusting of ethics to a constantly developing appreciation of the moral order is a delicate matter, and one fraught with enormous potential for error. As Gottfried Leibnitz noted in an age that was more certain of the moral order, but no less a creature of its ethics, than ours: "If geometry conflicted with our passions and interests as much as morality does, we would no less question and violate its laws." [9] Moreover, dualisms at best are difficult guides for living and we are discussing *the* basic dualism. We may live by our ethics; but we should set our course by the moral order as we come to know it. Particular difficulties obtain when our ethics are so demanding as to be improbable or impossible to attain under prevailing conditions as well as when our ethics demand much less than can be supplied under prevailing conditions. Human history is studded with examples of both extremes, the human tendency having been to career from the excesses of one extreme to those of the other. The pressures for change and the forces of resistance are massive enough to discourage greater moderation. The big picture also contains its compensations, however. Although there is no guarantee that good will always triumph, even a cursory acquaintance with the manners and mores of Medieval man suggests that the general trend in Western societies has been a closer approach to increasingly refined Judaeo-Christian moral insights.

Let this general position be applied bluntly to our focus on organizations. Both the Individualistic Ethic and the Social Ethic were adaptations to the possible or the convenient. And many supporters saw each ethic as a viable approach to their understanding of the moral order, although many manipulators made cynical capital of both ethics. The development of the Social Ethic in the 1920s and 1930s reflected an awareness that both conditions and knowledge had developed enough that—morally and practically—ethical change was possible and necessary. The Individualistic Ethic, that is, did not ask as much as could be given reasonably. Nor did it require as much as had to be given to organization members to encourage high output and high satisfaction under the more demanding technology of our era.[10]

Not that matters were cut-and-dried. There was nothing inevitable about the pressure for ethical change, and certainly not about the specific direction of that pressure. Nor did supporters of the Individualistic Ethic submit meekly. Indeed, they may be found today in ample numbers at any executive development program. Perhaps the only firm conclusion possible is that acting upon the Social Ethic a half-century earlier probably would have resulted in chaos. Both culturally and technically, we were not then ready for it.

Nor are matters now cut-and-dried, although the time is again ripe for developmental change in our ethical guides relevant to life in organizations. Technological changes at once require and permit a closer approach to our existing knowledge of the moral tradition than is encouraged by the Social Ethic. Research on behavior in organizations demonstrates that such change is practical and perhaps necessary to motivate high-level performance and satisfaction under the kinds of changed technological conditions that increasingly characterize our administrative and industrial organizations.

Let us, then, get on with it.

THE JUDAEO-CHRISTIAN ETHIC

A Derivation from Our Moral Tradition

Outlining a new organizational ethic is no trifling enterprise. Our understanding of the Western moral tradition derives from a number of sources: Judaeo-Christian theology; the humanistic doctrines of Graeco-Roman philosophy; and the peculiarly Western notion of the dignity and worth of man.[11] And one could reasonably spend a lifetime becoming acquainted in detail with any one of these sources.

Fortunately, a ready crutch is available. One of the happy products of the study committee of the Federal Council of Churches was an attempt to think through the Judaeo-Christian moral tradition. Of even greater interest, the effort was part of their series on ethics and economic life. The products of this effort may conveniently get us under way. The committee considered one goal *prima intra pares:* "The primary and over-arching aim of life is Christian love—by which is meant the love of God and of the neighbor. Implicit in this ideal of love is that the fulfillment of one's life is achieved through others." A number of "subordinate goals" relevant to economic life also were considered of "great importance." These subordinate goals are summarized in Table 1.

Table 1 does not stack the deck. No attempt will be made here to document the point in detail. However, evidence that the values are representative of our moral tradition could be drawn from many sources.[12]

These goals seem a reasonable enough guide for behavior in general, but they must be further refined for our present purposes. For it does not seem that all of these goals could be achieved in administrative or industrial organizations, at least at present. Moreover, there are no clear organizational applications of some of these goals.

The Judaeo-Christian Ethic will be consistent with the goals enumerated by the study committee of the Federal Council of Churches, then, while it is narrower in scope. Five values comprise that J-C Ethic.

TABLE 1   "SUBORDINATE GOALS" RELEVANT TO ECONOMIC LIFE

1. *Survival and Physical Well-being (Productivity).* Each individual should have access to the conditions necessary for health, safety, comfort, and reasonable longevity.
2. *Fellowship.* Each individual should have a variety of satisfying human relationships.
3. *Dignity and Humility.* Each individual should have the opportunity to earn a position in society of dignity and self-respect.
4. *Enlightenment.* The individual should have opportunity to learn about the world in which he lives. He should be able to satisfy his intellectual curiosity and to acquire the skills and knowledge for intelligent citizenship, efficient work, and informed living.
5. *Aesthetic Enjoyment.* The individual should have the opportunity to appreciate aesthetic values in art, nature, and ritual, and through personal relations. Many aesthetic values are attainable through both production and consumption.
6. *Creativity.* The individual should be able to express his personality through creative activities. He should be able to identify himself with the results of his own activity, and to take pride in his achievements, intellectual, aesthetic, political, or other.
7. *New Experience.* An important goal of life is suggested by the words variability, spontaneity, whimsy, novelty, excitement, fun, sport, holiday, striving against odds, solving problems, innovation, invention, etc. Each individual should have opportunity for new experience.
8. *Security.* Each individual should have assurance that the objective conditions necessary for attainment of the above goals will be reasonably accessible to him.
9. *Freedom.* Freedom is the opportunity to pursue one's goals without restraint.
10. *Justice.* The Christian law of love does not imply neglect of the self. The individual is to be as concerned about others as he is about himself—neither more nor less.
11. *Personality.* The preceding goals were stated in terms of the kinds of life experiences we wish people to have. These goals can be translated into the kinds of persons we wish them to be. Goals can then be regarded as qualities of human personality; accordingly, a desirable personality would be defined as one that is favorably conditioned toward the various goals.

From Howard R. Bowen, "Findings of the Study," in John C. Bennett, et al., *Christian Values and Economic Life* (New York: Harper & Row, Publishers, Incorporated, 1954), pp. 47–60.

They are listed below, with the numbers in the parentheses referring to the specific subordinate goals relevant to economic life to which each of the five values contributes:

1. Work must be psychologically acceptable to the individual, that is, its performance cannot generally threaten the individual (1, 3, 8, 10, and 11).
2. Work must allow man to develop his faculties (4, 5, 6, and 7).
3. The work task must allow the individual considerable room for self-determination (3 and 9).
4. The worker must have the possibility of controlling, in a meaningful way, the environment within which the task is to be performed (2, 6, and 9).
5. The organization should not be the sole and final arbiter of behavior; both the organization and the individual must be subject to an external moral order (5, 9, and 10).

This third ethic is offered without pretense of completeness, but it has several virtues. Thus the values directly imply conduct that has clear applications in both organization structure and managerial techniques. Moreover, the Judaeo-Christian Ethic is realizable in today's organizations, and this in the sense that approaching the five values can have very favorable consequences for productivity and for employee satisfaction. Supporting these summary conclusions will put the following analysis to a stiff test.

MAN IN TRADITIONAL ORGANIZATION THEORY

The Three Ethics as Yardsticks

Setting the Judaeo-Christian Ethic down raises questions rather than provides answers. To what significant organizational phenomena will the J-C Ethic be applied? In turn, do the organizational phenomena chosen reflect the common violation of the J-C Ethic? And if so, in what specific ways can violation be avoided while high levels of efficiency are attained? This is a key question. For unless alternative arrangements can be developed, all the criticism in the world will not prevail. That is, the critic must face the direct taunt: Put up or shut up.

The "traditional theory of organization" will structure our answers to these several questions. The focus has its strengths and limits. The traditional theory has been *the* guide for planning many organizations, and it deals with significant phenomena. Thus the traditional theory of organization is not a straw man. But it does provide a more extreme set of conditions than may sometimes exist in practice, and it hardly exhausts the organizationally relevant. Evaluating traditional organization theory in terms of the J-C values is meaningful, then, even if some modifications are necessary to fit particular organizing efforts.

Traditional organization theory—despite its limitations—has an immense advantage as a frame of reference for this analysis. One need not search for it. Indeed, one cannot avoid it. Almost any textbook on organization or administration is a probable source. Nor is there great disagreement about the properties of this theory. For present purposes, four "principles" may be emphasized. They prescribe that:

1. Authority should be "one-way"; it should flow in a single stream from organization superiors to subordinates.
2. Supervision should be detailed and the span of control should be narrow.
3. The organization of work should respect only the physiological properties of the individual, who is considered a social isolate.
4. Work should be routinized in terms of processes at the lowest levels and organized in terms of functions at the upper levels.

Whatever else, the incidence and prominence of the principles cannot be attributed to the J-C Ethic. Indeed, the two contradict one another in all particulars. Thus the classical theory calls for a routinized job at the lowest levels, a job whose performance is monitored closely by a supervisor with a narrow span of control, in an organization in which authority is a one-way relation. The contrast with the J-C Ethic could not be more sharp.

The point is not merely that the principles were built upon a different ethical set, but that the building was done implicitly and often unconsciously. For example, consider Frederick W. Taylor's treatment of man and his social relations. Taylor was painfully aware of the power of man-in-society, and sometimes pathetically so in his complaints that workers did not recognize the value of what Taylor was doing to them. Consequently, he tried to eliminate those characteristics of man and his social relations that were inconsistent with the System. That System was supreme and beyond moral judgment. This stretched matters too far.

Taylor thus reflected the tyranny of the positivistic assumption of a technical one-best way, and an age followed his example. He inflated a *method for analyzing work* into a *pattern for organizing men and work*. This presumed a great deal. The method was morally neutral, in itself. In contrast any pattern for organizing men is value-loaded, resting as it must upon some notion of what is morally desirable. The disregard of man-as-an-end captivated many. For example, the "boon of stupidity" has been cited by a testing expert as the most desirable quality of workers on some routinized operations. More to the point, the dehumanization of work has gone so far that morons and (believe it or not) pigeons have replaced "normal" human beings on some operations with marked success. These, of course, are extreme cases. Much work—both in industrial operations and in the so-called administration of paper—also leans in the same direction.

There is an alternative. One can have the best of the indubitably useful work analysis without forfeiting a moral evaluation of alternative patterns for organizing work. Indeed, the press of this argument is toward a coupling of the tools of scientific management with a pattern for organizing work and men that is acceptable on both ethical and on practical grounds.

The disregard of man-as-an-end may be established usefully from another point of view. The Individualistic Ethic and the Social Ethic both tolerate, if they do not wholeheartedly and unreservedly support, the traditional theory. Let us make the more difficult case. For example, the Social Ethic stresses two tactics, among others. The first is a long-run concern with training and developing personnel, a preoccupation that ill keeps company with the "root, hog, or die" bias of the Individualistic Ethic. The second tactic is greater use of a "supportive" style of supervision, in marked contrast to the authoritarian style congenial to the Individualistic Ethic and to the traditional theory of organization. Advocates of the Social Ethic still tend to support the traditional theory, however, despite their reservations about many of its facets. Evidence is everywhere, although one often must sniff carefully to discover it. For example, T. V. Houser noted that the greatest resources of any organization are the resourcefulness and initiative of its members, and that organization structure therefore must permit full use of these human capabilities. "*Although it is not the usual thing* to couple a discussion of the development of people with the structural form of organization," Houser concluded, "the two are closely interrelated." [13] That this coupling is not "the usual thing" implies worlds about the general acceptance of the traditional theory of organizations. At best, the Social Ethic only softens the outline of traditional structural arrangements and managerial techniques.

Despite such evidence of the general acceptance of the traditional theory of organization by advocates of both the Individualistic and the Social Ethic, substantial reservations concerning its efficacy must be noted. Consider the two base-problems discussed early in the chapter: husbanding power and inducing identification with the organization. Combination of the two ethics and the traditional theory of organization does not meet the challenge of these two base-problems. Indeed, the combination compounds difficulties implicit in the act of organizing and creates additional ones.

In the matter of managing the power over individuals in large-scale organizations—of freeing the individual from more or less complete subjection to massive forces beyond his control—neither the Individualistic Ethic nor the Social Ethic help the classical theory of organization meet the problems raised by pessimistic observers of the organizational revolution. The point may be established in two ways. First, neither ethic tames organizational power exercised over individuals. Indeed, on balance, both ethics heighten the dangers to freedom implicit in large-scale organization. This may be called failure by commission. Second, the combination of either one of the two ethics and the traditional theory of organization discourages resort to convenient ways of restraining the power exercised over individuals in large organizations. Or, at the very least, the efficacy of these approaches to restraint is reduced greatly. This is failure by omission.

Take the matter of failure by commission. Neither the Individualistic Ethic nor the Social Ethic curbs the power over the individual prescribed by the traditional theory of organization. That theory advises the total concentration of control over the work destinies of organization members in the hands of the chief executive, who parcels out responsibility as required to do the job. The principle of the unity of command reflects this dominant bias. The Individualistic Ethic sanctions such a monopoly of power, or at least the quest for it, in unambiguous terms. Patently, this provides no guarantee that power will be so managed as to increase the freedom of organization members.

The Social Ethic lacks even the attribute of forthrightness. It does stress such tactics as increased participation, and it shies away from overtly authoritarian supervision. But these emphases sit uneasily with the traditional theory of organization. Hence the common strategy of talking the language of the Social Ethic while acting the role of the traditional theory. Whyte, for example, fears just such an outcome will be common, the upshot being the restriction of individual freedom in the name of individual freedom. Certainly, long-extant habits make it easy to fall into diabolism without being aware of it. This writer recalls discussing certain changes in administrative practices, generally consistent with the Social Ethic, with the president of a medium-sized firm. Resistance to change by his employees? Not a bit of it, this sincere man explained. "They'll accept this human relations stuff," he said without appreciating the irony, "whether they like it or not."

Second, the common failure by omission also misses convenient opportunities to restrict the use of power over individuals in organizations. The traditional theory of organization—whether mediated by the Individualistic Ethic or the Social Ethic—tends to underutilize or misutilize three major approaches to controlling power:[14]

1. Through the operation of informal groupings that provide emotional support and mediate between the individual and the formal organization
2. Through ways of managing size that increase efficiency and the freedom of organization members, as by decentralization or organizing around discrete flows of work
3. Through the multiplication and expansion of interest groups that represent and protect organization members

The traditional theory does not cultivate such approaches to restraining power over organization members. Thus the authority relations in the traditional theory are those of person-to-person, and the limited span of control is designed to permit the close supervision of individuals necessary to reinforce these atomistic biases. Moreover, the traditional theory of organization strives to reduce the power of the individual to make him more responsive to formal authority. Hence the common attempts to destroy informal groups at work, to centralize formal authority, and even to control man's broader social relations via the New Machine so as to shape man's societal experiences to the requirements of the System. These are courses of action that undercut the three approaches above for moderating the effects of power over organization members.

The Individualistic Ethic strongly reinforces these potentials of the traditional theory of organization by sanctioning a wide range of entrepreneurial behavior designed to increase the administrator's power over organization members. The Individualistic Ethic also implied boundaries of a sort on entrepreneurial action. The organization member was a free agent too who need not accept conditions of employment that displeased him. This individual freedom for everyone was mitigated in practice, of course, by many factors that sometimes sacrificed the individual to overwhelming forces.

Failure by omission is not so starkly a feature of the combination of the traditional theory of organization and the Social Ethic. For emphasis upon the group is at the heart of the Social Ethic, and an underlying tension may exist between the sense of the traditional theory of organization and the spirit of the Social Ethic. However, this tension commonly is resolved in favor of the classical theory. For example, the power of an informal group may thwart the purposes of some supervisor, as well as support them. The Social Ethic neglects such cases because it places faith in group processes per se: it does not specify which products of group processes are acceptable. The manager is not likely to be so careless. Consequently, his devotion to the Social Ethic is likely to be lukewarm and his approach manipulative, and particularly so if his organization is based upon the traditional theory. This motivates Whyte to warn that the Social Ethic often produces a dangerous euphoria among members of an organization. Rather than freeing individuals from arbitrary power exercised over them, it can make individuals more willing participants in their own subjugation.

Employees have found ways and means of protecting themselves against the exercise of power. Labor unions, government action, informal groups restricting output, these typify common defenses. But note that they are all outside of work, if they are not the sworn enemies of management. There are various advantages and disadvantages of each of these means of controlling power in organizations, which need not concern us here. Basically, however, all neglect the fact that many dimensions of power can be controlled only by building restraints directly into the organization of work. This study is preoccupied with such a direct approach, and for good reason. The point is often made melodramatically, but the existence of our relatively free system of enterprise will depend in large part upon an enlightened management's success in building such restraints into the organization of work. The usual tendency, in contrast, has been to react to outside forces demanding restrictions on the exercise of management power, to resist these forces as long as possible, and to succumb to them only when necessary. No doubt such demands will not moderate until successful internal controls are developed, if then. The stakes of this line of work, in sum, are high.

Similarly, the traditional theory of organization leaves unresolved many of the problems of inducing identifications of members with a formal organization, if it does not aggravate them. General acceptance of the Social Ethic may encourage such identification. For the reasons outlined above, however, reliance tends to be placed on such punitive means for inducing and sustaining identification as the hierarchy and strict person-to-person discipline. This leads to a complicated tangle of intended and unintended consequences. For example, informal groups may develop among employees as a defense against the threat of both hierarchy and discipline. Indeed, this adaptation seems the general one, although there are many cases in which organization members behave submissively.

MAN-CENTERED ORGANIZATION

Toward Hard-headed Support

Such considerations come to an obvious point. There is ample reason to develop structure and techniques applicable in organizations that are consistent with the Judaeo-Christian Ethic. For the traditional theory of organization—which contradicts the J-C Ethic point by point—fails to meet significant problems of organizing, while it creates others. Even the brief sketches above should establish the point. If they do not, however, an ample literature certainly does the job.[15]

This implies an alternative to the pessimistic approach to the organizational revolution. This alternative may be sketched briefly. First, the Judaeo-Christian Ethic may be relied upon to describe the boundaries of behavior acceptable in organizations, to outline the conditions under which the formal organization should be supported and those under which it ought to be resisted. Second, specific structural innovations and managerial techniques must be developed that are consistent with the Judaeo-Christian Ethic. Moral injunctions are not enough, and never have been.

Structure and techniques must reinforce the more or less constant pursuit of the morally desirable in an organization context. Table 2 gives some feeling for the variety of "reinforcers" that will be of interest. The table thus presents two types of information: (1) the values which should underlie man-to-man relations; and (2) the structural properties and managerial techniques which approach the Judaeo-Christian Ethic and which behavioral research has shown to be associated with high output over the generality of cases. That is, Table 2 summarizes large aggregates of data from behavioral research. The findings do not always apply to individual cases. The behavioral findings are presented in the sense of central tendencies, of more or less dominant relations which have been isolated in the study of man in organization.[16]

The task, then, is there for the doing. Evidence supporting the usefulness of the several specific organizational ways of approaching the several values of the Judaeo-Christian Ethic will be reviewed in turn, one chapter being devoted to each of the five values. Especial attention will be given to describing and illustrating each of the structural properties and managerial techniques listed.

But the doing of the job can wait on the making of one further useful point. In addition to framing the analysis to come, Table 2 implies a subtle advantage. It directly meets a weighty challenge to the use of Judaeo-Christian ideals as criteria for moral behavior in organizations. Chester I. Barnard, for example, issued such a challenge and supported it with his extensive executive experience. Such ideals, he argued, were general and not easily applicable to the kind of concrete cases faced in

TABLE 2   STRUCTURAL ARRANGEMENTS AND MANAGERIAL TECHNIQUES
ASSOCIATED WITH HIGH EMPLOYEE SATISFACTION AND HIGH OUTPUT
THAT ARE CONSISTENT WITH THE JUDAEO-CHRISTIAN ETHIC

Values of the Judaeo-Christian Ethic Which Should Guide Behavior	Structural Arrangements and Managerial Techniques Associated with High Output and High Satisfaction of Organization Members
1. Work must be psychologically acceptable, nonthreatening.	1. Congruence of personality and job requirements a. testing for assignment decisions vs. in-or-out decisions b. compatibility of personalities of members c. self-choice of members
2. Work must allow man to develop his facilities.	2. Organizing around "work cycles" vs. "work units": job rotation, job enlargement for supervisors and operators a. training within work b. reciprocity as a goal
3. The task must allow the individual room for self-determination.	3. Managing dependence-interdependence-independence a. wide span of control b. supportive supervision c. motivating by growth vs. deficiency
4. The worker must influence the broad environment within which he works.	4. "Participation": group decision-making, Scanlon Plan, Multiple Management a. monitoring a discrete flow of work vs. a process b. organizing around small administrative units at low levels c. high supervisory power
5. The formal organization must not be the sole and final arbiter of behavior.	5. Decentralization vs. centralization a. monitoring a product vs. a function b. organizing around small administrative units at high levels

organizations. Moreover, these ideals are in the main concerned with person-to-person relations. Much behavior in organizations, he cautioned in contrast, is representative rather than personal. That is, organizational behavior is more a doing of things through channels in behalf of others than a doing of things directly for the self.[17]

The approach here avoids much of the barb of Barnard's point. For the stress upon structure and techniques consistent with the Judaeo-Christian Ethic will build ethical controls into the very organization of work that can be expected to guide the behavior of individuals over the generality of cases. Specific structural arrangements and managerial techniques will at once reflect the guidance of the J-C Ethic and will provide continuous direction for organization members. This constitutes an organizational answer to a problem of organization.

Footnotes: CHAPTER 3

1. Edward C. Bursk, *Business and Religion* (New York: Harper & Row, Publishers, Incorporated, 1959), p. vii.
2. Sylvia Kopald Selekman and Benjamin M. Selekman, *Power and Morality in a Business Society* (New York: McGraw-Hill Book Company, 1956), p. vii.
3. Francis X. Sutton, et al., *The American Business Creed* (Cambridge, Mass.: Harvard University Press, 1956), pp. 110–112.
4. Carl Dreyfuss, *Occupation and Ideology of the Salaried Employee,* trans. by Eva Abramovitch (New York: Columbia University, Department of Social Science, 1938), p. 17.
5. Sutton, et al., *op. cit.,* p. 112.
6. Abram T. Collier, *Management, Men, and Values* (New York: Harper & Row, Publishers, Incorporated, 1962).
7. Crane Brinton, *A History of Western Morals* (New York: Harcourt, Brace & World, Inc., 1959), pp. 3–10.
8. Sir George Schuster, *Christianity and Human Relations in Industry* (London: Epworth Press, 1951), pp. 121–122, for example, lists three main lines of thought that might conflict with the position here.
9. Quoted in Mary Sennholz (ed.), *On Freedom and Free Enterprise* (New York: D. Van Nostrand Company, Inc., 1956), p. 15.
10. William G. Scott, *Human Relations in Management* (Homewood, Ill.: Richard D. Irwin, Inc., 1962), especially pp. 22–41.

11. Selekman and Selekman, *op. cit.*, pp. 90–91.
12. Brinton, *op. cit.*, pp. 142ff; and E. S. Wengert, Dale S. Harwood, Jr., Lucian Marquis, and Keith Goldhammer, *The Study of Administration* (Eugene, Ore.: University of Oregon, School of Business Administration, 1961), pp. 40–65.
13. Theodore V. Houser, *Big Business and Human Values* (New York: McGraw-Hill Book Company, 1957), p. 20.
14. Selekman and Selekman, *op. cit.*, pp. 131–136; and Louis A. Vaccaro, "The Limiting of Power in Organizations through Delegation of Authority," *The Personnel Administrator,* vol. 9 (November–December, 1964), pp. 15 and 29.
15. Chris Argyris, *Personality and Organization* (New York: Harper & Row, Publishers, Incorporated, 1957).
16. For some of the qualifications necessary for more precise prediction, see Robert T. Golembiewski, "The Small Group and Public Administration," *Public Administration Review,* vol. 19 (Summer, 1959), pp. 154–156.
17. Chester Barnard, "Elementary Conditions of Business Morals," *California Management Review,* vol. 1 (Fall, 1958), pp. 1–13.

4

"The Proper Study of Mankind": Meshing Personality and Organization

"The proper study of mankind is man," Alexander Pope put the matter in an incisive epigram. This seems reasonable enough. If it is, however, the traditional theory of organization is unreasonable. Not without great effort, that theory stands foursquare behind the cozy notion that its own simple assumptions encompass the complex phenomena associated with men in organizations. This rephrases Pope to read: The proper study of mankind in organizations is the System. Only by accident, then, could the traditional theory of organization meet the first requirement of the Judaeo-Christian Ethic: to make work more acceptable to the employee and thus reduce its threat to him.

This chapter protests settling for virtue by accident, if at all, in several ways. It details the subtle and gross ways in which the traditional theory of organization has strayed from Pope's formulation; the analysis stresses the ersatz problems created thereby in "psychological testing"; and the argument documents the practical benefits of meshing personality characteristics with organization structure and managerial techniques in ways sensitive to the J-C Ethic. But more of this in due time.

For the present, we must be content with spotlighting the tendency for psychological testing to suffer from the guidance of the traditional theory of organization. It will take some doing to make the point satisfactorily, but that theory persisted in turn under the guidance of the Individualistic Ethic and then of the Social Ethic. That left open significant moral and practical questions in psychological testing under both ethics. Acting upon the Judaeo-Christian Ethic, however, provides a practical resolution of these difficulties.

FITTING MAN TO ORGANIZATION

Persistence and Simplicity

The traditional theory of organization could have followed one of two basic strategies in its handling of human resources. The emphasis could have been upon the fitting of appropriate structures and techniques to man and his diverse characteristics. But the emphasis was elsewhere. Fitting men to organizations has preoccupied both students and practitioners. Few have doubted whether the individual or the organization comes first. Lepawsky summarized the usual orientation toward the human in these terms: the ideal organization structure should be set up first, and then it should be staffed with individuals having the appropriate characteristics. Only a few writers, Lepawsky noted, "have warned that the obsession for organization should not stifle consideration for people and their capacities. . . ." [1] But stifled this consideration has been, in general, and with a vengeance that permits little optimism that the Judaeo-Christian Ethic will be served.

There were many reasons why the emphasis upon fitting man to organizations was convenient, and perhaps even necessary, in the early days of the development of the traditional theory of organization. Thus only now are we beginning to accumulate that knowledge of behavior necessary to make a strong case for fitting structure and techniques to man. The prissy orderliness characteristic of early work analysis therefore had a clear field. This orderliness always stemmed from a single-minded passion to develop some "whole" in the image of a grand *idée fixe;* and this orderliness often applied to human affairs those patterns of thought and design that were more appropriate to mechanics. Commonly, therefore, man's diversity was denied or neglected or suppressed. Hence the "well-oiled machine" of a Frederick W. Taylor. Most men were not enthusiasts for such orderliness, however. They were the bane of administrators of neat and precise systems. No convenient alternative to neglecting man's diversity existed, then, short of despairing of the entire enterprise of fitting man to organizations.

There is little despair about fitting man to organization in the early literature. Psychological testing was no more fortunate than other managerial techniques in this respect. For present purposes, to isolate our target more clearly, "psychological testing" may be defined broadly as employing "any problem or series of questions which has been tried out on persons of known ability; and it has been shown that the scores made by these persons correlate with their records in some form of ability." [2] Specifically, psychological testing has reflected such major assumptions at various times:

1. That jobs have a specific and unchangeable content, the performance of which can be prescribed precisely and once and for all
2. That a limited description of individuals suffices to predict their organizational effectiveness, the point being that:
   a. A one-best trait or aptitude (or set of them) will lead to effective performance by a specific individual on a specific job; and/or
   b. A one-best personality characteristic (or set of them) will lead to effective performance by a specific individual on a specific job
3. That all individuals have (or should have) such psychological properties that they will (or should) respond favorably to the same restricted class of motivators, punishment or the fear of punishment

Not all students and practitioners held all of these assumptions at all times, of course. There were heretics, albeit few of them; and even the most faithful might waver at a crucial point or two. But there was a discernible orthodoxy, and it included all of the assumptions above at various points in time. If the assumptions apply only in the sense of more or less, then, they apply rather more than less.

The logical orderliness of the traditional theory of organization cast a wide net of influence over psychological testing. No extended proof is necessary. For example, both assumptions 2a and 2b clearly assume that there is a one-best way to organize work. More specifically, the guiding hand of the traditional theory of organization in the development of psychological testing was as firm under the Individualistic Ethic as under the Social Ethic.

The "principles" motivated testing during the heyday of the Individualistic Ethic. The emphasis was upon limited sets of instincts, traits, or aptitudes, and they were to be discovered by simple paper-and-pencil tests or by the use of mechanical contrivances. The crowning glories of this early work were the famous Alpha and Beta intelligence tests administered to some 1,727,000 men in the armed forces during World War I. The chief advantage of testing this one aspect of the personality was professed to be the speed with which "officer material" could be isolated and the "mentally inferior" discarded. As a rough rule of thumb, this was reasonable, given the lights of that age.

Others pushed the approach so much further, however, that clearly more than a rule of thumb was at issue. They acted as if a leading idea of their age were impelling them. The "trait approach to leadership" that preoccupied research was a characteristic product, for example. The concept assumed the existence of a set of traits that sharply distinguished leaders from followers under all conditions, traits that some individuals had in abundance and others possessed hardly at all. The implied research problem was straightforward: isolate those traits. Individuals possessing them in high degree could be culled from large populations, and the problems of supervisory selection could be laid to rest forevermore.

Phrasing the problem of leadership selection in these terms followed the traditional theory of organization in many senses. Thus the trait concept presumed that leadership was fungible, that is, applicable over all situations. The omniscient head implied by the traditional theory could have been served no more faithfully. Moreover, these leadership traits allegedly were possessed by individuals in greatly differing measure. This provided patent support for the traditional theory's jealous safeguard of the unchallenged authority of some one supervisor over his several subordinates. Finally, the trait approach to leadership reflected that orderly, mechanistic view that pervades the traditional theory of organization. The following deadly earnest quotation, going back to 1919, eloquently expresses the kind of world view common among early testers: "The ideal employment method is undoubtedly an immense machine which would receive applicants of all kinds at one end, automatically sort, interview, and record them, and finally turn them out at the other end nicely labeled with the job to which they are to go." There was only one fly in this tester's ointment. It would be "many a day before this consummation is reached," [3] he lamented.

That such a consummation was even seriously considered must be counted as a triumph of sorts. For the approach had to be sustained in the face of substantial early evidence that reality was too complex to be trapped so simply. Bird, for example, reviewed some twenty studies that bore "some resemblance to controlled investigation." These studies had unearthed some seventy-nine traits, which conveys a rather clear message in itself. In addition, only some 5 per cent of the traits seemed to be common in four or more studies. Consequently, Bird reported that "surprisingly little overlap is found from situation to situation." [4] It was surprising, that is, in terms of the trait approach. A similar inadequacy characterized the search for instincts or specific aptitudes directly related to performance at work.[5] Such outcomes provided no great comfort for the traditional concept.

The influence of the traditional theory of organization also may be seen in the psychological testing induced by the Social Ethic. This may seem paradoxical, since the Social Ethic conflicts at a number of crucial points with that theory. Paradox or no, these nascent conflicts were buried deeply. The traditional theory of organization made peace on its own terms no less certainly with the Social Ethic than with the Individualistic Ethic.

The point is slippery enough to require illustration via one of the freshets of that watershed of the Social Ethic, the studies at Hawthorne beginning in the late 1920s. The Hawthorne studies did no less than undermine decades of intensive search for simple instincts, or traits, or aptitudes that could be related directly and consistently to job performance. The Hawthorne investigators put the matter in no-nonsense terms: "tests of dexterity and intelligence showed no relation between capacity to perform and actual performance." [6] The difficulties with the earlier approach were twofold. Early psychological testing measured only very limited aspects of the personality, and often just those aspects that were least important to success at the work site.[7] Relatedly, early psychological testing focused on the individual as an individual, shorn of the various social situations in which he might find himself. The Hawthorne investigators concluded oppositely that the relation of the individual with his immediate work group was *the* one single factor that best predicted the individual's probable performance on the job.

The Social Ethic was dedicated to avoiding both mistakes. Thus the employee's social relations became *the* central focus; and his ability to adapt in interpersonal relations became *the* lodestar of psychological testing. This dual emphasis upon group properties as well as upon individual qualities was reasonable enough. For example, highly qualified individuals might be members of a work unit that was restricting output or they might be members of a work unit that sanctioned high levels of performance. To know only the aptitudes of these individuals provides too little information. Consistent prediction requires (at least) knowledge of both individual skills and group properties.

Again, however, the useful approach of the Social Ethic was often distorted to fit the conventional wisdom about organizing. The traditional theory of organization thus protected psychological testing from inquiry rather than subjected it to scrutiny.

The coexistence of the traditional theory and the Social Ethic may be established in terms of three themes. First, efforts to act upon the Social Ethic in psychological testing commonly dead-ended in seeking support for the traditional theory of organization. For example, the measuring of employee attitudes is consistent with the Social Ethic, and a common finding of such measurement has been the extreme monotony inherent in much contemporary industrial and administrative work. Two major early opinions grew up around the "discovery" of monotony, and both supported the traditional theory as the model for organizing. The first view held that modern industrial work was necessarily repetitive and dull and, by implication, that one need not quarrel with necessity. This hardly urged a revolution in structural arrangements and managerial techniques. A second—and probably more popular—view amounted to about the same thing, but with an interesting twist. As Loren Baritz described and evaluated this second view:[8]

[It was argued that] no job was necessarily monotonous, that some people like repetitive jobs. Monotony, in this second view, inhered not in the job but in the relation between the worker and the job. . . .

This supposedly sophisticated view of monotony implied that management should and could do nothing about the nature of the job. The job was fixed, and management must therefore try to hire people who would not be distressed about working on meaningless and dull activities. . . . If management was to locate people who would not merely accept but would prefer monotonous work, the main personnel emphasis would have to be on selection techniques, and psychological testing was still the main prop of the "scientific" personnel department.

Psychological testing also was limited by the traditional theory to a narrow range of questions at executive levels. There its main goal was to isolate those individuals who could "get along with people," with an underlying one-best pattern being the common standard. But more of this later.

Other managerial techniques reinforced psychological testing in its support of the traditional theory of organization. Thus the Hawthorne studies led to a preoccupation with "adaptation" or "adjustment" to the work environment, the underlying notion being that the work environment is somehow determined irrevocably by technological necessity. This explains the use of "walking counselors" whose job it was to discover *and blunt* any employee *attitudes* that might inhibit "adaptation." These counselors were to steer clear of the *causes* of these attitudes. As one former counselor reported, she was instructed to deal "with attitudes toward problems, not the problems themselves." [9] In the most obtuse language, the counselor's job was to shift the employee's "frame of reference" so as to get the employee to see his alleged problem in a new perspective. An example illustrates this shifting of a "frame of reference": "In the case of the downgraded employee . . . her focus of attention shifts from alleged inequities, transfer and downgrading grievances, etc. . . . to her unhappy home life; then, when she returns to her original grievance, things do not look bad." [10]

A typical crowning achievement of the frame of reference approach demonstrates its strengths and weaknesses. Consider the military officer who resolves a complaint about the Jello at mess as a projection of an unsatisfactory love life. No doubt there are such cases. But what if the Jello had been bad, or the nature of work such as to cause difficulties that could not be dissolved into something else? These are the ones that got away from the "walking counselor."

Second, the knowledge of individual differences was put to a revealing use under the firm guidance of the traditional theory of organization. That is, differences in aptitudes (such as intelligence) had long been patent. Indeed, it had long been known that the performance of even a specific individual might differ very significantly over time, and at relatively uniform intervals. The "male cycle" of emotional (and productive) ups and downs already had received telling attention;[11] and the Social Ethic inspired considerable research on individual differences in what might be called "social skills."

Significantly, however, knowledge of these pervasive individual differences did not motivate the development of organization structure and techniques capable of making full use of them. With the exception of physiologically oriented work in "human engineering," rather, knowledge of individual differences usually has been used to cull rejects. *Iron Age* caught the spirit of the matter in an article entitled "Psychology Sifts Out Misfits." That piece described Armco Steel Corporation's "audit" of the "sociability" and other personality characteristics of its prospective and existing employees. As a consequence, the firm was able to reduce by 80 per cent the number of personnel hired who turned out to have undesirable or marginal personality characteristics. In addition, the audit was administered to some 20,000 employees as part of a personnel evaluation program to determine promotions and reassignments.[12]

There are many significant problems associated with this reject approach to individual differences, particularly when social skills are at issue, and this despite the neat uniformity promised by the approach. Some "good" employees at Armco no doubt were released along with the "bad," for example, since psychological tests have less than perfect discrimination. Morally, one must have great confidence indeed in whatever tests are employed for such "in or out" decisions. The decision is painfully final. Indeed, even if the tests measure what they purport to, and even if what they measure is related to effective performance, reservations still are in order. Such tests could lead to conformity born of the similarity among organization members that would burgeon beyond all reasonable bounds, thereby compromising the ability of the organization to perceive and to respond to change.

Far less of a risk is run if testing is used to assign individuals to work units in terms of compatible skills and characteristics. Thus personnel scoring low on a need for warm interpersonal relations might be grouped together rather than discarded. There are several kinds of compatible personalities, that is to say, not just one.

Third, that much psychological testing suffers from the one-best impress of the traditional theory of organization also is clear where the employee being tested is judged against some "profile" of characteristics that are allegedly associated with effective performance in specific jobs. One variation claims to judge the suitability of individuals for various jobs in terms of the time they spend in answering each of a list of questions. An effective salesman, it is argued, will have a different profile of times on the several questions than the effective plant manager. Sears, Roebuck employs a more complex variation on the profile theme. Figure 2 presents the ideal profile for executives at Sears. The typical Sears executive, for example, ranked higher than approximately 60 per cent of the people who have had their "theoretical interests" measured by the test in question. The aspiring executive at Sears need not produce scores that exactly fit this profile, but it is decidedly not to his advantage to gain scores that differ widely from the profile.

The reflected influence of the traditional theory is mischievous, on balance. As a general rule of thumb, this notion of a one-best set of aptitudes and personality characteristics might prove useful for some

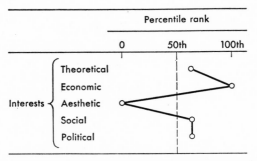

Figure 2. The Ideal Profile for Executives of Sears, Roebuck. From William H. Whyte, Jr., *The Organization Man* (Garden City, N. Y.: Anchor Books, Doubleday & Company, Inc., 1956). Copyright held and permission granted by Simon and Schuster, Inc.

purposes. Typists, for example, should have the usual number of fingers, and some ability to coordinate their movements. If not outrageous in such cases, however, neither does the one-best notion permit us to predict performance. Moreover, one can easily make too much of even a useful notion when applied to personality characteristics, as in the assumption that there is an "executive personality." Certainly we do not yet know enough to act cocksure.[13] Finally, there are many ways of effectively performing even jobs that impose the same or similar demands.

All of this permits relatively safe and brief summary. This history of much psychological testing grew as the traditional theory bent it. This has been to a self-defeating end in the main, both in framing awkward questions for research and in providing unfortunate guidance for applications.

TESTING THE ORGANIZATION MAN

Fad and Counterfad Rejected

The history of psychological testing must be written in terms of counterfad as well as fad. The preceding section thus requires qualification, for it deals only with the protagonist fad. Even among protagonists, moreover, unanimity in details hardly has been dominant. Roy Schafer put the matter directly in describing clinical psychology and testing. He wrote: "Because of its rapid growth, a boom town excitement has characterized clinical psychology until very recently. News of a 'good' test, like news of striking oil, has brought a rush of diagnostic drillers from the old wells to the new and has quickly led to the formation of a new elite. . . ."[14] In some respects such enthusiasm has proved valuable, but it has its negative features. Thus tests have been thrown into the breach before they were ready, or applied where they were not appropriate.

Overenthusiastic protagonists of psychological testing long have been legion. For them, testing holds allures aplenty. If appropriate tests could be developed, for example, many of the most troublesome personnel and industrial relations problems would disappear. Moreover, while early testing focused on employees performing lower-level tasks, increasing hope has been expressed for psychological tests as an aid in executive selection and promotion. This significantly increased the attractiveness of testing.

Many in authority in organizations were willing to ante up with such payoffs in view. As of 1954, nearly 32 per cent of the firms surveyed by the National Industrial Conference Board utilized psychological testing for their hourly employees, and 43 per cent of the same firms used tests for their supervisory and executive employees.[15] Considering the brief history of psychological testing, these data are impressive. This is particularly the case because large firms were by far the most likely to resort to testing. Matters did sometimes get out of hand, so great was the devotion. A point or two difference on some test scores sometimes was considered enough to decide an individual's job-fate irrevocably. Whether the devotion is extreme or moderate, at least as of 1960, the use of psychological tests was still growing, and particularly so in the larger companies.[16]

Antagonists of psychological testing, however, have of late come into their own. Whyte's challenging indictments in *The Organization Man* have spurred this reaction, which is a vocal one. The reaction has not all been mere talk, however. The Chance-Vought Aircraft Corporation ceremoniously burned the results of its psychological testing of employees accumulated over the years. And others are proud to be in the same ranks.

Neither the fad of acceptance nor the counterfad of rejection will settle matters, however, for both avoid significant issues that require attention. The point can be developed in terms of a brief catalog of Whyte's charges against psychological testing. Notice that Whyte's animus is directed against personality tests, as opposed to aptitude tests. That is, *The Organization Man* attacks testing that is oriented toward determining how "well adjusted" a man is, as opposed to determining whether he possesses certain specific skills. And Whyte's focus is upon the executive rather than upon the rank and file in organizations.

The Organization Man frames its case against personality testing in moral terms, and provides some interesting advice. Whyte does not let himself off easily just because he sees testing in such a tired and morally unfavorable state. He answers his own question in a revealing way.

"How much more must a man testify against himself? . . . Sensibly —the bureaucratic way is too much with most of us that he can flatly refuse to take tests without hurt to himself. But he can cheat. He must. Let him respect himself." [17]

That Whyte was led to this "solution" of the moral problem raised by testing testifies to the gravity of the charges he felt justified in directing at psychological testing. These charges may be abstracted conveniently:

1. In practice, personality tests are critical in the selection and promotion of executives.
2. In practice, the results of personality tests often are utilized in naïve ways by untrained executives.
3. By basic intention, personality tests measure the loyalty of an executive to his organization.
4. In effect, personality tests encourage conformity, particularly when ideal profiles for specific jobs have been developed.
5. In sum, personality tests are invalid in executive selection and promotion, if only because test performance commonly tells little about how specific individuals will perform at work and specific individuals are what a company hires and fires.

Whyte's wide-ranging indictment is difficult to evaluate fairly. It seems appropriate to conclude, however, that Whyte has raised many graver issues than are met by his recommendation of cheating. In part, some unhappy vaguenesses in his argument stand convicted. While deprecating the validity of personality tests, for example, Whyte argues that the tests encourage conformity in organizations via the selection of similar individuals. One cannot have it both ways. For the latter effect means that the tests do measure some persistent properties that have significant and predictable effects on behavior, and measure them with some reliability. Thus Whyte's own argument suggests that cheating is hardly an all-purpose remedy. It may hurt the respondent by condemning him to a job or work pressures that he deeply dislikes.

The questions left open by Whyte's advice to cheat are particularly prominent in his discussion of values in psychological testing. Thus Whyte correctly charges that psychological testing in all its phases cannot be "objective" or "value free," as some practitioners allege. He notes that: "Neither in the questions nor in the evaluation of them are the tests neutral; they are loaded with values, organization values, and the result is a set of yardsticks that reward the conformist, the pedestrian, the unimaginative—at the expense of the exceptional individual without whom no society, organization or otherwise, can flourish." This observation serves as a springboard for a summary generalization. "Not in failing to make the tests scientific enough is the error," Whyte notes; "it is, rather, in the central idea that the test can be scientific." [18]

Whyte's pronouncement reflects both acute observation and subtle error. For Whyte has fallen into the positivistic trap that he is so anxious that others avoid, as can be demonstrated with the help of our Chapter 2. Assume that Test A measures characteristics that may be labeled "conformist, the pedestrian, the unimaginative." Certainly, the *use* of Test A as a criterion of selection implies a value choice by management. This does not make Test A scientific or unscientific, however, and far less does it mean that testing per se must be either. The scientific status of Test A is determined only by its ability to measure reliably something real, that is, something that permits consistent prediction. This may be done scientifically, whether one likes the unimaginative or not. This type of work has been called empirical theory. Now values intrude obviously in a second type of work, goal-based empirical theory. Such a theory is a basis for applications. A sample proposition might state: If you want the conformist, the pedestrian, and the unimaginative, then you are well advised to use Test A to select personnel, and you may expect such consequences. One can complain that one must be foolish or immoral to want such behavior. The scientific status of the proposition is not influenced a whit thereby.

The point may be brought to a head. Whyte certainly is correct in noting that the *use* of psychological tests implies a value set, and that "organization values" often will be prominent among them. Could it be otherwise? Some value or values underlie any choice of a tool for use. Moreover, these organization values also have influenced the direction of early exploratory work on personality tests, as Whyte notes. Given the source of much of the research money, this is not earth-shaking, if it is accurate. But it hardly proves that personality testing is inherently unscientific.

Whyte's argument is far more remarkable for what is neglected than what is spotlighted, therefore. He does not concern himself with *why* psychological tests emphasize the conformist, the pedestrian, the unimaginative. That many tests do so is not some inherent characteristic of testing, but rather a reflection of prevailing organizational values. Moreover, since validatory work on existing psychological tests is incomplete, the influence of organizational values assumes even greater proportions. For one might understand their prevalence in testing if unshakable evidence demonstrated the superiority of the conformist, the pedestrian, and the unimaginative on the generality of tasks in organizations. But what sustains these values in the absence of such documentation? And what explains the money spent using the personality tests reflecting these values? Certainly cheating on personality tests is a pitiful challenge to these questions.

Let us hazard an explanation of Whyte's negligence while suggesting that he set too short a tether on his argument. There is a danger in imputing motivation to anyone's work, but Whyte seems to accept the traditional theory of organization as inevitable. This acceptance leads to some subtle difficulties. Consider Whyte's complaint that: "In return for the salary that The Organization gives the individual, it can ask for superlative work from him, but it should not ask for his psyche as well." [19] This pleasantly avoids a major motivation for testing, the difficulty of measuring performance under the traditional theory of organization. As subsequent analysis will demonstrate, its emphasis upon separate functions and minute processes opens significant possibilities for avoiding responsibility for error.

Psychological testing helps hedge against the derivative uncertainty or arbitrariness of allocating responsibility for performance. It helps choose individuals whose personality characteristics will not aggravate the difficulties inherent in the traditional theory of organization. Thus the traditional theory requires asking man for his psyche in order to encourage superlative work. Whyte's admonition, then, is in significant respects irrelevant to the realities faced in organizations patterned after the principles, if it is not truly irresponsible.

A conclusion is here for the taking. If the traditional theory of organization does in fact encourage psychological testing to seek the conformist, the pedestrian, the unimaginative, the obvious strategy is to demonstrate the less than universal adequacy of that theory and to spell out a more useful alternative theory that requires more of the innovative, the unorthodox, and the imaginative. If that is done, psychological testing will soon be seeking individuals with these qualities. Cheating on psychological tests has far less to recommend it as a grand strategy.

This conclusion aptly illustrates the senses in which fad and counterfad in psychological testing miss problems appropriate to our moral interests. These problems set the task for the four remaining sections of this chapter. First, these sections must demonstrate the usefulness of testing, both in practical ways as well as in the moral sense of increasing the acceptability of work and of reducing the threat work poses to the individual. Second, ways of testing so as to fit organization to man must be sketched. Third, an example of such a useful approach to testing will be analyzed. Fourth, managerial techniques and structural innovations must be sketched that permit psychological testing to reduce the threat in work and to increase its acceptability to employees, thereby approaching the first value of the Judaeo-Christian Ethic.

FITTING MAN TO ORGANIZATION

Some Successes and Outer Limits

As *The Organization Man* amply contends, unqualified praise for psychological testing is not appropriate. Its failures often have been spectacular. For example, psychologists applied their full arsenal of talents to predicting the success in training and practice of would-be psychologists. The results left much to be desired. As the psychologist Quin McNemar concluded:[20]

> If psychologists with ample funds and the best available personnel at their disposal cannot come up with a better solution to the prediction problem than achieved by this project, the question may be asked whether we haven't oversold certain psychological services.

One can easily be too severe with psychological testing, however, so much is severity in the air. Hence the moderate approach of this section. It illustrates a few successful applications of the testing of aptitudes and personality characteristics; but it will not be an unrelievedly rosy analysis in that these examples fail as they succeed. The senses in which this is the case will outline the orientation in psychological testing that is well designed to yield practical benefits as well as to meet the first value of the Judaeo-Christian Ethic.

Perhaps the most comprehensive attempt at testing for job-related attitudes involved the selection of pilots during World War II. It was also the most successful program ever attempted. The point is supported by these summary data on the number of dropouts from samples of pilot candidates chosen by three selection procedures:[21]

Selection Procedure	Per Cent Eliminated in Field Training
Physical test only	75
Prewar Army screening	61
Battery, 1944 model (upper three stanines)	36

The use of the 1944 battery to select candidates could serve both the purposes of the formal organization and the purposes of most of the individuals who survived the physical test but went on to be eliminated in the field training. Indeed, these data understate the usefulness of selection in terms of testing individuals on a number of flight-related aptitudes. Performance on the tests permitted assigning candidates to one of nine stanines. This rank proved a powerful predictor of performance in flight training. Figure 3 reflects just how powerful the tests were. Interpretively, individuals scoring in the highest stanine (9) completed primary pilot training, on the average, in 96 of 100 cases. Scorers in Stanine 1 were a far longer shot. On the average, three failures in this category would have to be suffered for each success. Figure 3 implied many useful guides for policy, and soon only individuals scoring in Stanines 7 to 9 were accepted for flight training. The choice was made as a complex function of the anticipated demand, the expected cost, and the resources available. The choice, then, required some more or less arbitrary judgments, which had to be made and are important. Successful testing decreased the error margin substantially, and testing's value was therefore high.

The choice of any cutting-off point on any psychological test used for selection purposes is a difficult and final one. Greater accuracy is always much to be desired. Such cutting-off points should be interpreted generously, then, particularly when small differences are at issue. Even

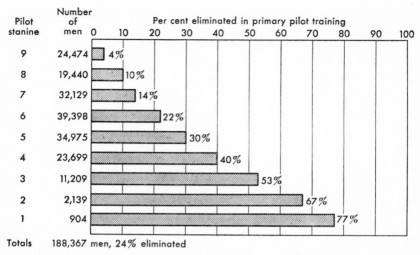

Figure 3. **Stanine Rank and Success in Primary Pilot Training. Based upon Donald E. Super and John O. Crites, Appraising Vocational Fitness, rev. ed. (New York: Harper & Row, Publishers, Incorporated, 1962), p. 25.**

the most generous spirit, however, must be restrained by one datum: performance demands that are very much greater than an individual's capabilities often will encourage despair, resignation, and less effort than the individual could expend.[22]

Some qualification of this position is necessary, but not much. Some individuals do rise to challenges to provide wholly unexpected performances. Indeed, we are beginning to learn how to isolate such individuals.[23] But for now we are pretty much left with this gross generalization: misplaced generosity in interpreting the cutting-off points of valid and reliable tests often will prove self-defeating, hurting just those who are to be helped. Certainly, whatever the other costs, man gains little from the "freedom" to face a challenge which he very probably cannot handle. This is the case even in an affluent society.

The point holds for tasks more humble than flying. Consider an assembly operation requiring some mechanical aptitude. One firm hired a number of applicants who passed a short and easy test of the required abilities, and it also hired untested applicants who seemed employable. Soon 49 per cent of the latter group left work. Only 7.8 per cent of the tested batch suffered the same fate.[24] Only a curious calculus could demonstrate that nontesting was preferable to testing in this case, whether for the individual or the organization.

It is a considerable jump from testing for aptitudes to testing for personality characteristics. This is a measured statement concerning a subject that has known little moderation. On one hand, many applications have not shown due respect for the difficulties involved. On the other hand, many critics of personality testing have transmuted difficulty into impossibility. *The Organization Man* makes the attempt to leap from testing aptitudes to testing personality characteristics appear quixotic. The leap (we are told) covers all of the territory "from the measurable to the unmeasurable." The purpose here is to put some fear of the difficulty of testing into the overexuberant advocate and to fault the rhetoric of the overzealous critic.

Many examples illustrate the usefulness of psychological testing of personality characteristics. Consider a relatively accessible example, the measurement of accident-proneness. The approach here is through Jenkins's Job Attitudes Survey which taps seven "syndromes," or basic patterns of related personality factors, that seem related to the tendency to have repeated injuries or accidents. These syndromes include:[25]

1. *Attentiveness.* The injury-repeater's attention tends to be more easily distracted than the safe worker's from the task he is working on.
2. *Judiciousness.* The injury-repeater reveals a relative unawareness or lack of discernment of the need for acting prudently.
3. *Group-dissociative independence.* The injury-repeater tends to feel less inclined to accept or comply with rules, standards, and social customs.
4. *Personal-social sensitivity.* The injury-repeater's feelings and attitudes are less easily swayed by either the feelings or actions of other people.
5. *Attitude toward pain.* The injury-repeater tends not to mind being in pain, and he may even get a thrill out of it.
6. *Self-assurance.* The injury-repeater exhibits a kind of self-confidence that militates against the feeling that any forethought or preventive care may be needed.
7. *Social orientation.* The injury-repeater tends to have aggressive, self-assertive attitudes towards others. He is not so likely to be interested in teamwork or cooperating in the achievement of group goals.

TABLE 3   SCORES ON JENKINS'S JOB ATTITUDES SURVEY AND ACCIDENT RECORDS

Safety Index Median	NN, % *	Neg, % †
High	81	31
Low	19	69
	100	100

* NN = no negligent accidents or no accidents.
† Neg = one or more negligent accidents.
From Thomas N. Jenkins, "Identifying the Accident-prone Employee,"
Personnel, vol. 38 (July–August, 1961), p. 59.

One attempt to validate the Job Attitudes Survey (JAS) suggests its usefulness. Using data from a large trucking firm, Jenkins classified drivers into two categories: those who had no accidents or were non-negligent participants in accidents during their period of employment by the firm, and those who had one or more accidents in which they had been negligent. Each driver then was tested on JAS, with a low score presumably indicating a great tendency toward accident-proneness. Table 3 tells an obvious tale: drivers with records of negligence had higher JAS scores than drivers with perfect safety records. The test was relatively successful in measuring what it purported to measure, then, and particularly so in the case of the accident-free drivers.

Some uses of such a test come to mind readily, assuming that other attempts at validation yield similar results. The trucking firm might hire only drivers scoring above the median in Table 3, with the expectation that a formidable proportion of these high scorers would compile no-negligence records. If the drivers in Jenkins's study are representative, the firm might expect to reduce the number of drivers hired who become negligent participants in accidents by some 50 per cent. Not all negligent drivers would be eliminated by this procedure, and some careful drivers would be lost. Varying the cutting-off point would determine how many fell into the two categories.

The choice and interpretation of some specific cutting-off point would depend on many factors, not the least of which is the level of certainty about whether accident-proneness is a more or less constant characteristic of individuals or whether it is more basically a result of a reaction to some current stress, either on or off the job.[26] The issue has not yet been settled, but Jenkins's work at least provides some reason for operating in terms of his conception at the present state of our relative ignorance.

Personality characteristics, then, are measurable. Other evidence of the apparent validity of particular tests for particular purposes might be noted, such as for the choice of personnel for work at isolated radar installations.[27] And the reliability of some tests over remarkably long periods of time can be documented,[28] a happenstance that suggests that whatever is being studied is not some fugitive quality somehow beyond measurement.

These brief illustrations are not a whitewashing of psychological testing, for they spotlight certain limitations of testing which cannot be neglected. Let these limitations be set down. First, the examples fit man to some structure or task. Many critics of personality testing stress the point and conclude that conformity is thereby encouraged, that "different" ideas are lost, and so on. Their charge is a serious one. Subsequent sections must accept the challenge to use testing and its results to guide the tailoring of structure and jobs to man, as opposed to discarding the man who does not fit the structure or the job.

Second, the most convenient psychological tests in general—and the ones employed illustratively above—are "actuarial." That is, as Saul Gellerman explains, they "aim for an objective measurement of the probability that a person will behave in a particular way." [29] The search is for probable mathematical relations between qualities that can be measured (like intelligence) and some properties whose prediction is significant (like performance on a particular job).

One pays a price for playing the heavy odds in *predicting* the likely behavior of many individuals under similar conditions, as opposed to *describing* a specific individual under all specific conditions. In the matter of accident-proneness, for example, high scores on the Job Attitudes Survey were gained by only 81 per cent of the nonnegligent drivers. Some 19 per cent were low scorers but careful drivers. It is not pleasant, even in the abstract, to sacrifice 19 per cent of the capable, unless one is content to play the game of claiming that the whole batch avoided accidents by blind luck. Moreover, seldom will the score of any individual on any psychological test permit definite predictions about his behavior, and an individual's score may vary considerably over several administrations of the same test. There are sometimes even great problems with the reliability of tests of physiological character- istics that use mechanical equipment.[30]

Hence this analysis is challenged to recognize and to compensate for the built-in limits of the actuarial approach. Meeting the challenge requires a view of testing that recognizes the limitations of an actuarial test in specific cases, and that evaluates all minor differences in scores as just that and nothing more. In addition, psychological testing should be used in assignment decisions, rather than for in or out judgments. That is, individuals might be assigned to various work teams on the basis of differences in their interests and personality characteristics, as well as in their aptitudes. Those low on sociability, for example, might be grouped with other lows. This contrasts sharply with rejecting all who score low on sociability, which puts a great deal of faith in one administration of one test and has other weaknesses in the bargain. The assignment approach is not congenial to the one-best bias of the traditional theory of organization, to be sure, but this is merely another datum urging the reevaluation of the traditional theory.

Third, personality testing can be a danger to privacy. Indeed, any test is an invasion of privacy of any individual who does not wish to take it. There also have been cases of more or less deliberate soliciting of deeply personal data which, to boot, are not particularly useful for operating purposes. Some "clinical methods" are most likely to dredge up such information. Projectives like the Rorschach Ink Blot Test, after all, were developed to aid in the treatment of the mentally ill and they are consequently oriented toward exploring the normally "private." Large amounts of data on sex, hostility, fear, guilt, and the like are thus gathered by projectives. But the effort seldom seems worth the candle. As Gellerman concluded: "What went on in a normal person's unconscious and what went on in his career did not seem to have the direct, pertinent relationship that the projective enthusiasts had hoped to find." [31] Nor does misguided enthusiasm of this kind exhaust the reasons for invasion of the private. Psychological tests have been used as a subtle espionage technique to limit the hiring of employees who had pro-union sentiments,[32] and this is not the worst of it.

The implied problems are consequential. Drawing a precise line between the private and the nonprivate seems inappropriate, however, even if it is possible. Basically, a positive approach seems more useful than drawing more or less arbitrary limits. As Gellerman observed: "The only sensible way to draw the line is not in terms of what is asked, but rather in terms of what is done with the answer." Let us follow this lead awhile. Basically, the positive approach involves making the testing experience increasingly helpful and decreasingly threatening. This might mean considerably less testing than at present, waiting on the development of highly reliable and valid measuring instruments that have demonstrated associations with performance. Certainly it implies the dominant use of testing in assignment decisions.

Invasions of privacy, then, may be limited by increasing the area into which the testor is freely admitted. And this increase will come as a result of restricting the use of tests to cases in which a legitimate and work-related need for information exists, by using tests in a rewarding way as much as possible, and by demonstrating to the individual the usefulness *to himself* of the testing he underwent.

Fourth, these first three limitations of psychological testing imply an increased sophistication in the development and use of psychological tests. This is not the old dodge that the limitations of science can be cured, but only by more science. There are two distinct but related tasks facing psychological testing, and this analysis takes on both of them. There is what may be called the "internal task," the development of tests of specific attitudes and personality characteristics that are significant in the sense that they are associated consistently with such important factors as job performance. The following section will outline the kind of work necessary for this internal task, building upon the critical analysis to this point. The more science in this work, the better.

Applications of psychological testing also face another task, a task in which science helps a great deal in some respects and very little in others. This has been called goal-based, empirical work. It refers to the scientific prescription of the ways and means of attaining those values that are desired. What is desired, the values to be achieved, cannot be generated by any scientific operation. Recall that scientific operations deal only with the existential, not the desirable. The Judaeo-Christian Ethic attempts to provide an *explicit* statement of values to give new direction to psychological testing, to replace the traditional theory which has guided much work in testing in organizations. If its rationale is destroyed and replaced by the Judaeo-Christian Ethic, that is to say, psychological testing will follow suit over the long run. This is not such a big "if." Here scientific work does a job: it will support the practicality under present conditions of approaching the J-C Ethic. The role of scientific work is only supporting, however. For the Judaeo-Christian Ethic rests upon a moral order that exists independently of our ability to act upon it at any point in time. It is merely a convenient datum, then, that we can now act on the J-C Ethic.

Whyte was both right and wrong, in sum. He was correct in emphasizing the relevance of values to the use and to certain stages of the development of personality testing; and he was painfully on target in noting that "organizational values" have on occasion captivated the scientist into neglecting or misinterpreting reality. No full-fledged personality testing, in short, can rest on science and nothing more. But Whyte was at least vague in arguing that the internal development of psychological testing was perforce unscientific. And he certainly was incorrect in implying that only the traditional theory of organization could guide the development of psychological testing or that only the Individualistic Ethic and the Social Ethic could underlay any workable theory of organization. Whyte oversimplified matters at best, and confused them at worst.

TOWARD THIRD-GENERATION TESTING

Some Directions for Development

The debate about psychological testing suffers from its preoccupation with the existing state of the art. Protagonists commonly are content with whatever magic existing tests have wrought, so great are the apparent uses of testing in the reduction of training costs or in the placement of individuals in jobs well suited to their tastes and talents. Antagonists happily accept this restrictive ground rule for debate, and vigorously score such features of existing tests:

1. The common lack of impressive correlations of tests with measures of performance
2. The ease of faking many tests whose intent is transparent

3. The invasion of privacy possible in testing
4. The ham-handed way in which test scores are sometimes interpreted
5. The tendency of some personality tests to deprive the organization of rare talents

Although controversy can have its many virtues, controversy in this case can be given useful direction by analyzing three generations of testing.[33] This will have the happy effect of imputing substance to the arguments of both protagonist and antagonist of testing, which takes off some of the polemical edge implicit in a right-or-wrong impasse. In outline, the criticisms abstracted above are not inherent in psychological testing. Rather they may be conceived as limitations of early generations of testing experience that later work must strive to eliminate. There is nothing sacrosanct here about the choice of three generations, of course. Some observers will settle for no less than six.[34]

The three generations of psychological testing may be outlined boldly. The first generation—going back to the years around World War I—utilized simple paper-and-pencil tests; the traits to be measured were narrow and atomistically conceived; the tests often were transparent and easily fakable; and validation was sparse. A second generation of testing was similarly hamstrung by a limited conception of its task but was far more refined in methods and techniques. This second generation, roughly, spanned the years between the two great wars. A third generation of testing, triggered by the need to meet the massive selection problems of World War II, reflects many evidences of improvement in concept and methods. Its broadened scope stresses aptitude and personality properties as they interact in specific situational contexts. Vastly more telling attention has been given to reliability and validity, in addition. And the greater subtlety of actuarial and projective tests poses a stiff challenge to the faker.

The usefulness of distinguishing generations of testing also may be demonstrated from the point of view of one particular problem of psychological testing, that of validity. J. G. Jenkins's treatment is a summary reflection of the emphases in validity over the years.[35] Thus the experience of World War I left students of testing with a deep respect for the *necessity* of validation; the following three decades saw many improvements in the *techniques* of validation; and the contemporary emphasis has been upon the *adequacy of the bases of validation.*

A firm conclusion may be built upon the foundation of generations of testing. Much psychological testing in organizations still reflects the firm impress of the first two generations of testing. The work of the third generation has not surmounted the major limitations of earlier work, and much less has it overcome the popularity of older tests. Thus Super and Crites could conclude in 1962 that:[36]

> Despite the great progress in psychological testing since its beginnings, knowledge of the characteristics which can be measured still leaves a great deal to be desired. . . . The measuring instruments we now use even for the most adequately measured traits such as intelligence and vocational interest are still not completely understood; those we use for measuring personality traits such as general adjustment, introversion, and the need for recognition are still in embryonic stages; and there are no methods of testing creative imagination, persistence, and certain other traits and abilities which are often assumed to be important and which laboratory studies and other types of investigations have suggested may actually exist.

The characteristics of third-generation testing that will improve upon this state of affairs and increase man's freedom in organizations are within our awareness, fortunately. Identifying the several major components of psychological testing helps structure matters. The analysis of Super and Crites will guide the way, if some liberties will be taken with their work.[37]

JOB ANALYSIS

Understanding the demands of a specific job is a prerequisite to the development of tests that will measure the aptitudes or personality characteristics that will tend to be related to successful performance and to the operator's satisfaction. This requirement often has been neglected despite its significance, which was demonstrated most forcefully by the testing program for pilot candidates during World War II. The program was both highly successful and based upon an intensive job analysis.[38]

SELECTION OF CHARACTERISTICS TO BE TESTED

Job analysis provides the test constructor with an idea of the aptitudes and personality characteristics necessary for successful performance. Perhaps "very rough idea" is more accurate. For just what apti-tudes and personality characteristics are relevant? We have some idea of what some of them are. But the ideal is some parsimonious set of properties, each of which measures a unique and distinct something. In practice, we are far from this ideal. Indeed, Cronbach likens the psychological tester to a hunter seeking a beast that no one has ever seen but whose existence is certain. The hunter must decide which of many animal tracks to follow, based upon some preconception—how-ever vague—of the characteristics of his quarry. And that preconcep-tion will be very influential in determining the quarry which the hunter will bag. As Cronbach explained: "Binet was in just this position. He knew there must be something like intelligence, since its everyday effects could be seen, but he could not describe what he wished to measure, as it had never been isolated." [39]

The test constructor today can rely on the expeditions of countless hunters. So matters are not in an impossible state, although they are difficult enough to be more than an ample test for even the most skilled investigator intent on isolating the characteristics relevant to perform-ance on some particular task.

SELECTION OF THE CRITERIA OF SUCCESS

The criteria of success selected will significantly influence the validity of any test. The matter is as complex as it is significant, unfortunately, what with the several distinctions between types of criteria and with the mixed evidence concerning the degree to which tests predict one or another of the criteria. Just as, unfortunately, the question of the ade-quacy of the bases for validation is commonly given short shrift.

TEST CONSTRUCTION AND STANDARDIZATION

We may gloss over the arduous labors of test construction with only a brief note about the need to standardize the test in terms of some meaningful reference group. There are pitfalls aplenty in the choice of such reference groups. Thus if some relevant aptitude test is standard-ized on a batch of persons experienced in some occupation, for exam-ple, convenient measures of the success of these individuals in their work often exist. But the question remains, "Is the test really meaning-ful for individuals who have not yet entered the occupation?" And if the reference group is composed of individuals who are not experienced in the profession, then what?

VALIDATION AND CROSS-VALIDATION

Validation involves the statistical analysis of the relations of test results and criteria of performance. Validation can be a delicate and tedious matter under the best of conditions, not the least touchy matter being the cross-validation of scoring keys based on the so-called "item validation" on a comparable batch of subjects to ascertain whether similar scoring of the second batch yields as high a validity as the original batch.

FACTOR ANALYSIS AND FACTOR VALIDATION

High correlations of test scores and criteria of performance, however, do not end matters. Such results merely raise a further question, that of the number of independent factors necessary to account for the observed relations. Normally, single tests lack precision: they are sloppy in that they measure some aspects of several significant properties. The goal of unidimensional tests may be approached via factor analysis. It is a sophisticated mathematical technique that permits a preliminary judgment of the more limited set of dimensions actually tapped by some battery of tests. The factors thus isolated, in turn, may suggest more convenient and efficient ways of measuring the intended qualities. For instance, test items may be dropped because they contribute little information of relevance, or new items or tests may be introduced to increase the predictive accuracy of the battery of tests. And all this is a very complicated and time-consuming business.

TOWARD THIRD-GENERATION TESTING

Compatibility as a Prototype

Even brief recitation of the components of third-generation testing counsels avoidance of two extreme positions. On the one hand, testing is not to be trifled with. Certainly the administration of a brief canned test or two, although it has captivated many in authority in organizations, must come off suspect. On the other hand, the strong temptation to chuck the whole testing business often has been felt.

Both trifling and temptation must be resisted. Thus no tests meet the above requirements; all leave appreciable room for improvement. However, several tests provide considerable hope for the relatively proximate future of serving organizational needs as well as that first desideratum of the Judaeo-Christian Ethic: to make work more acceptable and less threatening to the employee.

The focus here will be upon one of these promising approaches to testing major personality characteristics, Schutz's work with "general predispositions to action." His work has great promise of meeting many of the objections raised about the first two generations of psychological testing, although it hardly meets them all.

Schutz's basic intention was to isolate the "fundamental interpersonal relations orientations" of individuals, so as to assemble groups with specific properties. These orientations were thought to derive from the earliest experiences of a child with his siblings, peers, and parents, and they were considered so pervasive as to be retained fundamentally throughout adulthood. The orientations also were relevant to work in that persons with fundamentally opposed interpersonal orientations would experience great difficulty not only in "getting along" but also in "putting out" because of more or less conscious obstructionism.

Schutz settled on three basic predispositions, drawing upon a wide variety of applicable research.[40] If we avoid the complexities, these predispositions can be identified as:

1. *A power orientation,* intended to determine the predisposition of the individual to seek to become a powerful figure or to seek to be subject to a powerful figure
2. *A personalness-counterpersonalness orientation,* intended to determine an individual's predisposition to seek warm and close interpersonal relations, as (for example) in reacting to people in terms of their personal liking rather than in terms of their formal status
3. *An assertiveness orientation,* intended to determine the predisposition of an individual to make his views known in group situations

A longish questionnaire was designed to measure the degree to which individuals might be described in terms of these three orientations.

This was ambitious enough, but Schutz went on to make interesting use of the data measuring the fundamental interpersonal relations orientations of individuals. He used these data to study one aspect of the problem of the assignment of individuals to work groups, by varying the compatibility of the basic behavioral predispositions of group members. In combination with data on the intelligence of subjects, Schutz constructed three types of groups according to a complex design. In general, compatible groups were provided with a single "focal person" (FP) around whom group processes would be likely to center because of his high assertiveness, high intelligence, and low dependence. Focal persons with high scores on personalness were placed in one of the two varieties of compatible groups; and those with high scores on counterpersonalness were placed in the other variety. Incompatible groups were given two focal persons each, one high on personalness and the other high on counterpersonalness.

Without going into further detail, the overall working presumption was that compatible groups of both types would be able to mobilize very considerable forces toward the performance of a common task. An incompatible group, in contrast, would be more likely to dissipate large amounts of energy in intergroup conflict.

Some complex experimental work helps support the working notion that compatibility is of prime importance in organizing. A summary of several major results of this experimentation reinforces Schutz's guiding hunch. The effort has its limitations, particularly since it will be necessary to summarize the results of several major studies. This must detract from the richness of the available data, if it does not restrict the data to an interpretive straitjacket. The risk will be run, however.

Four major emphases suggest compatibility's relevance for life in organizations. First, both types of compatible groups had clearer and more stable leadership structures. Both Compatible-Personal (Com-Per) and Compatible-Counterpersonal (Com-Countper) groups cohered closely around their focal person (FP). Thus FP in compatible groups of both types was almost always identified as the "leader." Moreover, FP strongly tended to be chosen by his "main-support" member as a desired workmate and as "most liked." Incompatible groups, in contrast, had unclear and unstable leadership structures. For example, one incompatible group experienced such great disagreement about its leadership structure that members were forced into the daily rotation of certain tasks of headship.

Second, compatible and incompatible groups differed markedly in their "cohesiveness," that is, in their ability to stick together. Experimental work from other sources directly supports the conclusion.[41] As might be expected, incompatible groups tended to develop fractious ties. Thus one such group alternated between marked friendliness and an aloofness that implied little mutual involvement. In contrast, one Com-Per group developed such security that its members felt free to direct bantering aggression at one another and their task performance, thereby dissipating whatever tension existed and tying group members more firmly together. Such constructive byplay, of course, is one of the characteristics of close interpersonal relations. Similar aggression under other conditions might have disastrous effects.

Third, compatible groups were more successful in developing and enforcing standards of behavior. Both Com-Per and Com-Countper groups, for example, had records of high-level performance. Without exception, incompatible groups could not similarly control the behavior of their members. They were the poorest producers on all tasks. Members of one of these groups even gave up because the experimental task was "too hard." Since the incompatible groups possessed intelligence sufficient for better performance, much of their failure must be marked down to emotional difficulties induced by their low compatibility.

Fourth, these significant similarities between the two types of compatible groups developed despite other significant differences. Broadly, Com-Per groups developed what may be called a supportive, or democratic, atmosphere. Com-Countper groups might be, termed authoritarian in their basic behavioral style.

Not a few observers, including Schutz, were surprised that comparable performance could be attained in groups with such differing styles. The surprise is understandable, but it is inappropriate. For that surprise reflects the bias of the Social Ethic toward a supportive atmosphere, which is advocated to replace the authoritarian style consistent with the Individualistic Ethic. But even as things changed, they remained the same in an important sense. The bias toward a supportive atmosphere often is conceived in the same one-best way as the authoritarian style. This is inelegant. True enough, many (perhaps, most) individuals in the "American environment" prefer a nonauthoritarian atmosphere, and their performance might suffer in general if their preference were not met. Most observers have made a law of nature of what seems a preference of a majority of subjects, however. Certainly this law of nature did not apply to the Com-Countper groups. Nor were their members a part of that assumed majority whose experimental reactions support the Social Ethic. Real attention to the assignment problem, that is, permits making the best of what all people are.

Lest the rhetoric be too convincing, note that the available research is not up to the complete job sketched above for personality testing in organizations. Schutz made effective use of personality as well as of aptitude (intelligence) tests to measure qualities significant in the performance on the experimental tasks, for example, and his educated guesses were accurate enough. But the limits of the existing knowledge of task characteristics plagued his research. Even the relatively simple experimental tasks proved more than a match for the existing ability to isolate dimensions that differentiated tasks in terms of (for example) the degree to which successful performance requires harmonious interpersonal relations. The variegated tasks in the real world of organizations pose an even greater challenge.

In sum, while the study of compatibility overcomes the limits of much psychological testing in a number of significant particulars, it falls victim to these inadequacies in others.

Despite the brevity of the review of the major findings of Schutz's work, and despite the limitations of that work, research on the assignment problem via compatibility implies an intriguing potential for breaking the present general impasse in the testing of personality characteristics of relevance for organizations. Several factors contribute to this potential. Thus attention to compatibility improves upon the major presumption that there is a one-best constellation of personality properties, which presumption flies in the face of the commonplace observation that diverse individuals may successfully perform similar activities in the same organization. Being rid of the presumption also saves psychological testing from the question of what to do with the throwaways who do not fit some one-best personality profile. Compatibility has an immediate relevance to work, in addition, both directly and via hypothetical constructs that reach a wide variety of significant phenomena in organizations. Finally, testing for compatibility is complex enough to deter frivolous use, and the approach also is well designed for making nonpunitive assignment decisions. These last two characteristics make the best of the limits of the actuarial approach. With it all, testing for compatibility does not probe into areas usually considered private, such as the state of the testee's sexual life.

Most significant, the focus on compatibility permits fitting organization to man. If some men are pervasively differentiated from their fellows, the course of wisdom requires accommodating organization structure and managerial techniques to this fact of life. The task is a delicate one, and infinitely more difficult than crying that organization man is suffocating in his own collective offal or promising that man can live in some idyllic and uncomplicated state.

Emphasis upon compatibility has practical and moral advantages, then. The emphasis meets many of the objections to much testing. Moreover, high compatibility was associated with high output and high satisfaction of group members. That is a desirable combination.

Nor is compatibility a quality that can only be conjured up in the psychologist's laboratory. Consider a new plant, staffed with new employees, in a one-company town. Its work teams seemed highly compatible. "Morale was high, the accident rate was low, as were the absence rate, the scrap rate, etc. Production exceeded expectations and continued to show a gradual, steady rise." A cutback in the firm's operations, however, was necessary. Consequently, at least four or five men from each of the compatible work groups—which had ten to twenty members—were "bumped" to make places for other employees of the firm in the same town who had greater seniority. Compatibility was ill-advisedly disturbed. Although the bumping procedure was known to the men and accepted by them, awkward social dynamics were set in motion by it. These dynamics proved difficult to stop. We are informed that:[42]

The result was disastrous. Production rates slumped 50 per cent. Accident rates, absence rates, rate of scrap produced, all increased alarmingly. It took several months for the operations of this plant to recover to the point at which these various indices reached company standards. It was a matter of years before they again climbed above the standards for the company as a whole.

FITTING ORGANIZATION TO MAN

Structural Innovations and Supporting Techniques

This analysis would fall far short if it merely said a nice thing or two about compatibility and how it permits approaching the Judaeo-Christian Ethic without sacrificing organizational effectiveness. The very ability to say nice things about compatibility, of course, implies much about the inadequacy of the traditional theory of organization.

Matters go far deeper. Schutz's approach and psychological testing consistent with the traditional theory are at sixes and sevens. The authority relations prescribed by the traditional theory are appropriate for Compatible-Counterpersonal groups. But these authoritative relations —being based upon the criterion of formal status and being authoritarian in style—are hardly suitable for Compatible-Personal groups. The awkwardness of the one-best bias of the traditional theory, then, shows up in two senses. It preaches neglect of one type of compatibility, which is serious enough. In the bargain, it directs attention to an uncommon type of compatibility. Perhaps seven or eight individuals out of every ten tested thus far tend toward the personal orientation.

Seeking as it does to avoid falling short, this section outlines some of the broad structural relations necessary to capitalize on man's differences; and it also suggests managerial techniques capable of supporting such structure. Both structure and techniques are consistent with the Judaeo-Christian Ethic, as detailed analysis will show. From another point of view, this section previews the detailed analysis of the organizational environment within which man can be more free, and responsibly so in that his freedom is increased as he contributes more effectively.

Let the focus be upon the functions or processes emphasized by the traditional theory, to begin. Assume the integration of processes A, B, and C yields product P_1. The traditional theory prescribes the type of structure sketched in Figure 4, if we go no further up the hierarchy than the first level of supervision. Since several processes A, B, and C must be linked closely, it would be awkward (for example) to have S_A and S_C supervise Com-Countper work units while S_B supervised a Com-Per unit. This would be asking for trouble. The potential for conflict between the three units is great enough in the general case. In sum,

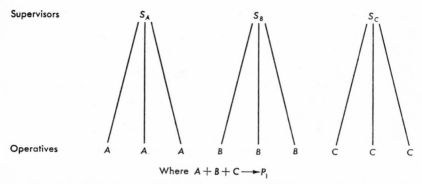

Where $A + B + C \longrightarrow P_1$

Figure 4. A Simplified Structure Prescribed by the Traditional Theory of Organization.

the traditional structure places a premium on the delicate and continuous cooperation of the three activities while it organizes them into separate units that need not have the same interests, and commonly do not. The ubiquitous result is interdepartmental conflict, a classic disease of organized life patterned after the traditional theory of organization. If the several units are staffed with individuals having sharply opposed personality predispositions, of course, interdepartmental conflict will be particularly intense.

Ways out of such difficulties do exist, but they have significant disadvantages. All work units might be staffed with Com-Countper individuals, for example, just as the traditional theory implies. The practical difficulty is the limited supply of such individuals. Make all of the units Com-Per, then? This seems reasonable enough, and the advice is implied by the Social Ethic. But what of the individuals who score high on counterpersonalness? Both approaches suffer from the punitive use of psychological testing for in or out decisions, a grave liability indeed.

The illustration permits generalization. All similar ways out of the difficulties encouraged by the traditional theory of organization are similarly self-defeating. When all is said and done, therefore, one still must redesign structure and techniques that consider individual differences while they avoid the pitfalls of blending such differences into organized effort. For compatibility under the traditional theory of organization is a costly accident, achieved only via high labor turnover as individuals search for more congenial surroundings; or it may be paid for in terms of chronic dissatisfaction as people chafe at their work. Either state of affairs is unfortunate. A single semiskilled hire in a large company might cost perhaps $500, a considerable burden indeed when turnover rates commonly run above 25 per cent per year. In the case of executives, their costly turnover commonly is due, not to any lack of technical skill, but rather to interpersonal difficulties that often suggest incompatibility. There is no convenient running away from compatibility.

If one cannot avoid the redesign of the traditional theory of organization, however, many of the benefits of compatibility may be achieved without an elaborate testing program. Those who cannot wait on inexorable progress in psychological testing may utilize some poor man's approaches to compatibility that often have the desired effects. Self-choice of members of a work unit is such a technique. It is hardly complex, and certainly not foolproof. But it seems capable of engaging many of the forces associated with compatibility, and it illustrates what is possible in the simultaneous serving of individual needs, organizational demands, and the Judaeo-Christian Ethic.

Self-choice is a simple technique that has been underexploited because the traditional theory of organization does not encourage its use. Elaborate psychological testing programs have gone on apace in ways consistent with that guiding theory while bucking a tide of research that provides little support for crucial aspects of the undertaking. In contrast, self-choice almost literally was not thought of until recently by students of organization. Early uses of self-choice were centered in emotional therapy, and the approach even there gained substantial support only in the 1940s and 1950s. Large-scale administrative applications of the notion—as in the assignment of troops in the Korean War—have an even briefer history.

This thumbnail history permits two conclusions. Thus, the literature investigating the subtleties of self-choice—and subtleties there are aplenty—is but little developed. Practice is markedly characterized by "above-choice," in addition, by which we mean assignment on grounds superficially convenient for management. Such grounds include alphabetical and random assignment. In contrast, self-choice taps factors that are behaviorally relevant for employees.

The simplicity of self-choice has much on its side. Even with ample discounting for the undeveloped state of the art, some evidence supports an important role for self-choice in enlarging the area of individual freedom in organizations while serving organization purposes. The comparison of self-choice versus traditional above-choice methods of assigning workers to teams on a construction project provides useful illustration. Some seventy-four carpenters and bricklayers were involved; and the work required the intimate cooperation of the two trades. After a period of nine months under an above-choice assignment of team members, the craftsmen were given an opportunity to name three choices for a work partner. Some two-thirds of the employees subsequently were assigned to work with their first or second choices. An experimental period of twenty months followed. Table 4 summarizes three crucial aspects of performance under the two conditions of above-choice. The table also presents the prior estimates by engineers of the magnitude of the costs thought to be reasonable.

The self-choice crews outdid the above-choice crews on all three measures of performance. Two of the comparisons—labor cost index and materials cost index—were significantly different at usually accepted levels of statistical significance. Differences in turnover are not so clearly due to nonrandom factors. The savings due to the self-choice condition ran to some 5 per cent of the total costs of production. In

TABLE 4   SELF-CHOICE VS. ABOVE-CHOICE IN ASSIGNMENTS TO WORK TEAMS COMPARED IN TERMS OF THREE MEASURES OF PERFORMANCE

Variable	Mean
1. Turnover:	
a. Before experimental period (9 months)	3.11
b. During experimental period (20 months)	0.27
2. Labor Cost Index, per row of housing units:	
a. Engineers' prior estimate	37.20
b. Before experimental period (9 months)	36.66
c. During experimental period (20 months)	32.22
3. Materials Cost Index, per row of housing units:	
a. Engineer's prior estimate	33.50
b. Before experimental period	33.00
c. After experimental period	31.00

The data are taken from Raymond H. Van Zelst, "Sociometrically Selected Work Teams Increase Productivity," *Personnel Psychology,* vol. 5 (1952), p. 182.

addition, the employees were more satisfied, if we judge from the lower turnover of the self-choice crews as well as from other evidence that cannot be reported here.

Self-choice has much to recommend it, then. Operational efficiency increased. The Judaeo-Christian approach also was more closely approached by the technique which increased the psychological acceptability of work and decreased the threat to the individual.

Nor is this the whole of it. The results are particularly striking because over 30 per cent of the craftsmen were assigned to work either with their third choices or with individuals they did not choose. These cases would profit little from self-choice, and probably would reduce the differences between the self-choice and the above-choice conditions. Consistently, the major difficulties during the experimental period occurred in the work units that were composed of third-choices or the mutually unchosen. Whatever led individuals to choose one another, then, it had a patent influence on behavior; and whatever it was that the workers perceived, that something eluded management.

This brief introduction to self-choice may seem to have done its job too well. Given the efficacy of self-choice, why bother with the traditional theory of organization? And is it really necessary to supplant the Individualistic Ethic and the Social Ethic with the Judaeo-Christian Ethic? The point seems solid enough, but only if we neglect one striking feature of the results in Table 4. The control of the group environment associated with high compatibility could be applied so as to restrict production, as well as to enhance it. No doubt some work teams in the experimental batch did use their group strength to restrict output, although they were a small minority. This probability makes the differences in Table 4 striking indeed.

These considerations go to a single point. By itself, self-choice cannot do the full job. Structural innovation will be necessary so that self-choice does not merely complicate the problems of control. The traditional theory of organization severely tempts self-choice units in organizations to utilize their group power at the expense of the formal organization and other work units. Let us go back again to the work units in Figure 4 organized around processes A, B, and C, and assume that all have been assembled by self-choice. Now if work unit B decides to use its power to restrict output, given high compatibility, it can exert much influence to that end. The heart of the matter is this. Only the three work units acting in close unison can raise output. That requires comparatively great social skills. However, one work unit may be able to force output down. Thus B's slower pace might lead employees at A to reduce their output, for why should they knock themselves out under the circumstances? Moreover, the alternative might be a nagging hostility between the two work units. And C can process only as much as B forwards to it.

Put it all together. There are great pressures implicit in the traditional theory of organization toward restricting output as the most convenient way of using group power to control the environment. Creating high compatibility in an organization patterned after the traditional structure only heightens these pressures.

The argument is not an artifact of the simplicity of Figure 4. That argument does not elaborately contemplate its own umbilicus. There are many examples in practice of the dynamics sketched above. Although details such as programs of payment and the like can encourage significant departures from the dismal generalization above even where the traditional theory of organization is respected, the traditional theory tends to level output downward. In the rubber industry, for example, relatively small units organized by processes—often at or near the end of some production line—can be the tail that wags the dog of thousands of workers performing operations earlier in the sequence. "Wildcatting," the calling of unauthorized strikes, is their major technique for influencing the pace of work at other stations. Relevantly, also, where the traditional theory of organization is commonly violated in appropriate ways, as is common in the electrical goods industry, the same phenomenon is far more rare.

Self-choice or no, then, concern with structural innovation cannot be avoided, and considerable attention will be given to various "appropriate violations" of the traditional theory of organization throughout this book. Here Figure 5 merely sketches the kind of structure that can contain the dynamics of self-choice and can make good use of both types of compatibility, Com-Per and Com-Countper. The individual units of organization are autonomous, and thus personality differences between the units are not as significant as in a Figure 4 structure. For example, S_1 could head a Com-Per unit; and S_2 might have Com-

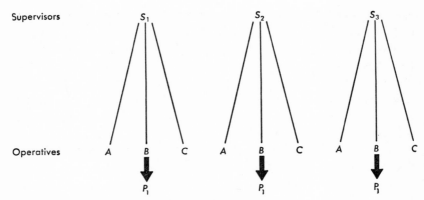

Figure 5. A Simplified Unorthodox Organization Structure.

Countper personnel. Performance would not suffer thereby. Indeed, it might be enhanced, for each unit of organization can raise output independently. Moreover, the performance of the three units is strictly and easily comparable, a datum that reduces the probability that high compatibility will be utilized to enforce restrictions of output.

FITTING ORGANIZATION TO MAN

Denouement and Prologue

Two conclusions wriggle out of the foregoing mass of detail, and demand note. First, available dimensions for both personality and aptitude testing leave much to be desired. The testing of intelligence may serve as an example. The technology is quite advanced in this area, but even intelligence scores have a mixed usefulness in predicting performance in organizations. There are sluggards who perform well enough, and many bright lights who do poorly. Intelligence scores commonly predict something like only 25 per cent of the variance in performance records. Indeed, a revolution in the scope and meaning of intelligence testing seems to be in full swing.[43]

Cries of utter despair are not in order, however. Although most measures of such basic personality characteristics have been crudely defined, testing for such personality characteristics has enormous potential for assuring that work is psychologically acceptable to employees. This is the case despite the cries of critics, such as William H. Whyte,

Jr., for whom testing means only a violation of the privacy of individuals.

There are risks in the use of testing, to be sure, and quackeries aplenty in its practice. But the payoffs—for individuals and for the organization—seem well worth the risks and the humbug. These payoffs seem particularly probable if effective attention is given to the redesign of organization structure and managerial techniques consistent with the Judaeo-Christian Ethic, and this to the ends that both structure and techniques make fuller use of man's diversity and that accountability for performance is made more certain.

Footnotes: CHAPTER 4

1. Albert Lepawsky (ed.), *Administration* (New York: Alfred A. Knopf, Inc., 1949), p. 239.
2. Harry W. Hepner, *Psychology in Modern Business* (Englewood Cliffs, N.J.: Prentice-Hall, Inc., 1931), p. 208.
3. Henry C. Link, *Employment Psychology* (New York: The Macmillan Company, 1919), pp. 184–185, 374–375.
4. C. Bird, *Social Psychology* (New York: Appleton-Century Crofts, Inc., 1940).
5. Loren Baritz, *The Servants of Power: A History of the Use of Social Science in American Industry* (Middletown, Conn.: Wesleyan University Press, 1960), pp. 25–26.
6. Fritz J. Roethlisberger, *Management and the Worker* (Cambridge, Mass.: Harvard University Press, 1947), pp. 445–446.
7. The work at Hawthorne, for example, emphasized the role of group standards in determining output.
8. Copyright 1960 by Wesleyan University. Reprinted from *The Servants of Power,* pp. 127–128, by Loren Baritz, by permission of Wesleyan University Press.
9. *Ibid.,* p. 105.
10. Quoted in Daniel Bell, *Work and Its Discontents: The Cult of Efficiency in America* (Boston: Beacon Press, 1956), p. 26.
11. Rexford Hersey, *Zest for Work* (New York: Harper & Row, Publishers, Incorporated, 1955).
12. Vance Packard, *The Hidden Persuaders* (New York: David McKay Company, Inc., 1957), p. 205.

13. Quoted in Marion L. Briggs, "How General Electric Uses Tests to Select Executives," *American Business,* vol. 26 (April, 1956), p. 24.
14. Roy Schafer, *Psychoanalytic Interpretation in Rorschach Testing* (New York: Grune & Stratton, Inc., 1954), p. 6.
15. National Industrial Conference Board, "Personnel Practices in Factory and Office," *Studies in Personnel Policy,* no. 145 (1954), pp. 12, 69.
16. Lewis B. Ward, "Putting Executives to the Test," *Harvard Business Review,* vol. 38 (July–August, 1960), p. 15.
17. William H. Whyte, Jr., *The Organization Man* (Garden City, N.Y.: Anchor Books, Doubleday & Company, Inc., 1956), pp. 221–222. Rights held and permission granted by Simon and Schuster, Inc.
18. *Ibid.,* p. 201.
19. *Ibid.,* p. 222.
20. Quin McNemar, quoted in George G. Stern, Morris I. Stein, and Benjamin S. Bloom, *Methods in Personality Assessment* (New York: The Free Press of Glencoe, 1956), p. 29.
21. Stuart Chase, *The Proper Study of Mankind,* rev. ed. (New York: Harper & Row, Publishers, Incorporated, 1956), p. 53.
22. Harry Stack Sullivan, *Interpersonal Theory of Psychiatry* (New York: W. W. Norton & Company, Inc., 1953), for example, has elaborated this tendency into a general theory of behavior.
23. David McClelland, John W. Atkinson, Russell A. Clark, and Edgar L. Lowell, *The Achievement Motive* (New York: Appleton-Century-Crofts, Inc., 1953).
24. A. R. Michael, "Tests Help Cut Turnover Rate 74% in Five Months," *Factory Management and Maintenance,* vol. 109 (May, 1951), pp. 78–80.
25. Thomas N. Jenkins, "Identifying the Accident-prone Employee," *Personnel,* vol. 38 (July–August, 1961), pp. 56–57.
26. Alan A. McLean and Graham C. Taylor, *Mental Health in Industry* (New York: McGraw-Hill Book Company, 1958), p. 171.
27. Morgan W. Wright, George C. Sisler, and Joanne Chylinski, "Personality Factors in the Selection of Civilians for Isolated Northern Stations," *Journal of Applied Psychology,* vol. 47 (February, 1963), pp. 24–29.
28. Mabel K. Powers, "Performance of Measured Vocational Interests in Adult Males," *Journal of Applied Psychology,* vol. 40 (April, 1956), pp. 69–72.
29. Saul W. Gellerman, *People, Problems and Profits: The Uses of Psy-*

chology in Management (New York: McGraw-Hill Book Company, 1960).

30. Lee J. Cronbach, *Essentials of Psychological Testing,* 2d ed. (New York: Harper & Row, Publishers, Incorporated, 1960), p. 309.

31. Gellerman, *op. cit.,* p. 194.

32. Baritz, *op. cit.,* pp. 158–159.

33. Saul W. Gellerman, "A Hard Look At Testing," *Personnel,* vol. 38 (May–June, 1961), pp. 11–15.

34. Stern, Stein, and Bloom, *op. cit.,* pp. 9–18.

35. Cited in Donald E. Super and John O. Crites, *Appraising Vocational Fitness: By Means of Psychological Tests,* rev. ed. (New York: Harper & Row, Publishers, Incorporated, 1962), p. 32.

36. *Ibid.,* p. 8.

37. *Ibid.,* pp. 29–53.

38. *Ibid.,* p. 31.

39. Cronbach, *op. cit.,* p. 163.

40. See W. C. Schutz, "What Makes Groups Productive?," *Human Relations,* vol. 8 (November, 1955), pp. 429–431.

41. E. F. Cross, *An Empirical Study of the Concepts of Cohesiveness and Compatibility,* unpublished honors' thesis, Department of Social Relations, Harvard University, Cambridge, Mass., 1957.

42. McLean and Taylor, *op. cit.,* p. 62.

43. Jacob W. Getzels and Philip W. Jackson, *Creativity and Intelligence* (New York: John Wiley & Sons, Inc., 1962).

5

The Human Use of Human Beings: Organizing for Individual Development

Man does not enjoy freedom as an abstract right. He nourishes it and feeds upon it, and then only to the degree that his many activities provide room for the expression of his talents, and his nature, and his personality within the boundaries of morality. As these activities demand too little of man, his freedom is impoverished in fact; as these activities demand too much of man, his freedom turns to despair; but as these activities permit increasing self-actualization of what individual men can be, men are increasingly free and the second value of the Judaeo-Christian Ethic is realized.

Consequently, man's experiences in organizations must loom large in determining the degree of freedom that he enjoys in important sectors of his life. Man spends that much of his time getting along in organizations, being influenced by them, and perhaps trying to avoid their reach. Designing work so as to make the most of men cannot be avoided, then, either as a practical or as a moral matter. This was the essence of Wiener's plea for *The Human Use of Human Beings*.[1]

The traditional theory of organization falls far short of unleashing man to his fullest. This and the following chapter document and amplify the point, focusing upon the individual job and the ways superiors and subordinates interact at work. The view in these two chapters is microscopic. Chapters 6 and 7 to follow provide a macroscopic complement. They focus on broader relations, such as the linkage of many jobs and the employee's influence over the total organizational environment within which he works.

The narrow perspective and the wide will be preoccupied with these two issues: the use made of human beings in organizations; and ways of making both more moral and more economic use of human beings.

Some sense of the detailed analysis to come, if the example is extreme, may be suggested by this exchange between an interviewer and an old-time foreman:

Interviewer: "How do you handle a new employee?"
  Foreman: "I jest stand there . . . and stare him down to kinda show
    how dumb he is."
Interviewer: "And then?"
  Foreman: "Then I spit. . . ." [2]

The foreman made relatively inhuman and ineffective use of the human beings in his organization. There are ways and ways of improving matters. Some of these have been profitably exploited with benefit to all parties, as they were on a grand scale during World War II when a million foremen passed through the Training Within Industry program and were sensitized to what should have been patent all along: that they were dealing with human beings in complex social situations rather than with isolated individuals standing insecurely and self-consciously about.

This analysis proposes to go beyond introducing managers and students to some obvious facts. Indeed, it will venture into some relatively complex considerations of structural arrangements and managerial techniques suitable for the more effective and human use of men in organizations.

"GREAT IS WORK, FOR IT HONORS THE WORKMAN"

An Opposed Tradition

Much of life can be approached usefully in terms of extremes. Thus the *Talmud* announces that: "Great is work, for it honors the workman." And so work sometimes is, and so it sometimes does. The vast majority of workers in an automobile assembly plant had an extremely different slant on the matter, however. "The work isn't hard," one of them observed. "It's the never-ending pace [of the assembly line]. . . . The guys yell 'Hurrah!' whenever the line breaks down, you can hear it all over the plant!" [3]

The approach via extremes will be taken here. Work will be described for what it is under the traditional theory of organization, and for what it might be if it were grounded in a different set of guiding propositions. Let us, then, get on with describing what work has become.

We often describe our world as radically new, but work has not become what it is in a historical flash. Thus a fully automated flour mill was in operation near Philadelphia before the Revolutionary War. And the historian of antiquity Xenophon tells us that among the Persians in large towns "there are places even where one man earns a living by only stitching shoes, another by cutting them out, while there is another who performs none of these operations but only assembles the parts." Even in those long-ago days it was clear to Xenophon "that he who devotes himself to a very highly specialized line of work is bound to do it in the best possible manner."

Xenophon's conclusion rightly enough charts the major path taken by orthodox thought about organizing work. True, only the late nineteenth century saw specialization raised to the dignity of a philosophy of life, to the stature of what Friedmann called a "semi-mystical belief" that the "scientific rationalization" of work implies the "breaking down of jobs, increasing the output of the 'semi-skilled' worker . . . with a lowering of the cost. . . ." [4] Even then, specialization did not make it on its own. It had the support of the leading ideas of its time. Darwinian thought gave enormous impetus to rationalization via specialization, for example, for its heyday coincided with the first attempts in this country to analyze work in detail via scientific management. A strained analogy encouraged the support of the one by the other. It did not escape such famous students of social organization as Émile Durkheim that the place of an organism on the evolutionary ladder was determined by the degree to which it possessed specialized organs for specialized purposes. There are difficulties aplenty with this uneasy analogy. Given the heady wine of the evolutionary approach, however, no one need be surprised that it was extended to work.

There were many inducements to be careless in this way. The extension of a hypothesis about biology to human organization was encouraged by this basic notion: evolution implies progress. Since progress was thought desirable per se, following an evolutionary path would solve the nagging value problems of how men ought to live. The great machine of evolution would grind inexorably toward an increasingly desirable condition. Curiously, this notion was shared by such vastly disparate types as an Andrew Carnegie and a John Dewey, although they differed widely in their profundity of argument and in the speed they attributed to evolution. This fascination with progress gave an easy go-ahead to the specialization of work. Specialization was its own solution to such questions of value that plagued an emerging large-scale economy: How should the worker be controlled and motivated? What is a fair day's pay for the specific job z? This is not overdrawing a point. Many were the observers who saw an end to all labor-management conflict as the evolutionary goal of the rationalization of work. The vogue of positivism, or scientism, enormously encouraged such a happy conclusion.

The neglect of value limits precluded the raising of this significant question: Specialization to what extent, for what purposes, in which organizations? The proper question not having been asked, important answers went unformulated. It was not long in the biological realm, by way of contrast, before it became clear that evolution was not unidirectional. Species could evolve themselves into extinction as well as into "higher types."

The issue was not joined so clearly in matters organizational, nor so early. It has become increasingly clear that different approaches to the division of work can have radically different consequences, however, and all of them may be dubbed "specialization." The division of work can contribute to the freedom of the individual. It can increase his control over his environment by making him more the master of his work and by making the individual's contributions significant and identifiable. This might be called true specialization. The specialization of work, however, also can tyrannize man. It can subjugate the individual to his work, depriving him of the meaning of work as well as of the social status that derives from relevant and identifiable contributions to the public weal. The consequences of such a division of work are hardly sanguine. As Durkheim observed:[5]

In fact, if [the individual] does not know whither the operations he performs are tending, if he relates them to no end, he can only continue to work as a matter of habit. Every day he repeats the same movements with monotonous regularity, but without taking any interest in them and without understanding them. . . . One cannot remain indifferent to such a debasement of human nature.

Such are the fruits of specialization without limits. It might be called false specialization, or routinization.

The worst commonly has been made of specialization. That the organizational cards have been definitely stacked to favor routinization is attested to in extreme form by the work of many millions; and many more millions labor at work that approaches the extreme form. Friedmann, for example, tells of the workers on an assembly line who fill liquor bottles. One of the workers, time after interminable time, places a bright, decorative label on the neck of each bottle. But she does no more. A worker farther down the line does the actual sticking on of the label.

The bias toward routinization is not a matter of indifference. Thus it creates considerable difficulties, many of which have a moral significance. Consider only this brief list of consequences associated with routinization:

1. The worker loses control of work, as in being paced by a machine or assembly line.
2. The simplification of work reduces the possibility of the employee developing skills that can lead to his advancement.
3. The simplification of work also depersonalizes work in that skill-content tends to be reduced and equalized, thus undermining the

hierarchy of skills that (for example) can constitute a promotion ladder and can give social meaning to work.

4. The simplification of work reduces the degree to which the individual can meaningfully participate in organizational affairs through his work.

5. The simplification of work often prevents the individual from completing a task that is meaningful to him.

6. The routinization of work implies monotony.

7. The routinization of work often requires that the individual work alone or, at least, there are few positive incentives for individuals in separate organization units to integrate their contributions into a smooth flow of work.

These consequences overlap and reinforce one another in complex patterns in operating situations. Some may be more important in one case, others of little significance. But they tend to occur together. Whether alone or in combination, however, one thing is clear. These consequences clash sharply, point by point, with the Judaeo-Christian Ethic.

The bias toward routinization and its consequences did not occur by accident. This is a crucial point. Both reflect conscious guidelines that are held by the vast majority of professionals in the field of job design. These guidelines both conform to pattern and surprise. Thus, as might be expected, they are grounded in basic criteria that may be summarized as "minimizing *immediate* cost and maximizing *immediate* productivity." This is according to form. Three assumptions of much work analysis hardly permit any other criteria: a technical bias; the convenient notion that meeting technical demands also implies a solution of all relevant problems of value; and the general neglect of longer-run human costs in early thought about organizing work. The guidelines do have their surprising side, however. Although firmly held, they are supported by little research specifying those conditions under which they will hold and those conditions under which they will not be applicable. This statement, which leads to the lifting of an incredulous eyebrow, must be qualified.

No doubt technical problems once were so great that it would have been impossible to meet human characteristics as well. Guidelines with a technical preoccupation could hardly be avoided. But today ample evidence supports the usefulness of designing work to suit human capabilities, as in reducing noise levels or in providing for operator comfort. Yet the guidelines remain virtually unaffected by knowledge of man's diversity. This does merit a tilted eyebrow.

This summary paragraph makes some significant claims, and they require careful investigation. Following sections will test the common guidelines of job design against the available research. To facilitate matters, a bare sketch of these guidelines follows, as does a listing of the ground rules of the test to which these guidelines will be put later. It is about time that these guidelines were set down specifically, of course. For they have often been alluded to.

Job design must be basically tripartite, to begin.[6] The basic individual steps required for (let us say) producing a dish must be determined. Moreover, appropriate methods for these tasks must be specified. Finally, the several steps must be somehow allocated to jobs, each of which then can be assigned to one or more employees. Outlining these three components of job design is not mere finickiness. Conceivably, the analysis of required steps and methods design might be restricted to technical considerations only, while such engineered tasks might be combined into jobs following rules that served human needs. Job design, however, is not content with half a loaf. Similar guidelines are utilized in both the specification of methods *and* in job design. Thus the content of the individual tasks, or steps, into which work is broken down is commonly determined by such guidelines:

1. Specialize the skills required
2. Minimize the skills required
3. Minimize the learning time required
4. Equalize workloads
5. Conform to existing layout of facilities, the nature of the equipment, and union restrictions

A similar approach is taken in combining the individual tasks into jobs. Jobs commonly are formed so as to: limit the number and variety of tasks; make the job as repetitive as possible; and minimize the training time required for any job.

The test of the usefulness of these guidelines will be approached in terms of four emphases. First, the following analysis will not be anti-machine or anti-organization. Certainly there has been a surplus of reactionary pipe dreams, and particularly by individuals whose revulsion to industrial life was fed by their lack of knowledge of the factory environment and of the expectations of the industrial worker.[7] Any dark inevitability of the sacrifice of the human to the machine seems overdrawn. Some industrial jobs permit variety aplenty; and many more jobs can be designed to yield similar human benefits. The record is not some monolithic gray that can only get darker; and matters certainly are not beyond all improvement. What DeMann called "joy in work" need not of necessity be denied the industrial worker or his clerical brother. Providing the opportunity for more workers to have a creative experience at work, however, will not come easily.

Second, although the immediate emphasis will be upon lower-level administrative and industrial work, we will range more widely. For the organization of work at low levels will affect relations far up the hierarchy. Moreover, the traditional approach to organizing work implies basic notions about motivating effort, and the impact of these notions will be felt both high and low in organizations.

Third, the effort here is not do-goodish. This is meant in three senses. There is little question that man has been considered marginal in the organization of work. The characteristics of the existing technology, the properties of the materials to be worked with, and narrow technical considerations have called the tune to which the employee was to jig. We cannot shuck the many generations of such bias as one does soiled undergarments, however. We still know too little of man's characteristics to take on the full job of fitting a new technology to him. There also is an enormous capital investment in the existing technology, which forces men to adjust to the technology in varying degrees. Capital cannot be willed into existence or even printed into existence by the Treasury Department. Despite this unavoidable datum, we do know how to organize work more satisfactorily than is usually the case. This approach intends to get what can be got when it can be gotten.

Moreover, the radiance of some ultimate vision will not blind this analysis to short-run costs. Evidences of the mischief of such exuberance are everywhere. "Safety first," for example, proved more compelling when it became clear that "safety pays." The easy way out is cynicism which notes the foot-dragging implications of such a position. But no enterprise—public or private—can very long set its cap to doing the uneconomical. Therefore this analysis will demonstrate that an approach to the Judaeo-Christian Ethic pays, and may demonstrate it to a fault. The point is not that ethically one should only do what benefits him, whatever that means. Rather, the point is that the profitable is likely to be the most probable. And this analysis faces enough problems without lengthening the odds against it.

Finally, for the first time in history longer-run costs of organizing work cannot be neglected with impunity. Our economy and technology call these debts due too quickly. Innovative cycles in products and technology have been accelerated that much, and no relief is in sight. Indeed, matters will only get more serious. In any case, work has left an unattractive legacy to this new organizational age, if observers like Adam Smith are anywhere near the mark. Smith put the effects of routinized work upon man in no uncertain terms. "The understandings of the greater part of men are necessarily formed by their ordinary employments," he explained. "The man whose life is spent in performing a few simple operations . . . has no occasion to exert his understanding. . . . He generally becomes as stupid and ignorant as it is possible for a human creature to become." [8]

Two reactions to the Smithian prediction emerge from a contrast of the organizational yesterday and the organizational today. Whatever the grievous longer-run consequences of man coming to such an end, a simpler technology did not imply great longer-run costs in the here and now. Indeed, the economy could use large numbers of just such stunted people. Thus Taylor put this as one of the "very first requirements" of a pig-iron handler: "so stupid and so phlegmatic that he more nearly resembles an ox than any other type." Conditions have changed radically. For example, the pace of change in many industries is so great that periodic retraining is necessary. Moreover, an employer in general must make do with his own work force, particularly given labor-management agreements. Despoiling one's pool of trainees is increasingly unreasonable, therefore. Relatedly, the more certain an employee is of his employment, the less likely he is to accept unsatisfactory conditions of work. In some countries, worker reactions have gone far indeed.

There seems an obvious solution: bargain with the employee to accept the deprivations of work by offering him greater leisure. But this solution has mixed consequences, if it is not self-defeating. The sociologist C. Wright Mills considered that mass leisure was replacing the "gospel of work" that once amounted to a middle-class ethic. The new ethic of leisure brought with it an "almost absolute split between work and leisure," and so captivated the society of employees that leisure became the standard by which work is judged. Thus leisure now "lends to work such meanings as work has." [9] Mills may have put matters too sharply, but his point stands. It applies, not only to industrial labor, but also to "white-collar work" as well as to supervisory and executive effort. The longer-run costs of work can never be solved by neglect. Prevailing conditions merely make that point very obvious.

Fourth, this analysis feels itself on the frontier of a revolution. At one time technical problems were so awesome and behavioral knowledge so diffuse that the Judaeo-Christian Ethic could not be approached. In Sir George Schuster's terms, very few individuals were able to combine in significant measure these two aspects of work: work as a bread-winning activity and work as a means of achieving the rewards of creative activity. Although the combination even today is not commonplace, enough is known to increase the odds in its favor. This analysis will outline managerial techniques and structural innovations that will permit achieving greater creative activity at work, by arranging matters so as to meet Schuster's list of facilitative conditions. These conditions include:

1. Giving the individual responsibility for his job and providing sufficient freedom for him to express himself in his work
2. Permitting the individual to work as a member of a team with a sense of comradeship and of joint responsibility
3. Giving the individual an understanding of the place of his work in the broader scheme of things
4. Providing jobs that at once give some satisfaction with the skill they require and do not require overtaxing effort
5. Assuring that the individual is unfettered in his legitimate efforts at work by managerial action
6. Giving the individual fair and adequate payment for his work[10]

This revolution implies new structure and techniques for organizing. Thus the present attempt tries to bring the worker psychologically closer to his work, and to do so straightforwardly by rewarding the individual at his workplace. The more typical approach to problems of work is indirect, as by slick advertising campaigns designed to create the illusion of belongingness in the XYZ Company. We follow Friedmann in pursuit of that "integration which attracts the individual into the productive collectivity and obtains his loyalty," then, and this by allowing the organization member to expand "further his physical energies of production and his mental energies of technical participation, ingenuity and initiative." [11] This approach seeks this integration by giving satisfaction in work to men as they contribute, rather than by creating verbal illusions aimed at getting without giving.

THE ANATOMY OF WORK, I

Testing the Traditional Guidelines

A first step toward approaching the second value of the Judaeo-Christian Ethic—that work must allow man to develop his abilities—seems clear enough. One question aptly sets the task. Are the traditional guidelines for job analysis both sufficient *and* necessary for organizing work? A "no" answer on either count opens up the opportunity and the challenge of developing alternate guidelines that are more sensitive to the J-C Ethic.

The leading question is not a simple one, to be sure, but neither is it beyond answer. Strictly comparable evidence bearing on the sufficiency and necessity of the classical guidelines is scarce, but Louis Davis provides some interesting and typical data in his comparison of four types of job design.[12] The four job designs were:

1. *Line Job Design* (L.J.D.). An assembly operation, paced by a conveyor, typical of classical job design in all respects except that workers rotated between hard and easy work stations every two hours. This deviation from routinization was due only to the inability to equalize skill requirements at each of the nine work stations.
2. *Batch Job Design.* The conveyor was eliminated and workers set their own pace. No other changes from the Line Job Design were made.
3. *Individual Job Design* (I.J.D.) *No. 1.* Each worker performed all nine operations at his own station. In addition, the employee con-

trolled the sequence of assembly, procured necessary supplies, and inspected his own output.

4. *Individual Job Design* (I.J.D.) *No. 2.* Job content was the same as in No. 1. The location was changed, however, and the experimental period was longer.

The traditional guidelines of job design did not come off uniformly best in Davis's experiment. The Line Job Design did live up to some of the claims of maximizing immediate output. As Figure 6 demonstrates, all three alternative job designs fell below the average output of 100 achieved under the Line Job Design.

Beyond this point, the advantages of the Line Job Design either disappear or at least seem problematic. Consider only four points. First, the lower output in the unorthodox job designs may be explained in part by the fact that employees had only six days' experience with Individual Design No. 2, as compared with an average of some four years of experience with the Line Job Design. That this is no quibble is patent in Figure 7. The average daily productivity under the two Individual Job Designs rose so consistently that on the last experimental day productivity surpassed the average of 100 attained by the Line Job

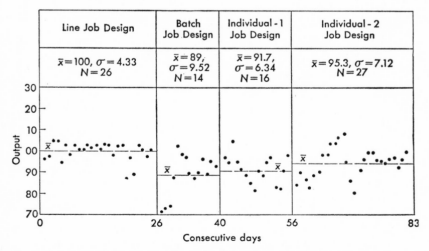

Figure 6. Average Daily Productivity Indexes for Four Job Designs. (N = number of days in each job design period.) From Louis E. Davis, "Job Design and Productivity: A New Approach," *Personnel,* vol. 33, March, 1957, p. 425.

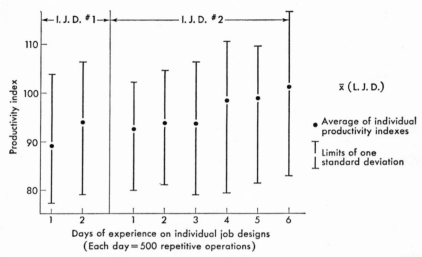

Figure 7. Trends in Daily Average Individual Productivity Indexes on Individual Job Designs. From Louis E. Davis, "Job Design and Productivity: A New Approach," *Personnel*, vol. 33, March, 1957, p. 426.

Design. Because of overlapping experimental assignments, this trend does not show up in Figure 6. Note that this level of output in the Individual Job Design was achieved despite the fact that employees inspected their own finished product and procured their own supplies.

Second, the Line Job Design placed a ceiling on output that was anchored toward the level of the slow(est) worker. Figure 6 reflects the point clearly in the narrow range of productivity scores. The conveyor's steady pace can fall anywhere in this range: too fast for all but a few or too slow for all but a few. As a practical matter, the pace tends to be set nearer the minimum of the least efficient worker than the maximum of the most efficient. The three alternative job designs permitted far fuller play to individual differences, in contrast. Figure 6 shows that the output records of some individuals on the Individual Job Design were 30 or 40 per cent higher than the average performance under the Line Job Design.

These pacing liabilities of the traditional guidelines for job design have been accepted as unfortunate but unalterable laws of nature. Thus one hears little of the argument that precisely accurate and unchangeable standards can be developed by time and motion methods. In contrast, such "standards" often are viewed merely as a basis for negotiation between management and union.[13] Relatedly, many managements apparently have been content to settle for middling motivation of their employees.[14] Management's posture has complex sources. The very organization of work tends to impoverish work itself as a positive motivator. Moreover, traditional techniques for motivating effort—individual incentive systems, for example—often do not have that direct relation to effort once widely assumed, and/or such techniques are difficult to administer.

Responding to such pressures has less to recommend it than eliminating them. Whatever the pace of a conveyor, for example, that pace will ill suit some employees. Of even greater significance, *different* individuals will achieve their optimum output at different paces of work.[15] Finally, when work is far below the individual's capacities it is not likely to be taken seriously.

Work must be so organized, then, to provide for individual differences while preserving the administrative simplicity of salary systems when everyone is working at the same speed. The implied challenge goads the following effort, and it can only be met successfully by the cumulative lessons contained in existing research.

Third, to an appreciable degree, the Line Job Design paid for its productivity with defective workmanship. This is not an attractive bargain. Indeed, it is tolerable only to one with a myopia that emphasizes the reduction of *immediate* cost and the increase of *immediate* output. Apparently that myopia existed in the present case. The point may be supported by considering the number of kinked assemblies produced under the four job designs. This provides a useful and direct measure of workmanship. The level of defective work under the Line Job Design was low enough to satisfy management, but there was much room for improvement. Thus Individual Job Design yielded only one-quarter of the kinked assemblies produced under conveyor-paced work. The improvement is striking, and particularly so given the brief experience with the three alternative job designs and the relatively high levels of output achieved under them.

Fourth, the comparisons above probably overstate the advantages of classical job design. The Line Job Design in this case was not a pure reflection of the classical guidelines. Necessity mothered job rotation. This introduced some variety into the work, and probably made it more palatable for the operators. The cost was the great difficulty of assigning personal responsibility for production, since the workers moved from "hard" to "easy" tasks. A "pure" Line Job Design—in which each employee would perform only a single and simple task—was not possible. Without job rotation, therefore, the apparently unavoidable skill differences would require a complex wage program. The desire to keep the wage program and its administration simple explained the violation of classical job design.

It is significant, and unfortunate, that other "violations" of the classical guidelines were not attempted. The Line Job Design was *not* clearly superior in all relevant respects, and particularly so when compared to Individual Job Design. Moreover, Davis also notes a number of other attractive features of Individual Job Design. That design

1. Increased the flexibility of the production process
2. Permitted the identification of individual deficiencies in productivity and quality
3. Reduced the service functions of the department such as materials delivery and inspection
4. Developed a more favorable attitude toward individual responsibility and effort—after experience with Individual Job Design, workers disliked the lack of personal responsibility characteristic of Line Job Design[16]

The traditional guidelines for job design limp badly, in sum. Even studies yielding more friendly results point up similar inadequacies. In one experiment, most workers preferred repetitive work because it permitted daydreaming. Even so, over one-third of the workers did not find such features desirable. Moreover, individual differences were prominently reflected in the revealing fact that not all workers achieved their maximum output at the same conveyor speed! This much is clear, therefore. The classical guidelines for job design do not provide a model appropriate under all conditions, or even under conditions commonly encountered in organizations. Moreover, the criteria of maximizing immediate output and minimizing immediate costs leave too many factors of importance unprovided for. Work design can hardly be tethered short of considering a much broader range of criteria of effectiveness.

THE ANATOMY OF WORK, II

Toward Making the Job as Big as the Man

The test of the classical guidelines for the design of work provides substantial encouragement that approaching the Judaeo-Christian Ethic at work is not foolhardy. The test also conveys another message: variations in job design affect a wide network of relations. Variations in design significantly enlarge or restrict the content of jobs; they imply significantly different organizational relations as (for example) inspection and materials handling services are provided by the operatives themselves or by separate "staff" units; they imply changed relations between supervisors and employees; and they permit widely different degrees of freedom for the employee.

These contrasting pairs of structural arrangements and managerial techniques must be analyzed. The immediate focus will be upon the possibilities for increasing the scope of low-level jobs, an approach that flies in the face of the classical guidelines of job design and the routinization they prescribe. The aim is to describe an alternative to the excesses preached by the traditional theory of organization and practiced in many organizations. Rather than harking back to some supposedly idyllic state where everyone does everything, however, the effort here tries to make the morally best of a significant proportion of the existing technology.

Let "job enlargement" be described in general, to begin. Figure 8 illustrates two extreme alternatives to organizing a simple set of operations. The letters a, b, c, and d designate the component tasks; and the rectangles contain the task or tasks assigned to individual jobs. The *work cycle* in both cases is the same, *abcd*. Following David Cox and K. M. Sharp,[17] the total work cycle may be defined as that set of operations necessary "to advance one material unit of production by one whole stage in the process of manufacture." The unit cycle consists of a or b or c or d in Figure 8*a*; and of *abcd* in Figure 8*b*. Job enlargement, in these terms, means designing unit cycles to include more (or all) of a work cycle.

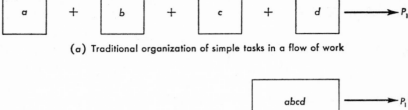

(a) Traditional organization of simple tasks in a flow of work

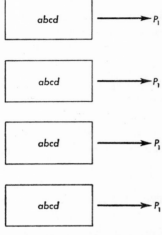

(b) Job enlargement of simple tasks in a flow of work

Figure 8. Two Approaches to Organizing Simple Tasks into Jobs.

Although no uniform opinion exists about which extreme to approach in organizing, most professionals in job design are of one mind. Their dominant opinion was articulated by one manager in discussing a simple process for manufacturing electrical goods:[18]

The ideal would be for each [operator] to have only one connection to make. Many of our workers, when they first come, prefer simple work, consisting of a small number of elementary operations. When the work they have to do grows, when they have to weld, for instance, or to make connections, their output falls. Besides, even if well trained, they will have moments of hesitancy which makes it difficult to plan, and in particular to time, their operations.

This opinion did not have complete currency, however, even in the manager's small circle. One employee was interviewed during the slump season when each operator made all thirty required connections, as opposed to the five connections made during times of greater demand. He said: "It's much less tiring and more interesting."

One can easily become enamored of the general case. Before suggesting the broad range of consequences of job enlargement, the experimental evidence will speak for itself in support of one or the other of the organizational extremes sketched in Figure 8. A great mass of such evidence exists, but attention will be focused here on but two examples of job enlargement of lower-level jobs. One comes from an administrative context, the second from an industrial environment. Both examples come to the same point: enlarging the unit cycle often motivates effort and usually simplifies work relations.

Detroit Edison, a public utility, has pioneered the use of job enlargement in its lower-level clerical operations. J. Douglas Elliott, an Edison executive, sparked this innovation in organizing work in his firm.[19] The problems induced by classical job design were obvious enough, he explained, and efforts to relieve them had ranged from color dynamics to recorded music. Unfortunately, these commonly inspired techniques have a common fault; they stop short of changing the job, and thus avoid the heart of the matter. The Detroit Edison program of job enlargement was not tethered so short. It had three objectives:

1. To reduce job monotony, by increasing the content of the job and thus the freedom of the individual
2. To utilize the intellectual capabilities of employees to a greater extent, by challenging them more at work
3. To decrease overspecialization or routinization where they have been applied so as to create duplication and to complicate work

If these objectives were achieved, Elliott observed, increased production and reduced costs normally could be expected.

Detroit Edison's approach to job enlargement may be illustrated by considering one case in detail. Following Figure 8a, Detroit Edison originally had three separate organizational units for machine work—tabulating card, key punch, and calculating—in its customers' billing department. The work flowed within and between these units, as is typical of the Line Job Design. The flow of bills then went through two separate and repetitive bill-checking points. Again, Figure 8a was followed in spirit. One checking job involved the comparison of completed bills against other records to verify accuracy of billings. Five employees were assigned to this operation. The second check was a quick examination of the same bills for one particular type of discrepancy. One employee performed this operation. All five organizational units were sources of employee discontent. The sequence of remedial actions is enlightening:

1. To relieve the monotony of the checking operation to a degree, job rotation was inaugurated, the smallish effect being to give six employees a different repetitive job every sixth working day.
2. The two checking jobs then were combined into one enlarged job.
3. As improvements in equipment and procedures were made, the dual check was no longer necessary, but to simplify the checking operation would leave a very monotonous job.
4. Therefore, the specialized checking operation at the end of the production line was discontinued, and the activity was given to the machine operators who prepared the bills and who were subject only to a quality-control check of their efforts.
5. The three specialized machine jobs in the separate organization units, however, began to take their toll in low morale and lack of flexibility in operations, since it was difficult (for example) to assign responsibility for error when each unit handled only one of the three interdependent machine operations.
6. Each unit, then, was reorganized to handle all three machine operations, and a new machine-job classification was established requiring that each operator be able to perform all three machine operations as well as the checking operations.

There is a kind of inner logic to job enlargement that tends to force appropriate changes at related points in a flow of work, as is also the case with the classical guidelines. There is a crucial difference. Job enlargement tends to bring together related operations so as to minimize the problems of integrating them. Classical job design tends to fragment related operations. One must choose his inner logic with care, therefore.

Integration seems preferable to fragmentation. Following the classical guidelines proved costly at Detroit Edison, for example, while job enlargement had more sanguine results. As Elliott noted of assigning the check of billings to the machine operators: "It is normally the responsibility of machine operators to check their work, anyway; so they were given more to watch for and the final responsibility for the general appearance of the bill. The machine operators have renewed interest in their work and are now doing a better job of printing their bills, further reducing the need for a final examination." Enlarging the machine-job classification to include all three machine operations also has its attractive compensations. Flexibility in assigning work is increased, for example, since the operators can be assigned by supervisors to any task necessary to smooth out the flow of work. Absences, machine breakdowns, and the like consequently can be adapted to swiftly. In addition, the unorthodox structure reduces the supervisory burden. For the employees often know where they are needed, and they have a common responsibility for the total flow of work. The common responsibility also has increased the teamwork of the operators, only one sign of which is the rotation of operators between the several machines "according to their own collective choosing." [20]

A firm conclusion seems possible. Allowing man freedom to develop more fully and to utilize his faculties via job enlargement—that is, approaching the second value of the J-C Ethic—can be achieved without sacrificing either the planning of work or its effective performance. Indeed, increasing the unit cycle of work so as to approach (or coincide with) the total work cycle simplifies work relations, permits greater flexibility, reduces the number of separate units of organization whose contributions must be integrated into a flow of work, and encourages the involvement of the individual with his work. This is not to say that all workers will be more satisfied with an enlarged job. A minority of subjects in many studies, and a majority in some (particularly women) prefer narrower jobs.[21] But at least the bias should be toward job enlargement, if a monolithic bias there must be. At best, psychological testing will be so well developed and the organization structure so adaptable that the needs of both majority and minority may be met.

Faith in the efficacy of allowing man more freedom at work through job enlargement need not rest on a single case from a single firm. Many other industrial and clerical applications provide ample support for faith in the possibility and efficacy of freedom at work. Sometimes by design, sometimes by accident, and often with regret that conditions prohibit using the guidelines of classical job design, job enlargement has been used in industrial work with generally consistent results. IBM consciously developed such comprehensive programs, for instance, on milling jobs.[22] As originally organized, the work was highly repetitive and required integrating the efforts of many overspecialized workers through elaborate supervisory controls. But these controls did not save work from delays such as those caused when one overspecialized worker waited for another to finish. The original organization of work required only that the milling-machine operator insert a part, engage the machine to start the cut, and remove the piece when the machine stopped automatically. He repeated this over and over. When a new part was scheduled, the operator stepped aside. He waited for a setup man, also overspecialized but more skilled, who installed an appropriate fixture and adjusted the speeds and feeds for the new part. The operator also waited while a process inspector checked the first few samples from the new setup. Only then did the machine operator resume his routinized task of putting a piece in, pushing a lever to start the cut, and taking the finished piece out. The total work cycle, then, required at least three specialized hands. Their integration often was not perfect, with consequent losses of time. Additional difficulties sometimes resulted because the operator had no responsibility for inspection. A long run of defective output might result before an inspector noted that a dulled tool (for example) was producing pieces which exceeded permissible tolerances and before the appropriate specialist could set matters right again. This reflects Figure 8a with a vengeance.

The enlarged milling-machine job was less slavish to the classical guidelines for job design. When a new job is to be run, the operator himself checks the blueprints and specifications. He then sets up his own machine, checks the sample parts from his own setup, and makes any appropriate adjustments. When the run is started, the operator makes his own periodic quality checks and is responsible for keeping his cutting tools in proper condition. This describes a condition under which even the relatively humble in organizations can attain a significant measure of freedom as they exercise their own capacities, and this while avoiding the close and constant oversight associated with routinized work.

Greater freedom at work need not be bought at exorbitant cost. In fact, the consequences of industrial job enlargement seem as generally favorable from the standpoint of costs as from the standpoint of the Judaeo-Christian Ethic. Relying heavily on the IBM experience, the following four factors are particularly significant. First, workers became more satisfied. Job enlargement means more variety, more clear individual responsibility for a total work cycle, more interest in work, and fewer aggravations implicit in supervisory efforts to integrate the efforts of numerous specialists. Second, better quality is achieved, while losses due to defective parts and scrap drop sharply. Third, total production costs are lowered somewhat, despite the fact that the enlarged jobs carry higher wage rates. Fourth, cost savings and less idle time accrue from reducing the number of specialists whose efforts must be integrated in a work cycle. Walker presents more or less typical data bearing on this reduction of overhead and service costs in one plant.

Year	*Number of Setup Men*
1940	1 for 22 operators
1943	1 for 11 operators
July, 1946	1 for 48 operators
January, 1950	none

The sharp increase in the proportion of setup men between 1940 and 1943 coincided with the rapid growth of IBM, when the guidelines of classical job design should have been most appropriate. Rather than facilitating operations, however, problems were compounded by increasing the proportion of setup men. Hence the job enlargement program, which by 1950 had eliminated all setup men.

This introduction to job enlargement has been painted with a broad brush. A few qualifying features must be stressed lest the reader think that some all-purpose glory road toward greater freedom at lower levels in organizations has been sketched.

To begin, job enlargement is not universally applicable. One knowledgeable observer estimated in 1950 that perhaps 500,000 industrial workers could have their jobs enlarged.[23] This is no insignificant number, although it is but a small fraction of the 25 to 30 million employees in semiskilled industrial and mining work. Any such estimate is chancy in the extreme, but 500,000 is probably in the lower range of possible estimates for industrial work. If nothing else, this estimate was based on a pessimism about the possibilities of enlarging jobs on assembly-line work. Numerous successful applications of the technique have been made under just these conditions, however, although long after the half-million estimate was made in 1950. In addition, many other jobs could profit from job enlargement, as in clerical or administrative settings.

Moreover, job enlargement is not appropriate under all conditions. Some reasonable provisions must be made for workers likely to be displaced by the resulting economics. Recall the setup men in IBM. An expanding firm, then, is an appropriate setting for a job enlargement program. Workers are unlikely to cooperate themselves out of a job. Relatedly, employees must be rewarded for accepting the retraining usually implied by job enlargement. This is no particular problem, since the enlarged job commonly merits a higher wage rate.

Nor is job enlargement some all-purpose managerial tool. If it is applied by management without enthusiasm and conviction, its chances of success are markedly diminished. If nothing else, job enlargement requires significant changes in supervisory habits. Such changes will not be encouraged by lukewarm managerial commitment.

Finally, job enlargement is but one element in a situational analysis of the particular nature of the work involved, the personalities of the operatives, and the specific changes made in the job and the ways they are made. Volumes of research are required to etch in the details of such situational relations. The trick seems to lie in increasing the worker's control over a work cycle in contrast to, let us say, the introduction of variety into work by rotating individuals through several unit cycles of different work cycles. In the latter case, the employee may feel more estranged from work than ever when the novelty wears off. Relatedly, it may be impossible to assign responsibility for performance when such rotation is relied upon.

The situational nature of job enlargement has many ramifications. What might be an effective program for one batch of employees might fail for another batch. The import of this section will hold in most cases, therefore, but not all. Everything is not in flux, however. Increasingly, the development of testing techniques will permit more precise predictions. Here the point may be established only in raw form. Table 5 presents some relevant data showing that employees in one sample tended to evaluate routine jobs less favorably, while jobs with greater content were given more enthusiastic reception. The differences, incidentally, are statistically significant. Of 100 cases, approximately 70 fit the above generalization. These are relatively good odds. The cases that do not fit the generalization include both employees who preferred routine jobs as well as employees with abilities or aspirations far beyond the confines of even the most enlarged jobs. Various studies yield various results, but Table 5 illustrates the orders of magnitude most commonly encountered.

TABLE 5   THE NUMBER OF OPERATIONS PERFORMED ON AN ASSEMBLY LINE AND THE DEGREE OF INTEREST IN THE JOB

Operations Performed	Very or Fairly Interesting	Not Very or Not at All Interesting	Total
1	33	67	100
2–5	44	56	100
5 or more	70	30	100
Total	147	153	300

From Charles Walker and Robert H. Guest, *Man on the Assembly Line* (Cambridge, Mass.: Harvard University Press, 1952), p. 54.

The cases which elude our generalization also can be accounted for in large part. Thus the nature of the job is not the only determinant of employee satisfaction. Various advantages relevant for particular workers can overcome grave liabilities of the jobs they perform. Reynolds and Schister, for example, report that five factors contribute most to employee satisfaction and turnover: (1) the physical characteristics of particular jobs (2) the degree of independence permitted the employee in doing his work (3) the adequacy of wages to cover the employee's living costs (4) the fairness with which he feels he has been treated by company officials (5) the degree to which the work interests him.[24] Only factors 1 and 5 have clear and direct connections with job enlargement, although 3 and 4 often will be favorably affected by job enlargement.

Two conclusions seem appropriate. First, we should not be surprised to find that programs of job enlargement are significant for most employees. The point may seem petty to some since the differences between many enlarged jobs and overspecialized jobs are so "obviously" slight. However, numerous studies reflect a world of psychological difference between (let us say) jobs with five operations and those with ten. Second, job enlargement might be of little or no significance, as in the case of an individual with strong economic drives.

Qualifications and all, job enlargement seems a useful managerial technique. This underscores the simplicism of the claims of universality of the guidelines of classical job design, as well as of the traditional theory of organization from which they derive. Put differently, job enlargement demonstrates that the Judaeo-Christian Ethic may be approached without sacrificing the efficiency of operations, if indeed job enlargement does not lead to significant short-run economies as well as to longer-run advantages.

THE ANATOMY OF WORK, III

Organizing for Training in the Process of Work

The inner logics of job enlargement and the guidelines of classical job design again clash headlong on the question of employee training. This should not be surprising, but the clash can still be adumbrated usefully.

Again, the contrast is of extremes. Job enlargement patently rests upon the effectiveness of the training which supports it and upon the predisposition of the employee to be trained. One-shot efforts will not suffice, for programs of job enlargement tend to develop by successive additions to unit cycles of work. Invariably, enlarged jobs are upgraded in the process, and thus impose increasingly greater demands on the employee. Training must be more or less continuous, therefore.

Classical job design and the traditional theory of organization do not bother with opening broader training vistas to employees. Indeed, the traditional goal is to confine the individual ever more narrowly.

Baldwin and Shultz put the matter forcefully in outlining the classical rationale in terms of three propositions:[25]

. . . (1) break the work process down into the smallest possible components, (2) fit jobs into a rigid structure that emphasizes the duties and the boundaries of the job rather than its part in the process, and (3) put everyone possible on an individual or small-group incentive system gearing pay to output on the particular job. This philosophy inevitably has tended to identify the individual with an ever more narrow task, giving him positive incentives to restrict his interests and no incentive at all to think beyond his immediate work environment. . . .

These are not merely words. Overspecialized and routinized work commonly can be mastered in a matter of hours or days, or at most in a few weeks. Table 6 documents the point from the early experience of the Ford Motor Works. Some 79 per cent of the employees had a very brief training period. Not all work has been subjected to such extreme subdivision, but the Ford experience reflects the model after

TABLE 6   LENGTH OF TRAINING AT THE FORD MOTOR COMPANY

Length of Training	Percentage of Workers
1 day	43
1–8 days	36
1–2 weeks	6
1 month to a year	14
Up to 6 years	1

From Julius Hirsch, *Das Amerikanische Wirtschaftswunder* (Berlin: S. Fischer, 1926), p. 344.

which work was commonly patterned. Circumstances might not permit a close approach to the model in specific cases, but this is considered unfortunate. Professionals at job design had few doubts of what work should be like, ideally. Nor did they bandy words about the consequences of extreme specialization. Thus Frank Gilbreth, a pioneer in the analysis of work, provided this terse summary. When the employee learned to perform his limited set of operations correctly, Gilbreth noted, "his vocational training is finished, whatever his age." [26]

The inner logics of classical job design and job enlargement do not stop at the level of the operators. These logics influence structure and techniques far above that level, as in the two opposed ways of organizing the supervisor's job depicted in Figure 9. Figure 9a presents the orthodox structural relations for a hypothetical task *abcd*. The difficulties induced by the orthodox structure, in outline, are that each supervisor monitors but a single process. More and more activities once performed by supervisors are taken over by "staff" (as S_D in Figure 9a) or by labor unions, over neither of whom the supervisor has direct control; and this flight of much of the substance of the job of the first-level supervisor, plus the narrowness of the process supervised, leaves little room for anything but trivial decision-making. Indeed, so extreme have been these trends that some observers conclude the first-line supervisor

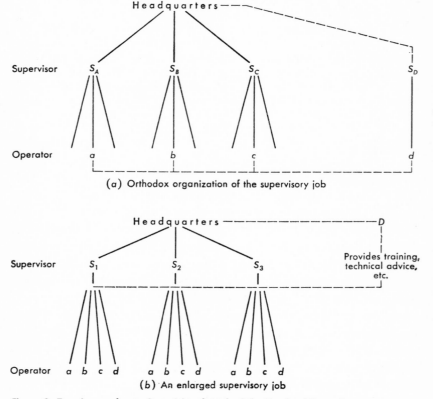

(a) Orthodox organization of the supervisory job

(b) An enlarged supervisory job

Figure 9. Two Approaches to Organizing the Job of the First-level Supervisor.

is destined to be a "socio-emotional specialist" handling only interpersonal problems, with little responsibility for such matters as scheduling, hiring and firing, discipline, and the like. Foremen tend to regard this trend with some hostility. They are the "men in the middle," forced at once to apply policies in whose formulation they had no hand and to motivate employees over whom they have less and less leverage.

The above sketch of the supervisor's job is no caricature. Detroit Edison provided this circumscribed role for their first-level supervisors, for example:[27]

It was the duty of the so-called "front office," consisting of staff men in addition to the department head and his assistant, constantly to study routines and procedures and to write directives as to how the work was to be done. All the supervisors had to do was to follow instructions, although they may have been consulted on procedure changes occasionally. The front office was fully responsible for such functions as preparing the budget and keeping all cost statistics, hiring and firing employees, making wage adjustments, handling employee grievances, and shifting employees between groups to expedite the work during peak periods and absences. In addition, the department head or his assistant had to be consulted by the supervisor in handling personnel matters such as granting time off and scheduling vacations.

This is a faithful rendering of the model sketched in Figure 9a. The training of first-line supervisors posed no great problems under these narrowly defined conditions.

The common supervisory pattern may be unwieldy and expensive, but it is not inevitable. Detroit Edison illustrates both points. The firm moved toward the structure in Figure 9b. The various activities once performed by the front office were delegated to the first-line supervisors. Thus the supervisors could make procedural changes in their own work units without clearance, when these changes did not affect other work units and when they did not violate established policies.

Following Figure 9b prevents supervisory action from being hamstrung by detailed procedures or clashes among interdependent units. Simply, each supervisor monitors an entire work cycle and each supervisor's unit therefore is more autonomous than in a Figure 9b structure. S_1 thus supervises all operations necessary for the entire work cycle $abcd$. S_a oppositely supervises only one of the necessary unit cycles for the larger work cycle. S_1 has far more opportunity to tailor procedures and work pace to the particular characteristics of his work unit without fouling the activities of other units. That is the central characteristic of the unorthodox organization of the job of the first-level supervisor.

The benefits of supervisory job enlargement in simplifying work often are substantial, but they do not come without training. The case is patent for the first-line supervisors, and hardly less so in the case of their superiors who can frustrate the most comprehensive program of job enlargement. Consider one chain store that has a policy of job enlargement for its sales personnel. Each salesgirl in effect manages a department of her own, consisting of one or more counters. These "departmental managers" sell, build displays, order merchandise, and (we are told) "in most ways take complete charge of their department." The program met with varying degrees of success. Where employees favored the program, a wide chain of favorable consequences was observed. Turnover was only 28 per cent; average service was six years; and employee satisfaction was high. Employees in three stores expressed strong dislike of the department manager system, however. Turnover in these stores averaged a considerable 168 per cent; average service was 2.5 years; and salesgirls were markedly dissatisfied, and this despite the facts that they liked selling and had salaries 15 per cent higher than the girls in the other stores studied.[28]

These may seem embarrassing data, for both sets of stores had similar programs of job enlargement. Matters may be explained without embarrassment, however. Training was deficient in the stores that disliked the department manager system, and the girls had little information about the system. Why this was so cannot be settled with certainty, but several contributing factors seem to have reinforced one another. The store officials "interfered" with the department manager system. Moreover, many new employees did not "believe in" the system and, since their turnover was so great, there were new employees aplenty. Both factors imply the need for training, and for store officials as well as for the salesgirls.

The structure in Figure 9b imposes its demands for training rather lightly. It not only requires greater training, but it facilitates training at work. This is an unusual combination, for nature is not in the habit of being so cooperative.

The training advantages of a Figure 9b structure are considerable. Basically, the first-line supervisor will have his managerial mettle tested at work. Experience at Sears, Roebuck suggests that such a structure spotlights the more capable, challenges those who can improve, and exposes the less capable. The point is credible. For the more of a total work cycle controlled by a supervisor, the easier it is to assign responsibility for performance. Extreme specialization provides more places to hide because a number of supervisors monitor routinized unit cycles of work that contribute to a total cycle. Moreover, the danger of allowing the supervisor some scope at work is reduced by the Figure 9b structure. If one of the supervisors in such a structure grievously bungles, output at a maximum would fall by $1/N$, where N is the total number of units performing the same or comparable total work cycle. A similar bungle in a Figure 9a structure could reduce output to zero at a minimum. For each organizational unit provides only one of the necessary processes for the work cycle abcd, and a breakdown in any one unit affects all other units. There are ways of getting around such a possibility, but they are expensive ways. Freedom is less risky in a structure congenial to job enlargement.

A Figure 9b structure also positively facilitates the training of employees at work, and not only in the sense that it permits job enlargement. Since the individual identifies with a small organizational unit that handles a complete work cycle, he is encouraged to expand his interests beyond his own particular job. Relatedly, job rotation is convenient in such a structure. For any one supervisor can monitor his own program; no supervisor need worry about losing his best men to other supervisors; and the supervisor has a direct stake in the success of the program of rotation. Such considerations do not apply, at least with equal force, to a structure patterned after Figure 9a. Moreover, job rotation in a Figure 9b structure does not face great difficulties in assigning responsibility for performance. It is all in the family, and one can only shift responsibility to one's immediate organizational brothers. This is a powerful deterrent to buck passing and shoddy work; and derivative psychological and social identifications reinforce performance along the entire flow of work. In a traditional structure, in contrast, similar identifications often serve to fragment the flow of work. For "my" unit performs but one operation; "their" units perform others; and no one has any clear responsibility for the total integration of these operations at the first level of supervision.

There are other routes to the same end, but they seem reserved to the relative few. An intense awareness of the broad organization and a deep identification with it could facilitate many of the jobs above. "Selling the company" to employees thus may be worthwhile in some cases. In general, however, employees are "locals" as opposed to "cosmopolitans." They tend to identify with smaller, more immediate work units. This "water cooler in the corner" theory of what motivates employees is supported by much evidence. Hence the great usefulness of a structure congenial to job enlargement and job rotation.

The questions implied in this contrast of the training demands of traditional job design and job enlargement may be put bluntly. Can training as an ongoing concern be neglected as being of minor significance in today's organizations? If not, can training sufficient for today's needs be provided outside of work? If not, should the organization structure be such as to facilitate training in the process of work?

Appropriate answers to these questions may be sketched with confidence. An outline will do for a beginning. Training cannot be neglected; in most cases it is not sufficient to make training supplemental to work; therefore, by elimination, work must be organized so as to facilitate training and development.

Several factors support this compound conclusion. First, any help in training provided by the organization of work must be welcome. The total training job is that big, a point supported by these data from a medium-sized company and its training demands that resulted only from internal transfer and promotion. Two students observed that: "In a company employing approximately 6,000 workers, 13.5% of the employees were transferred to jobs requiring some training, and 9.5% were promoted to jobs requiring, in some instances, extensive training. This was not an abnormal year for this company." [29] In addition, training usually is required by each change in methods and by the introduction of new products.

At least, then, a structure that discourages a positive orientation toward training must have significant compensating advantages. If that structure gives operators and supervisors positive incentives to restrict their attention to some narrow task—as the traditional theory of organization tends to do—these compensating advantages must be enormous.

Second, even if repetition has made the point trite, we live in an age of revolution in processes, systems, and products in industrial and administrative organizations. The training burdens will be correspondingly great. Increasingly, training (as Heron notes) "must be part and parcel of the work itself," a point established firmly during World War II when 40 million Americans took on jobs new to them.[30] That training also should be increasingly supplied and/or directly monitored by the immediate supervisor. Nor can we wait until the individual has moved into a relatively high-level position in an organization. Suitable habits must be established early, and these habits are necessary at levels both high and low in many organizations. Friedmann describes a humble case in point. Photographs of workers plunging fruit into a sugar solution showed that inefficient movements were common. A three-month program taught inexperienced workers to move their hands in ways that were more efficient and less tiring. Output increases of some 88 per cent were recorded. More central to the present point, Friedmann also reports that: "Young workers already accustomed to the old movements were re-educated and attained an increase of 27%. . . . But the re-education turned out to be useless among the older women workers." [31]

Again, a premium must be accorded the organization structure that both facilitates and rewards attention to the broader flow of work rather than commitment to a narrow task. Emphasis on the narrow task understandably results in so great a psychic investment by the employee that he often will resist giving it up, no matter how burdensome or ineffective or tiring. And, the truth must be told, "giving it up" has become increasingly necessary under contemporary conditions. There is no sign that matters will change in the near future.

Third, automation raises pointed challenges to training, and thus to the organization structure within which training must take place. This is the case in a number of significant senses. New jobs will be spawned by automation and these with characteristics only dimly envisioned, with all this implies for training. Many of these new jobs will be highly skilled, if indeed the skill level of the entire "job mix" is not raised appreciably. Therefore automation may imply merely gigantic training problems or really stupendous ones. Most significantly, automation implies habits of thought that are at extreme odds with the rationale of the traditional theory of organization and classical job design, which rests upon discontinuous and highly specialized methods of production. Baldwin and Shultz summarize matters in these terms: "[Automation] requires a new way of thinking . . . that emphasizes continuous movement of work through a total process rather than stop-and-go progress, thought of as the sum of independent operations." [32] Stop-and-go progress, of course, is implied pointedly by the individual processes and functions emphasized in the traditional theory of organization.

What precise effects automation will have upon work are not yet clear, but some educated guesses may be made. Baldwin and Shultz see seniority as one casualty, for example. They observed that automation implies "the development of a work force willing and able to adapt itself to the changing needs of an evolving work process [and this means] more than application of seniority protections to broader units of work. As a standard for continued employment, 'ability to learn' would gradually replace 'ability to do' the job." [33]

A conclusion by way of denouement seems appropriate. The structure based on the traditional theory of organization is firmly grounded in the ability to do some narrow job. That structure, at least at the lower levels, is not up to motivating or determining the ability to learn.

Fourth, the wisdom of organizing work so as to decrease or eliminate the need for substantial training must be suspect, even if the factors discussed above were unimportant. The matter is a complicated one, but one facet permits easy illustration. Employee satisfaction will significantly help determine long-run costs, and high satisfaction is not the most likely outcome of overspecialized work. "Deskilling," for example, reduces the ability of a job to serve as a springboard for promotion because jobs are more or less uniformly simple. This robs man of an important component of both status and satisfaction, the "steady process" (in Cox's words) "of training graded to the operator's capacity, which presents difficulties but ensures that they will be overcome."

Such an interpretation seems to fit available data. On one assembly line, for example, fully two-thirds of the workers interviewed in one department desired transfer to some other job in their department. Their choices for a new job are significant, reflecting as they do the hunger for a job with more content and scope: about half of the men wanted repair or utility jobs; one-quarter had set their caps for supervisory positions; and the remainder would settle for any production job as long as it was not on the main assembly line, which reflected the most extreme devotion to the guidelines of classical job design. Significantly, few of the discontented traced their desire for mobility to higher pay. Their typical explanations seem appropriate: "On the job I want, I could do a lot of different things." "It would give me a chance of learning more." "It would be easier, not so much work." [34]

The relevance of employee satisfaction must be put in perspective. The workers quoted were well paid, their workplace was modern and safe, their lavatories were sparkling. But to paraphrase one of them: "These things are well and good, but it's what you do most of the time that's important." It is important, indeed, and one can entertain grave doubts about neglecting the important. Do we really want to create a kind of well-paid proletariat, bored with their work and seeing no way out short of an early retirement? The answer is not obviously in the affirmative and, at least in many cases, it need not be. Organizing for training in the process of work suggests a way out of this unattractive cul-de-sac, and a profitable way in the bargain.

A real choice exists, then, between the inner logics of classical job design and of job enlargement under a wide variety of conditions. This choice need not sacrifice either technical demands or the moral demands of the Judaeo-Christian Ethic. The following chapters will stress structural arrangements and managerial techniques which will facilitate this task. Immediate attention will be devoted to generalizing the import of the analysis just completed.

MAN-CENTERED ORGANIZATION

Reciprocity as a Goal

Man is a model-building animal; he seeks to express what he knows in ever more compact and generalized form. The formula $E = mc^2$, in this sense, epitomizes man at his most human. This and the preceding chapter imply a particular challenge to this preoccupation of man with giving order and meaning to his experience. The challenge cannot be avoided, but neither can we be more than suggestive.

Much of the previous analysis straightforwardly implies the importance of "reciprocity." This is no surprise. More or less obviously, giving in order to get is at the heart of life. Indeed, eminent observers have called reciprocity "*the* vital principle of society." [35] Reciprocity need not mean an equal exchange of benefits between two or more actors, but the balance must be mutually agreed upon. Cultural beliefs and attitudes determine this mutually acceptable balance. The balance is dynamic: it might remain virtually unchanged for long periods of time, but change is more characteristic.

Reciprocity can be tied in to the broad framework of this analysis. The balance in organizations during the heyday of the Individualistic Ethic was decidedly in management's favor. Many factors reinforced this state of affairs, but influential opinion agreed that matters could hardly be otherwise. No wonder that the early organization of work was not overly sensitive to human needs. Reciprocity, as then defined, did not demand anything more.

The emergence of the Social Ethic over the last decade or two, in similar terms, reflected the growing opinion that reciprocity demanded a new balance, one tilted decidedly more toward the employee. This seems almost inevitable, given that (as Drucker argued) this is the age of the employee as an earlier period was the age of the small businessman. Just as reasonably, the balance was effected first by rewards outside of work. Pensions, recreation programs, increased wages, and better working conditions; these and other considerations were thrown on the scales of reciprocity. The organization of work was left basically undisturbed.

The present argument for a closer approach to the Judaeo-Christian Ethic implies that a still further adjustment of the reciprocal balance is necessary, and that this adjustment must come in significant part through changes in the organization of work. This analysis is in a real sense a fulfillment of a long historical development. The Individualistic Ethic applied only narrow technical considerations to the organization of work; the Social Ethic often was well intentioned, but it was brought up short by its own serious limitations; and the Judaeo-Christian Ethic attempts to get the most for men and for work.

The attempt to reconcile the demands of work and those of man has much to recommend it, even under conditions of advanced rationalization of work. Consider the Saint-Jacques Works and one brainchild of the French industrialist Charpy. The organization of work at that plant was patterned after the guidelines of classical job design, with output tied to a definite rhythm. But there was a human qualification on all this technology: the work rhythm was fixed by agreement with the workers and could be changed during the day. The urgency of the work on order, the level of orders on hand, and the physical and climatic conditions were among the factors that would influence the pace agreed upon. Charpy saw much of value in this approach. As he observed: "The workers willingly adopt this style of work. . . . This irregular pace is infinitely more logical and more humane than continual production at the highest possible speed, which . . . raises serious objections from the physiological point of view." [36]

Much evidence supports Charpy's position. Without management action or awareness, workers often will struggle to wrest greater reciprocity from their work. Employees may "blitz" on certain jobs, that is, sharply increase their speed so as to gossip or rest until the line again catches up with them. Where such adaptations are possible, management's failure to seize the initiative in organizing work is an opportunity lost, if indeed informal practices do not depend upon conspiratorial arrangements or upon a supervisor "looking the other way." Moreover, the variable states of the human organism are known well enough. Indeed, variations in emotional tone and efficiency are so universal as to suggest that (to chance a bad pun) irregularity is the natural state of man.[37]

These specific illustrations hardly do it all. They should suggest ways in which work can be made more sensitive to man, however, and the senses in which work commonly is caught in the web of a logical system that does not know man.

Figure 10 goes beyond the specific case. The sense of the figure both guided and was reinforced by findings derived from a study of a midwestern utility company by a research team from the Menninger Clinic.[38] Their findings, while tentative enough, suggest the generalized

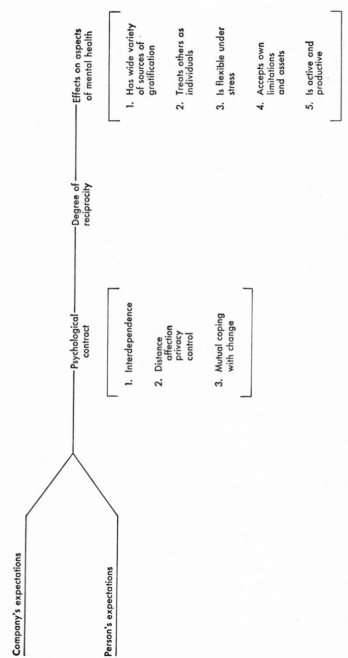

Company's expectations

Person's expectations

— Psychological contract —

— Degree of reciprocity —

— Effects on aspects of mental health

1. Interdependence

2. Distance
   affection
   privacy
   control

3. Mutual coping
   with change

1. Has wide variety of sources of gratification

2. Treats others as individuals

3. Is flexible under stress

4. Accepts own limitations and assets

5. Is active and productive

Figure 10. A Schema for Viewing Reciprocity in Organization. From Harry Levinson, Charlton R. Price, Kenneth J. Munden, Harold J. Mandl, and Charles M. Solley, *Men, Management and Mental Health* (Cambridge, Mass.: Harvard University Press, 1962), p. 159.

usefulness of structural arrangements and managerial techniques that give fuller play to reciprocity in organizations.

The schema in Figure 10 may be considered with profit. In sum, the Menninger team was struck by the significant interplay of the expectations of the firm and the expectations of its employees. These expectations—written and understood, consciously recognized and implicitly acted upon—constitute what the research team called the "psychological contract." This psychological contract might be more or less viable, depending upon the degree to which it implied reciprocal fulfillment of the expectations of both firm and employees. The degree of reciprocity was conceived as having significant effects, in turn, not only on the productivity of individuals, but also upon their mental health.

The schema cannot be exploited fully here, but the psychological contract poses clear problems for reciprocity and implies sharp challenges for the development of organization structure and managerial techniques. The Menninger team found "social distance" an important element in the psychological contract, for example. Employees brought to work with them strong preferences for various social distances, and these preferences had to be coped with at work by employees and supervisors. Paralleling Schutz's approach to compatibility, the Menninger research team considered that affection, privacy, and control by both employees and superiors were the primary components of social distance. To the degree that the preferences of employees for various social distances could be met in the organizational context, reciprocal benefits for both the employee and the firm were likely. The Menninger team concluded that of the several aspects of behavior considered to be mentally healthy the degree of reciprocity was related most closely to item 5 in Figure 10, that is, to being active and productive. The team concluded that reciprocity also was related to productivity in three ways:[39]

1. Reciprocation makes the task the focus of the employee-management relation.
2. Reciprocation implies the resolution by individuals of certain significant psychological conflicts, particularly those related to dependence. The individual, consequently, can draw greater psychological support from his environment.

3. Reciprocation frees much of an employee's energies from coping with psychological conflicts and makes these energies available for productive effort. Investment of such energies in performance, however, will depend on the work being satisfying enough for the individual.

Reciprocity seems significant enough, even in these hurried terms. Thus the concept proved useful in analyzing the productivity differences between two offices. Its application also seems far broader. Consider the list of conditions thought necessary to permit reciprocity to develop in some fullness, by way of suggesting its ties to the specific structural innovations discussed above and to those to be introduced later. The Menninger research team outlined these eight conditions, or "opportunities," that facilitate reciprocity for most individuals:

1. To plan at least some part of one's work life; an area of freedom to function
2. To model one's self on authority figures in the company
3. To act on the organization, to shape it to some extent to one's own values
4. To experience oneself and the organization as confronting stress together
5. To obtain the gratification of psychological needs for dependence and support
6. To be controlled, or to have personal controls enhanced, by the demands of the company
7. To have the feeling of a fair-share partnership with the company
8. To be stimulated, which includes the experience of growth and change[40]

The point hardly needs bringing home, but let us do the proper thing. These opportunities facilitating reciprocity for most individuals lean heavily on the crutch of the structural arrangements and managerial techniques associated with job enlargement and with training in the process of work. These unorthodox arrangements no less serve individuals who may have extremely different needs, as, for instance, those who are high versus those who are low on "freedom to function." To assign both highs and lows to the same organizational unit seems unwise under most conditions, for the structure and techniques that facilitate reciprocity for some employees would be inappropriate for others. Given the traditional theory of organization, neither can one safely staff some units with highs and other units with lows. If the several units must be integrated in a flow of work, conflict could be intense.

The unorthodox structure sketched in Figures 8b and 9b does not stumble in this case. Highs might be assigned to one unit and lows to another. Appropriate structural arrangements and managerial techniques also could be employed for each unit. The crucial factor permitting such liberties is the relative autonomy of the units of organization where supervisory and operative jobs have been enlarged.

The possibility of a high degree of reciprocity at work also provides a way out of what is one of the most significant binds in thinking about organizations, one's view of organizations and mental health. Sigmund Freud. This set an unfortunate standard. Thus some adventuresome mental health mostly as a negative matter, as one of loosening the bonds of "conscience" if not of destroying inhibitions on behavior altogether. The individual without repressions was mentally healthy for Freud. This set an unfortunate standard. Thus some adventuresome Freudians have explained that there is really nothing wrong with this country that a little less "sexual privatization" would not cure. Baldly, it has been observed that resisting the desire to possess another's wife can cause mental problems. "Society" therefore is adjudged guilty of placing so unwise a stumbling block in the way of individual self-expression, and a destruction of the relevant taboos is advised. Mowrer's brilliant collection of essays, *The Crisis in Psychiatry and Religion,* puts the matter more elegantly.[41] But he comes to the same critical point stressed here.

Given the wide acceptance of this doctrine, little wonder that the literature is so pessimistic about the possibility of individual freedom in organizations. One cannot have the organizational equivalent of a host of free-floating spirits: there will be constraints on behavior in organizations, by definition. Ergo, organizations can hardly be conducive to Freudian mental health. No doubt, the traditional theory of organization and classical job design are not above reproach. Yet they merit reproach, not because they detail constraints on behavior, but rather because they detail the wrong constraints, those that hinder reciprocation under today's prevailing cultural definition of the acceptable balance in organizations. Moreover, one cannot claim a cheap victory by asserting that the traditional theory of organization and classical job design are the only models for organizational relations. They need not be, nor are they the most useful of alternative models.

Reciprocity at work provides a way out of the unrelieved pessimism of common prognoses about life in organizations grounded in the simplistic notion that restraints on behavior are unhealthy. The Judaeo-Christian Ethic sketches the moral boundaries that will guide the restraints on behavior in organizations. This may steal a march on psychiatry. For the present ferment in that area is seriously concerned (among other matters) with the moral rootlessness of the Freudian concept of mental health.

Footnotes: CHAPTER 5

1. Norbert Wiener, *The Human Use of Human Beings* (Boston: Houghton Mifflin Company, 1950).
2. Quoted in Stuart Chase, *The Proper Study of Mankind,* rev. ed., (New York: Harper & Row, Publishers, Incorporated, 1956), p. 166.
3. Quoted in Daniel Bell, *Work and Its Discontents: The Cult of Efficiency in America* (Boston: Beacon Press, 1956), p. 172.
4. Georges Friedmann, *The Anatomy of Work* (New York: The Free Press of Glencoe, 1961), pp. ii, iv.
5. Émile Durkheim, *The Division of Labor in Society* (New York: The Free Press of Glencoe, 1947), p. 371.
6. Louis E. Davis, "Job Design and Productivity: A New Approach," *Personnel,* vol. 33 (March, 1957), pp. 419–420.
7. *The Communist Manifesto* (London: Labour Party Centenary Edition, 1948), p. 134.
8. Adam Smith, *The Wealth of Nations* (New York: Modern Library, Inc., 1937), p. 734.
9. C. Wright Mills, *White Collar: The American Middle Classes* (Fair Lawn, N.J.: Oxford University Press, 1956), p. 236.
10. Sir George Schuster, *Christianity and Human Relations in Industry* (London: Epworth Press, 1951), p. 33.
11. Georges Friedmann, *Industrial Society: The Emergence of the Human*

Problems of Automation (New York: The Free Press of Glencoe, 1955), p. 363.

12. Davis, *op. cit.,* p. 421.

13. Adam Abruzzi, *Work, Workers and Measurement* (New York: Columbia University Press, 1956).

14. George Strauss, "Some Notes on Power-equalization," in Harold J. Leavitt (ed.), *The Social Science of Organizations* (Englewood Cliffs, N.J.: Prentice-Hall, Inc., 1963), especially pp. 53–54.

15. For evidence that there is a tendency, at least in some kinds of work, to set the pace near the minimum output of the least efficient worker, see Howard J. Rothe, "Output Rates among Butter Wrappers," *Journal of Applied Psychology,* vol. 30 (June, 1946), pp. 199–211. Concerning the datum that different workers may achieve optimum output at different work paces, see Friedmann, *Industrial Society, op. cit.,* pp. 165–166.

16. Davis, *op. cit.,* p. 427.

17. David Cox and K. M. Dyce Sharp, "Research on the Unit of Work," *Occupational Psychology,* vol. 26 (April, 1951), p. 90.

18. Friedmann, *The Anatomy of Work, op. cit.,* pp. 14–15.

19. J. Douglas Elliott, "Increasing Office Productivity through Job Enlargement," *Office Management Series,* no. 134 (New York: American Management Association, 1953).

20. *Ibid.,* p. 10.

21. M. D. Kilbridge, "Do Workers Prefer Larger Jobs?" *Personnel,* vol. 37 (September–October, 1960), pp. 45–48.

22. Dause L. Bibby, "An Enlargement of the Job of the Worker," in *Proceedings of the 17th Conference, Texas Personnel and Management Association* (Austin, Tex.: University of Texas, 1955), pp. 29–31; and Charles R. Walker, "The Problem of the Repetitive Job," *Harvard Business Review,* vol. 28 (May, 1950), pp. 54–58.

23. Walker, *op. cit.,* p. 57.

24. Lloyd G. Reynolds and Joseph Shister, *Job Horizons: A Study of Job Satisfaction and Labor Mobility* (New York: Harper & Row, Publishers, Incorporated, 1949), p. 9.

25. George B. Baldwin and George P. Shultz, "Automation: A New Dimension of Old Problems," pp. 124–125, in Industrial Relations Research Association, *Proceedings of the Seventh Annual Meeting* (1954).

26. Quoted in Friedmann, *The Anatomy of Work, op. cit.,* p. 87.

27. Douglas, *op. cit.,* pp. 6–8.

28. Herbert E. Krugman, "Just Like Running Your Own Little Store . . . ," *Personnel,* vol. 34 (July–August, 1957), pp. 46–47.

29. William McGehee and Paul W. Thayer, *Training in Business and Industry* (New York: John Wiley & Sons, Inc., 1961), p. 10.

30. Alexander R. Heron, *Why Men Work* (Stanford, Calif.: Stanford University Press, 1948).

31. Friedmann, *Industrial Society, op. cit.,* p. 287.

32. Baldwin and Shultz, *op. cit.,* p. 125.

33. *Ibid.,* pp. 125–126.

34. Walker and Guest, *op. cit.,* pp. 56–57.

35. Alvin W. Gouldner, "The Norm of Reciprocity: A Preliminary Statement," *American Sociological Review,* vol. 25 (April, 1960), pp. 161–162; and L. T. Hobhouse, *Morals in Evolution* (London: Chapman & Hall, Ltd., 1951), p. 12. For a parallel analysis, see George Parthemos, "Obligation: A Framework for and a Preface to Substantive Work," paper read at the Southern Political Science Association, November, 1962.

36. Quoted in Friedmann, *Industrial Society, op. cit.,* pp. 170–171.

37. Rexford Hersey, *Zest for Work* (New York: Harper & Row, Publishers, Incorporated, 1955).

38. Harry Levinson, Charlton R. Price, Kenneth J. Munden, Harold J. Mandl, and Charles M. Solley, *Men, Management, and Mental Health* (Cambridge, Mass.: Harvard University Press, 1962).

39. *Ibid.,* pp. 141–142.

40. *Ibid.,* pp. 129–130.

41. O. Hobart Mowrer, *The Crisis in Psychiatry and Religion* (Princeton, N.J.: D. Van Nostrand Company, Inc., 1961).

"They Go But Faintly to Work, ... With One Buttock": Self-determination in the Micro-environment

There seems much in the French saying that: "The more things change, the more they remain the same." To which the pessimist might add: if indeed they do not get worse. Consider Voltaire's observation of long ago concerning factory hands. "They go but faintly to work, as they say, with one buttock," he noted with decorum. "They," of course, never said it exactly that way, but Voltaire's meaning is clear. Work commonly violated the third value of the Judaeo-Christian Ethic—which prescribes that the individual control significant aspects of his immediate work environment—and man sensibly protected himself by lukewarm commitments to his work.

Matters had not changed for the better by 1946, apparently, which year saw Henry Ford II quoted that his firm was getting some 34 per cent less output than in 1941, as measured by direct labor costs on comparable products and processes.[1] General Motors announced a similar decline of 37 per cent, approximately 43 per cent of which was attributed to ineffective management, as through poor organization, inadequate tooling, and the like. The remainder, in management's opinion, could be traced to reduced effort by employees.[2]

Such data have occasioned much debate and nostalgic harking back to an era when all employees were loyal and industrious to a fault. At best, however, comparative data tapping the "will-to-work" over time are sparse and difficult to interpret in the bargain. Whether the pernicious trend suggested above did occur, therefore, cannot be established definitely. Organizational folklore in this particular cannot be supported or rejected by empirical data.

CONTRA THE TRADITIONAL THEORY OF ORGANIZATION

Further Directions

A more moderate position seems less contentious. It may be laid bare in terms of three propositions. Whatever the long-run trends in the will-to-work, first, pervasive ideas about organizing operate so as to alienate the individual from his work. Lewis Way put the matter forcefully in *Man's Quest for Significance:* "Given no responsibility, [the worker] showed none; treated as an automaton, he behaved as such." This puts matters too broadly for all workers, of course. Often the relevant ideas about organizing are applied only in much diluted form, and their perniciousness is thereby reduced. Whatever the degree, however, the tendency is the same. Second, the present strategy is to determine whether these ideas about organizing are the universal verities they are often presumed to be. Third, to dispel any possible mystery, only qualified support can be marshaled for the traditional theory of organization, and thus for the structural arrangements and managerial techniques consistent with that theory.

Each of these three introductory propositions may be discussed briefly. Leading ideas about organizing curb the individual's opportunities to influence his immediate work environment, first, and encourage him to approach his work in the anatomically curious way described by Voltaire. Frederick W. Taylor gave direction to generations of thought in this particular, as in others. He noted that his system demanded of the worker "not to seek to increase production by his own initiative, but to perform punctiliously the orders given down to their slightest detail." [3]

Taylor's basic demand might not have been troublesome, given his belief that work standards could be determined with absolute accuracy, once and for all. This positivistic ideal has proved far out of reach, however. In fact, it is basically unreachable. Any work standard must be a composite of (at least) what both worker and time-study man consider reasonable, and "reasonable" cannot be defined in the absolute, narrowly technical sense that Taylor implied. Such value phenomena were submerged by positivistic enthusiasm, and the vital weakness was clear even in Taylor's advice to pig-iron handlers that he did not want them exhausted after a day's work, but only "properly tired." Hardly an absolute standard this!

The fugitive nature of work standards creates significant problems. Not infrequently, for example, a rate will be set by a time-study man. An employee might then change his notion of what properly tired means, thereby earning wages far above those considered reasonable by the time-study man. These mistakes tend to be quickly corrected, as by reducing the per-piece price. The consequences tend to be unfortunate. As one observer noted: "This has happened to a million workers in American industry . . . since the war began. It makes workers wary. It makes them hold back. It causes great masses of them habitually to work way below their productive power. *Here is the greatest single loss of human energy in American life.*" [4]

The restriction of the employee's initiative thus often will have consequences precisely opposite those Taylor intended. His dictum, therefore, requires this reworking: "The worker must not so much perform punctiliously the orders given down to their slightest detail, but seek to increase production by his own initiative."

Second, such considerations suggest reasons aplenty for an aggressive investigation of alternative ways of increasing the will-to-work. Thus the problems of work are simply there; they will remain for many decades, at least; and they are not likely to improve by themselves. Avoidance therefore is not an acceptable strategy. Heron drew the proper conclusions after World War II. He stressed contemporary man's incomparable potential for freedom in his new mobility. Consequently, the forces that once held a man to one job were much diminished; and the sanctions which caused men to work steadily (and perhaps fearfully) lost much of their power. Instead of bemoaning these data, Heron concluded, "we may better spend our time in searching for the positive inducements to work effectively." [5]

Over-reaction is as dangerous as avoidance, however. We can careen wildly beyond a reasonable readjustment unless "positive inducements" are built into work. The inequities of the Individualistic Ethic hardly sanction an extension *in extremis* of the Social Ethic. There is considerable evidence that we have been just this immoderate, having rejected the good along with the bad in thinking about work. Adriano Tilgher put his finger on precisely such evidence.[6] "It is certainly a serious matter," he noted, "that in the country which till yesterday was the veritable Holy Land of this new faith [in work], in the United States of America, the religion of work should seem paradoxically but inevitably to be producing a religion its exact opposite, the religion of recreation, pleasure, and amusement." This seems serious, if only because there is so much to be done to which the religion of recreation contributes so little.

Third, commonly used structural arrangements and managerial techniques encourage men to approach work with "one buttock." The point will be approached via a multidimensional analysis of the will-to-work as a product of such forces acting simultaneously:

1. The personality characteristics of organization members
2. The formal organizational arrangements, such as job design, company policies, and incentive plans
3. The quality and style of supervision
4. The social relations that exist at work

Interpretively, a low degree of reciprocity between these four factors will be associated with a low will-to-work.

The multidimensional approach to the will-to-work permits both summary and preview of this analysis. As for summary, Chapter 4 provides information necessary to meaningfully consider personality differences in organizations, while Chapter 5 dwells on the problems of classical job design at lower levels of organization. By way of preview, this chapter stresses the style of supervision. It also outlines an alternate pattern for organizing work that can provide social relations more congenial to employee personalities while it simplifies significant problems of supervision. The bias of Chapter 6 is still toward lower-level operations, then, but not unrelievedly so. Chapters 7 and 8 will stress similar factors as they apply in the bigger picture of entire organizations. In all three chapters the continuing aim is to restore some degree of order to the research literature. There is ample reason for impatience with the literature. Typically, one study will report that in Company A the turnover of employees on repetitive work was greater than those on nonrepetitive work. In the same study, however, Company B's experience will show only minor tendencies of this kind.[7] This chapter will try its hand at reconciling such results.

DEPENDENCE AS AN ORGANIZATIONAL DISEASE

Some Wages of the Traditional Theory

Understanding the tendency of traditional notions about organizing to curb the will-to-work may begin conveniently at the broadest level. That specialization implies the dependence of the employee seldom has escaped practitioners. Extreme specialization of work commonly has been accompanied by the introduction of structural arrangements and managerial techniques whose purpose it was to bind the employee unalterably to the "system," to ensure his dependence upon it. Nor did leading proponents of classical job design shrink from raising such practices to the level of a principle. Planning and execution should be radically separated, Taylor prescribed, and management was to be the repository of all work-relevant knowledge. The worker once possessed this knowledge and skill, but that would have to be changed. The new worker was not to "seek to increase production by his own initiative but [should] perform punctiliously the orders given down to their slightest detail."

The traditional theory of organization reeks of dependence as an ideal. That ideal applies to jobs both high and humble, although the ideal might be approached closely only under more or less unusual circumstances.

The emphasis upon dependence deserves close inspection, for considerable evidence shows it to be an awkward principle. Indeed, the limitations of dependence are most apparent where it is approached most closely. On an automobile assembly line, for example, employee satisfaction fell as dependence was increasingly organized into work. Even the minority of workers who found their jobs satisfying fit this generalization. Thus all employees with nonrepetitive jobs—the repairmen and the utilitymen—expressed satisfaction with their jobs. Where repetitive jobs provided human advantages, satisfaction was also likely to be high. Such human advantages are typified by the possibility of social interaction to break the monotony. Only a rather small percentage of employees enjoyed repetitive jobs without such advantages. One such worker noted: "I like doing the same thing all the time. I'd rather stay right where I am. When I come in in the morning, I like to know exactly what I'll be doing." [8]

This pattern seems typical, and its effects are not limited to factors, like satisfaction, that imply mostly long-run costs. As Charles Walker and Robert Guest have demonstrated, the more closely work enforces employee dependence via the classical guidelines of job design, the greater is the rate of absenteeism. [9]

So much having been said about the general trends, exceptions should not cause great surprise. Any one batch of employees can contain a majority of individuals with personality characteristics well suited to classical job designs. Such employees will be in a definite minority in larger populations, however.

Much other evidence reveals the sharp and unfavorable reaction of most men at all organization levels against unilateral dependence upon management. Unionization, for example, seems motivated in no small part by a widespread desire for multilateral reciprocation. Workers certainly organized into labor unions for economic reasons, but psychological and social motives were just as compelling. Thus they sought to participate in making decisions that vitally affected them in their work and community life. [10] The formation of labor unions need not reduce the employee's will-to-work, but other adaptations certainly do. Consider the time-hallowed practice of "dogging it" at work. Stanley Mathewson documents the existence of such practices among office workers and executives, as well as among factory workers. So resourceful were employees in developing protective practices even against "speedups," that Mathewson concluded that underwork and restriction of output were greater problems than overspeeding and overwork. [11] To the same point, the experiences of the sociologist Donald Roy with various factory operations permit us to assign an order of magnitude to the potential for, and the practice of, such restriction. As a very green hand, Roy was able to waste (by his own estimate) an average of 1.35 hours out of every 8-hour shift over six months of factory employment. He quickly got the hang of things, however, raising this to two of every eight hours in his last two months. Nor was this the end of it. On some jobs, Roy estimated the "potential quota restriction" at some 2.7 hours per day.[12] Abandoning output restrictions, then, could have increased production by at least 21 per cent and perhaps as much as 57 per cent.

Many of these reactions against dependence seem paradoxically desirable, however. They seem desirable, that is, compared to the behavior characteristic of the extremely dependent person, the person who habitually and almost desperately relies on the support and protection of others. These individuals, as Saul Gellerman describes them, often are agreeable and contented enough, if they are not charming. But these assets soon peter out. Gellerman makes the point sharply. "Dependency can show up in many different ways," he notes. "Most often, it affects what people *don't* do: it makes them unwilling to take chances, to exert extra effort, to use their imaginations or to display initiative." [13]

These diverse findings support a common point: the bias of the traditional theory of organization toward dependence falls short on two basic grounds. Employees are not generally predisposed to respond to intense pressures to act dependently without murmur or unconscious defense. The "rate-buster" does appear in organizations alongside the "rate-setter," but the latter is more common. No wonder that rate-busters can be characterized in the following terms. They tend to be hostile and aggressive toward others; they are often prejudiced and narrowly inflexible; they reflect a distrust of most of their fellow employees; and they are motivated largely by economic rather than social considerations.[14]

Nor do uniformly favorable consequences result when individuals can be conditioned to act dependently. Given contemporary needs for change and training, dependence can prove very troublesome even in low-level positions. Indeed, the single, biggest cost-saving suggestion in a giant industrial concern came from a floorsweeper. The more significant rub, perhaps, is that structural arrangements and managerial techniques appropriate for inducing and sustaining dependence reinforce one another, affecting not only the employee but various levels of supervision as well. If an employee's early experiences reward dependence, moreover, can that lesson be unlearned easily later? A probable defense against great pressures toward dependence, finally, is a more or less stubborn resistance to adaptation at work. This always makes work enervating, if not positively dangerous, under conditions of advanced technology. I have in mind one case in which automatic controls were installed and employees were constantly reminded that they should not think, but merely consult the procedures manual and act accordingly. This is precisely what the employees did, even when an unanticipated malfunction that could have been remedied quickly went unattended because nothing in the procedures manual covered the situation. Dependence can have its great costs, then, and perhaps even under those uncommon circumstances when almost every contingency can be provided for and when employee adaptations and adjustments cannot materially aid performance.

This disregard of some obvious points is not merely cavalier or careless. Rather it implies that the emphasis upon dependence in the traditional theory is a logical derivation from the several properties of the System, as opposed to a description of man as he is, or indeed of man as he must be to act effectively under the generality of conditions encountered in organizations. If either realistic description or prescription had really interested early students of job design and organization structure, their treatment of dependence would have been far more complicated. Such a more complicated view would emphasize that man may be considered as being simultaneously somewhere along each of several dimensions of dependence-independence. These continua may be described, following Chris Argyris, in terms of the dynamic tendencies of individuals to develop from:[15]

1. A more passive state as infants to a state of increasing activity as adults
2. A dependent state as infants to a state of relative independence as adults, while acknowledging healthy dependencies
3. A capacity for few behaviors as a child to a capacity for many complex activities as an adult
4. Having erratic, casual, shallow, and momentary interests as an infant to having deeper and more intense interests as an adult
5. Having a short time-perspective as an infant to having an extended time-perspective as an adult

6. A state of subordination in the family to a state of aspiring for positions of equality or supremacy relative to their peers
7. A lack of awareness of the self to increasing awareness and control over the self as an adult

The basic organizational problem is the tailoring of structure and managerial techniques in ways that will facilitate these developmental tendencies rather than obstruct or divert them. The traditional theory of organization does not measure up well.

Particular attention in the design of structure and techniques must be accorded the supervisor's role in handling dependence. Dependence is a more or less constant phenomenon, universal in organizations as everywhere else in human life, touching everyone. At the same time, individuals seek to achieve some continually changing balance of dependence, interdependence, and independence in their several organizational relations with superiors, peers, and subordinates. Achieving such a balance in organizations is no less difficult than in other areas of life, if it is not more difficult. Organization superiors at all levels will play crucial roles in the degree of reciprocity achieved, for they are *the* legitimate authority figures after all. Superiors can at once meet an individual's legitimate dependence needs, encourage interdependence, and guide employees toward independence.

Two aspects of superior-subordinate relations of particular importance in the management of dependence will concern us immediately. The structure that channels supervisory behavior and the supervisory style encouraged by that structure are the next analytical targets. They demonstrate that the traditional theory of organization prescribes structure and style that are at once inappropriate for the mastery of dependency needs, ineffective in inducing interdependence, and generally inhibit the individual's progress toward independence.

THE SPAN OF CONTROL

The Tyranny of Logic Illustrated

The simplistic emphasis upon dependence in management thought no doubt encourages many men to approach their work "with one buttock." Anything more is psychologically dangerous. Reciprocity must suffer from the emphasis upon dependence; and most individuals can only give of themselves over the long run as their needs are met. Man thus is bigger than the work given him by the traditional theory. Therefore man could hardly give all of himself to it, even if he wanted.

Whether self-defeating or not, however, the bias toward dependence has been shaped by, and has itself shaped, logically consistent structure and managerial techniques in its own image. Consider the common prescription of a limited span of control. The traditional advice is to have but a few subordinates reporting to any single superior. The precise number deemed appropriate varies only within a narrow range. A common rule of thumb advises that the number of subordinates reporting directly to each superior should approach three toward the top of an organization's hierarchy, and perhaps seven to ten at the lowest levels. Figure 11 sketches an organization based upon the limited span of control, as it was found in a number of medium-sized stores in the Sears, Roebuck chain.

The limited span of control is common in practice and orthodox in theory. Challenges have shaken the prevailing orthodoxy.[16] But they

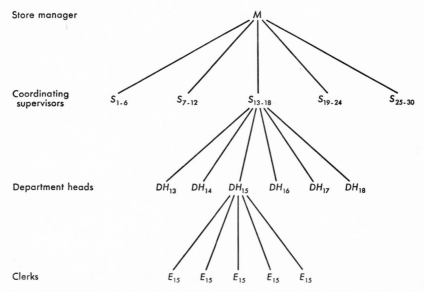

Figure 11. Sales Organization of a Sears, Roebuck Store with Traditional Span of Control.

have not laid it low, probably because one could not think of a structural arrangement better designed to induce employee dependence upon management. All the properties of the traditional theory of organization are at home with a limited span of control. For example, the emphasis upon specialization implies problems of integrating the many separate pieces into which work is commonly fragmented. A narrow span of control is well suited in logic to this delicate job.

If often respected (and particularly at the verbal level), the prescription of a limited span of control is grounded in nothing more solid than logical consistency whose *idée fixe* is dependence. It is supported only by an ineffectual lick and a far-fetched promise. In addition, considerable evidence demonstrates that the concept often adversely affects both short-run and long-run efficiency. These adverse effects are not clearly overbalanced by the "principle's" contributions to effective performance.

The indictment may seem too broad. It is not. Thus the most ambitious proof of the necessity of a limited span of control is the simple mathematical demonstration by V. A. Graicunas dating back to the 1930s. Graicunas observed that as the number of related individuals was increased arithmetically, the number of possible interrelations between them increased exponentially. The increase in these possible interrelations was particularly sharp when six or more individuals are involved. This is interesting enough, but it proves nothing about a *desirable* span of control. At best, the demonstration proves that *if the efforts of several supervisors are closely interrelated* (as the traditional theory requires) a limited span of control may be necessary to prevent matters from getting extremely complicated. But this merely demonstrates that the traditional theory of organization is congenial to a limited span of control, which information any list of the "principles" provides directly.

No more convincing is the other evidence offered of the significance of the number 6. People (it was alleged) could remember six consecutive digits with tolerable efficiency but experienced increasingly great difficulties as the string of digits was lengthened. True or not, the relevance of the datum in supporting a desirable span of control is obscure in the extreme. Of such flimsy stuff was the argument for the validity of the limited span of control.

Practice in organizations gives even less support to the limited span of control. Let several factors be listed briefly, by way of an introduction to a more extended discussion of one important aspect of organizational life that reflects unfavorably on that "principle." First, the flat prescription of a limited span of control must be suspect, as must all monolithic guides. There may be operations that absolutely require a narrow span of control, and there will be individuals who can work well only under conditions of constant stimulation or goading by supervisors. The traditional concept is well suited to such operations and to such personalities. However, there will be operations and personalities aplenty to whom this structural arrangement is ill suited, and here the monolithic traditional concept fails.

Second, the general acceptance of the limited span of control demands nothing less than clear proof of the superiority of organizations with a limited span over otherwise comparable organizations that are less in debt to this principle. No convincing demonstration of the efficacy of a narrow span of control exists, nor has one been attempted. That is not surprising, given that the traditional theory of organization has been less concerned with validating its underlying properties than with logically contemplating its own umbilicus.

Third, a narrow span of control places some obvious and significant barriers in the way of the effective functioning of organizations. Although far more research is necessary, well-established findings plus relatively straightforward inferences permit considerable boldness. For example, chains of communication become attenuated quickly in organizations having a narrow span of control. Figure 12 can serve as a bench mark for comparison. This structure requires only three levels of organization; the Figure 11 structure requires four levels for a comparable number of employees. This is the margin by which communication can be complicated, time lags between problem perception and action can grow to significant proportions, and organizations can settle into that lethargy vilified as "bureaucracy."

These unhappy consequences are not inevitable under the narrow span of control, but they are encouraged by powerful circular forces. Consider the position of the department heads in Figure 11. The coordinating supervisors are not likely to delegate substantial powers of decision-making to the department heads or to give them considerable

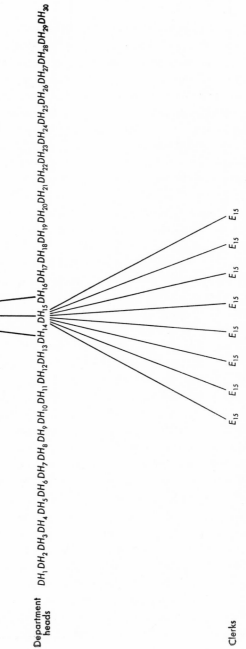

Figure 12. Sales Organization of a Sears, Roebuck Store with a Wide Span of Control.

latitude in running their own operations. The narrow span of control does not prohibit department heads from having considerable discretion, but it gives only faint encouragement to it. If one were really interested in encouraging substantial delegation, a narrow span of control would have little to recommend it. Bluntly, the coordinating supervisors in Figure 11 must have something to do. Most supervisors would get the powerful message implied by a limited span of control. The derivative weakness in the positions of the department heads, in turn, would encourage them to make more extreme demands for the dependence of their own subordinates.

A host of factors reinforce such a reasonable adaptation, and push it toward costly extremes. Given that only trivial matters are delegated to a department head, his employees are not likely to take him all that seriously. This datum implies great problems in supervising employees, problems that are likely to involve the coordinating supervisors as well as the department heads. The department head must walk a tightrope. He must maintain acceptable levels of output and discipline, while the narrow span of control helps deprive him of useful leverage for influencing his subordinates. One gambit often resorted to is "sweetening" upward communications, but the tactic has self-defeating limitations. Commonly, department heads will be very selective in the information they communicate to their superiors. They will minimize problems they face and emphasize successes, and they may plant information that does not reflect favorably on their colleagues.[17]

Sooner or later, the coordinating supervisors will be burned by such "administered news." The likely consequences are greater surveillance and more carefully hedged delegation to the department heads. The allegiance of the department head's subordinates will be further strained, if efforts are not made by superiors to "encourage" the flow of information from these subordinates. And the nasty circular process is complete.

No direct demonstration of the point is available, but efficiency often will be affected unfavorably by such dynamics. Two emphases suggest the nature of the complete argument. First, the narrow span of control tends to inhibit training in work. For if a coordinating supervisor is available, if not anxious, to pull a department head's chestnuts from the organizational fires, relations of dependence may flourish. Problems will be kicked upstairs, thus depriving the department heads of valuable training opportunities. Second, the supervisory job probably will have narrow scope, given the limited span of control and the emphasis in the traditional theory on departmentation by functions and processes. The consequences seem unfortunate. As several studies show, much mischief can result from the temptation to use a narrow span of control to limit the power of supervisors, "power" referring to the degree of control over the immediate work environment. In one case, sharp differences between the productivity of work units only emerged when supervisors were distinguished in terms of their influence with superiors. High supervisory power was associated with effective performance.[18] Similarly, a number of departments in one organization were ranked in terms of their productivity. The "top" one-third of the departments then were compared with the "bottom" third. The top departments accorded their department heads more power over "what goes on in your department" than the low departments accorded their immediate supervisors.[19]

These costs have been avoided, at least under a wide variety of conditions, as in the Figure 12 structure which depicts the broad span of control that developed in some medium-sized stores of Sears, Roebuck. These stores were comparable to other Sears stores that developed a narrow span of control, as depicted in Figure 11. Consistent with Sears policy, the individual store managers were allowed to develop the intrastore organizational structure they desired. No true believers in the narrow span of control, then, were the Sears policy makers.

Such variations in the span of control can be consequential, even given the hesitancy befitting the undeveloped state of the literature. Thus the Sears stores with broad spans of control had more employees considered promotable to higher positions than the stores with narrow spans of control.

These findings seem reasonable enough in terms of past discussions of training, supervisory power, and dependence. First, Figure 12 structures provide significant opportunities for training of department heads. The manager in such a structure must delegate with zest, and as a general rule he must allow the department heads considerable room to tussle with their own problems. These define conditions well suited to training on the job. Substantial prior training also is required. The combined effect is the early elimination of those unable to profit from the opportunities. In contrast, inadequacies may be hidden more easily where superiors are more anxious to help run a subordinate's affairs, as under a narrow span of control. The training opportunities and delegation associated with a broader span of control, second, would enhance the power of the department heads. Third, subordinates consequently could develop viable patterns of dependence-interdependence-independence with superiors who control enough aspects of the immediate work environment to make necessary accommodations to individual needs. Moreover, supervisors with high power are likely to sympathize more with the needs of their subordinates toward self-actualization.

Supported by structural arrangements and training, that is, the department heads in a Figure 12 organization need not puff themselves up by demands for the dependence of their subordinates. Low-power supervisors, sorely enough beset, will tend to reject such efforts by subordinates as a threat to the supervisor's already shaky position. Some experimental evidence also supports the point.[20]

Some reservations are in order. If other conditions are favorable, a narrow span of control may be very useful for training purposes. But "other conditions" seldom seem favorable. For a narrow span of control is normally a part of a set of related structural arrangements and managerial techniques derived from the traditional theory of organization—such as an authoritarian style of supervision—and these tend to bring out the worst in the narrow span of control.

The advantages of a broad span of control are not there simply for the taking, in any case. Other conditions must complement it. For example, a wide span of control could breed chaos in the absence of nonarbitrary measures of performance and of a structure that facilitates such measurement. In this sense, a broad span of control patently makes most sense under conditions of job enlargement. There the individual units reporting to any supervisor are relatively autonomous, the comparative performance of the several units may be ascertained with speed and confidence, and broad delegation to supervisors and to employees is consistent with both job enlargement and a broad span of control. In this case as in others, structure and managerial techniques which approach the Judaeo-Christian Ethic are mutually reinforcing.

Personality characteristics imply no less a challenge to the choice of an appropriate span of control, as Sears experience shows. Wishing to gain the advantages associated with a broad span of control in some of its stores, management took an apparently reasonable step. Some of the managers who had developed a narrow span of control in their stores (X-type) were transferred to stores in which a wide span of control had existed; and some managers who had developed a wide span of control in their stores (Y-type) took the places of the X-type managers.

This reflected a human desire to have the best of both worlds, but that full-blown desire was frustrated. It was thought that Y-type managers would in short order convert their stores to a broad span of control; and the force of existing structural arrangements was to have forced a change upon the X-type managers. The surmises were 50 per cent accurate. Y-type managers did inaugurate wide spans of control, and gradually eliminated the level of coordinating supervisors that had existed. X-type managers did not play the game. They built up an intermediate level of supervision where none had existed. The press of events did not permit psychological testing of the transfers, but descriptive accounts strongly suggest that the personality characteristics of the X-type and the Y-type managers differed significantly in expected ways. Whyte noted that a Y-type manager had an optimistic view of people, and he was at once trusting of their abilities and helpful in their development. Managers of X-type stores were more pessimistic, and they tended to feel that trust and help were not appropriate because "it was very difficult to get hardworking people any more." [21] Expecting the worst of their employees, the latter managers often found their fears justified.

Chapter 4 permits a shorthand description of such apparent personality differences. X-type managers have a supervisory style that can be designated as "authoritarian," while Y-type managers are "supportive."

This analysis may be brought to a point. A broad span of control seems widely applicable. Many jobs would require no significant changes if the span of control were increased (as in the Sears stores), and a broad spectrum of jobs can be appropriately redesigned (as by a program of job enlargement). Relatedly, a large proportion of organization members in this country have personality characteristics that tend toward the Y-type described above. Many employees, and perhaps a heavy majority, are not predisposed to meet the demands of a narrow span of control. This will be the case particularly when it exists along with an authoritarian supervisory style. The odds favor such a coexistence, as the following section will show.

Although existing evidence does not settle all questions, a devotion to dependence via a narrow span of control has little to recommend it as a universal strategy. At the very least, the monolithic prescription of a narrow span of control is grossly insensitive to individual differences. The case may be demonstrated from the standpoint of immediate dollars-and-cents costs, as in the less-favorable sales records of those medium-sized Sears stores whose organization is sketched in Figure 11. It also is the case in longer-run senses, as in the training and development of a higher percentage of employees considered promotable in the Sears stores whose organization is sketched in Figure 12.

The lack of support for a narrow span of control also extends to ultimate values, as they are approximated in the Judaeo-Christian Ethic. The dependence consistent with a narrow span of control hardly does faithful service to that increase of freedom to control the immediate job environment called for by the third value of the J-C Ethic. Tersely, a narrow span of control is a jealous master. It implies monolithic dependence and thereby fosters the neglect of individual differences.

The same point may be put otherwise. The wide span of control not only facilitates approaching the Judaeo-Christian Ethic, but it also can have a wide range of useful consequences in contemporary organized activity. Thus a broad span of control permits a more sensitive response to individual differences than does a narrow span of control. This is no mere logical surmise. For example, the organization of the Sears, Roebuck colossus has spans of control at the three levels immediately below the level of the president that approximate fifteen, fourteen, and forty-nine as one descends the hierarchy, we are told.[22] Consequently, there are but two or three levels of authority between the responsible corporate officials and their store managers. With all this, some of Sears's medium-sized stores had a narrow span of control, with only some five or six subordinates reporting to each superior. As Figure 11 shows, that is, there were as many or more levels between a clerk in one of these stores and his store manager as there were levels between the president of Sears and the store manager! The store managers, in part by virtue of a wide span of control, have the freedom to utilize a narrow span of control in their own stores. Aggressive readers should not leap to the conclusion that this implies the restricted freedom of employees who might not prefer such a span of control. The manager's freedom in this case stops short of gross neglect of the personality predispositions of his employees. Thus the Sears managers are responsible for maintaining effective performance, as compared with similar stores. Moreover, Sears utilizes an employee morale survey technique to guard further against the single-minded pursuit of short-run productivity at the expense of morale or of the neglected training of subordinates.[23]

MANAGERIAL AUTHORITARIANISM

Uses, Pathologies, and an Alternative

Like all of life, organizational phenomena come in "syndromes," clusters of related structural arrangements and managerial techniques. It is always somewhat uncomfortable, then, to consider a single element of the authoritarian syndrome prescribed by the traditional theory of organization. Dependence, a narrow span of control, and an authoritarian style of supervision are the major interacting components of this syndrome as surely as fever and milky white spots are part of the measles syndrome.

This section focuses on the third element of this cluster of related structure and techniques, upon an "authoritarian"—or "directive," or "nonsupportive"—style of supervision. An authoritarian style of supervision may exist independent of the traditional biases toward total dependence of the employee or a narrow span of control. But these factors will commonly occur together, if in varying degrees of unrelieved severity. Their complementarity fairly leaps through this description of one supervisor's behavior:[24]

He loved to yell at people and he did not like to delegate authority. His immediate subordinate had been in that job seven years and in all that time he had not been allowed to make any decisions. If he did they were countermanded immediately. The boss would go out in the field and see something that didn't quite suit him and the boys would say, "_____ told us to do it that way," and he would say, "Don't pay any attention to that s.o.b., he won't be here long."

Here was a man made to the mold of demanding dependence and utilizing a narrow span of control. This neanderthal type has many more sophisticated brothers. Verbal nothings—about the "organizational team" or the "family"—commonly are used to sugarcoat the underlying goal of the total dependence of the employee upon management reflected in such structural arrangements as a limited span of control and in such managerial techniques as an authoritarian style of supervision. The harsher realities are brought to the surface only when the employee does not do precisely as his superiors have already decided he must do. If anything, this authoritarian type is more insidious than his less inhibited counterpart.

Name-calling is a limited technique, and conceptual baptism does not determine an appropriate style of supervision. Let us lay bare the bones of the authoritarian style of supervision so that its efficacy in organizations may be determined. At least these four characteristics underlie the description above of an authoritarian style of supervision, whether primitive or sophisticated:

1. A low degree of participation by subordinates in decision-making
2. A high degree of punitiveness as, for example, in supervisory reactions to error
3. A high degree of person-to-person pressure for output
4. A high degree of emphasis upon "structure" and a low degree of emphasis upon "consideration," as in pointed countermands of actions taken by subordinates to demonstrate who is "the boss"

These characteristics may be taken to define an authoritarian style of supervision for our purposes. The opposed extremes of these characteristics—high participation by subordinates in decision-making, for example—may be taken to describe a "group-centered" or "supportive" style of supervision.

Tests of these major properties of the authoritarian style of supervision, to put matters flatly, hardly encourage fervent devotion to the traditional theory of organization. One could demonstrate that all the characteristics above tend to be associated with low output and other unattractive consequences. Less ambitious use of the available evidence will be attempted here. Consider the degree of pressure for output, by way of illustration of what a broader survey would show. Thus ten of eleven departments in one organization whose supervisors applied *high* pressure for output were *low* producers. In the same organization, nine of ten departments whose employees reported *low* pressure were *high* producers.[25] Predictions based upon the efficacy of the authoritarian style of supervision were incorrect in over 90 per cent of the cases. This is not a strong showing.

Other awkward consequences of the authoritarian style of supervision may be illustrated at greater length by considering its emphasis upon "structure" and its neglect of "consideration." Following Edwin Fleishman,[26] consideration by supervisors may be defined for present purposes as "mutual trust, respect, and a certain warmth and rapport between the supervisor and his group"; and "structure" may be taken to indicate a supervisory role largely conceived in terms of assigning tasks, planning ways to get work done, and pushing for production.

The traditional theory of organization pays a stiff price for its preoccupation with structure, thus defined. For as the consideration of a supervisor increases, the grievance rate among his employees *decreases*. Similarly, as the supervisor's emphasis upon structure increases, so does the grievance rate.

Do not rush to the implication that structure therefore must be neglected if low grievance rates are desired. Figure 13 suggests the sharp limits of this pessimistic approach, summarizing data obtained from many supervisors. The figure permits these constructions. If consideration is low, it makes little difference whether structure is emphasized or not. Grievance rates will be high. Where consideration is moderate, low grievance rates can be achieved only if supervisors make few demands for structure. As a supervisor increases his structure, the grievance rate zooms upward. These are dark enough tendencies, but there is a way out that can satisfy both the needs of most employees and the formal organization. When consideration is high, increases in the degree to which a supervisor demands structure have but a small influence on the grievance rate.

This review has a double-barreled implication. The authoritarian style of supervision and the traditional theory of organization get little

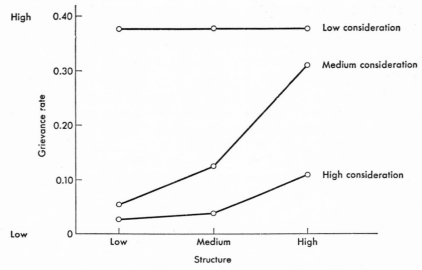

Figure 13. The Effects of Various Combinations of "Consideration" and "Structure" upon Grievance Rates. From Edwin A. Fleishman, "Patterns of Leadership Behavior Related to Group Grievances and Turnover," *Personnel Psychology*, vol. 15, Spring, 1962, p. 50.

support. They stand embarrassed on two counts. They put the emphasis in the wrong place, on structure as opposed to consideration. Moreover, no monolithic guide is sensitive enough to account for the delicate variations sketched above, no matter where its emphasis.

Existing research does not flatly recommend the usefulness of a group-centered style of supervision and organizational arrangements consistent with it. To put that temptation behind us, let four points be emphasized. They will provide more useful direction for the following analysis.

First, there may seem a cart-and-horse problem implicit in the findings illustrated, but the difficulty is spurious. Some have argued that supervisors of high-producing units exert little pressure for output because it is already high. The supervisory attitude, that is, might result from high output rather than contribute to it. This reverses the direction of the causal arrow, crudely. The point is significant. For if supervisory attitudes are considered the dependent variables, if they are caused by various levels of output, one must despair of answering the question of how to induce high output. Understanding has no real alternative to according substantial significance to supervisory attitudes and practices, while recognizing that high output may serve to reinforce them. This alternative seems fruitful: direct evidence demonstrates that changes in supervisory attitudes and practices can influence output. As three researchers concluded: "It is difficult to see how such personal values and characteristics [of supervisors] could be produced solely by virtue of having groups who produce at a higher rate. . . . It seems logical that differences in group motivation are related to differences in supervisory practice and philosophy." [27]

Second, much independent evidence supports the reasonableness of attaching real significance to the supervisor's style. To put one aspect of the matter directly, the resort to an authoritarian style of supervision implies the frustration by the supervisor of significant needs of most employees. Ideally, a supervisory style should facilitate the reaching by each employee of some working balance of two opposed forces, those in the direction of dependence and those in the direction of independence. Any working balance should have such components: decreasing dependence upon organizational superiors; growing interdependence between peers, superiors, and subordinates in an organization; and an increasing area of active independence for the subordinates. There is no avoiding an ever-changing resolution of these forces-in-opposition since they derive (as Mason Haire observes) from the "fact that the infant is born with a set of needs, but is dependent on an agent to satisfy them." [28]

Overemphasis upon any one of these three components seems ill-advised. Emphasizing dependence probably would threaten most individuals, perhaps reducing their security to the degree that their work was affected and their initiative to supply the adjustments required by their work was stifled. An unrelieved emphasis upon independence, oppositely, makes cooperative activity in organizations chancy in the extreme.

There seems an available middle road in which the supervisor must play a crucial role. Thus Haire outlines three supervisory techniques that seem appropriate to the task of making dependency "as easy to live with as possible." They are:

1. The superior must provide a wide range of relevant knowledge for his subordinates.

2. The supervisor must maintain an atmosphere of approval at work, including particularly the freedom of the subordinate to make mistakes, profit from them, and be responsible for them.
3. The superior must maintain consistent discipline.

These three conditions tend to assure that dependence relations will not hamper subordinates. Haire also notes the need to facilitate the independence of subordinates. Three additional directions seem most useful for appropriate supervisory action:

4. The supervisor should "provide opportunities for growth and expansion of the individual's social and egoistic need-satisfactions."
5. The superior should seek to secure the subordinates' participation in an increasing variety of job-relevant matters.
6. The superior should seek to provide a real right of appeal to his decisions.

The supervisor hewing to the traditional theory of organization, in contrast, is enjoined to emphasize structure. This encourages neglect of points 2 and 4 above, particularly. Moreover, since the traditional approach directs that the employee is to follow orders punctiliously, inattention to points 1, 5, and 6 is probable.

But enough of this: a conclusion is there for the making. Most individuals will find an authoritarian style of supervision of limited help in resolving their dependency needs, if it does not aggravate matters. Low output and high grievance rates are convenient means by which the employee could compensate himself psychically for such neglect of his nature and needs. But the argument also has this positive implication. A group-centered or supportive style of supervision helps most individuals grapple with their dependence needs in organizations.

Third, such findings should surprise some, for they reflect a topsy-turvy world where the unexpected happens. Ordinarily this would be puzzling, but there is no problem here. Our expectations need changing, simply. The traditional theory of organization assumes a model that is false to man as he generally appears in organizations. It should be no surprise when structure and techniques built upon this notion lead to consequences that are the opposites of those expected. What is surprising is that man is adaptable enough to labor as well as he does under conditions so alien to his needs.

The falseness of the model of man in the traditional theory may be demonstrated by establishing that not all individuals respond positively to such features of the traditional theory as an authoritarian style of supervision. Table 7 presents some relevant data for subjects with differ-

TABLE 7   PERFORMANCE ON AN INTELLECTUAL TASK UNDER VARIOUS CONDITIONS OF ATMOSPHERE AND INTELLIGENCE

Condition	Efficiency Criteria	
	Questions Per Problem	Per Cent Problems Solved
Permissive atmosphere—bright subjects	15.5	100.0
Authoritarian—bright	18.5	87.5
Authoritarian—dull	24.5	75.0
Permissive—dull	31.0	37.5

From Allen D. Calvin, Frederick K. Hoffman, and Edgar L. Harden, "The Effect of Intelligence and Social Atmosphere on Group Problem-solving Behavior," *Journal of Social Psychology,* vol. 45 (February, 1957), p. 64.

ing levels of intelligence. Interpretively, the "dull" subjects under the authoritarian condition performed nearly as effectively as the "brights" under the same condition, despite the greater capacity of the latter to perform the intellectual task involved. The performance differences between the brights and the dulls under permissive conditions, in contrast, was very marked. An authoritarian supervisory style might show up as sharply superior to a permissive style, given the proper subjects and task,[29] but such a relation is unlikely. Apparently, both personality characteristics and/or task characteristics are usually more congenial to a supportive style. Many tasks have been overspecialized, or routinized, and performance of them might require only "speed as a skill." But the human personality demands more of work than work often does of the personality.

Fourth, these findings concerning the relative effectiveness of alternative styles of supervision often are interpreted narrowly. Thus the reader may go on convinced only that the supervisor should, as a general rule, emphasize consideration, low pressure for output, and the like. Or the reader might concentrate on longer-run considerations, such as the development of psychological testing to such a degree that it can isolate those specific individuals who will perform a specific task most effectively under a specific style of supervision. This breakthrough would permit the resolution of many assignment problems, but waiting on it hardly meets problems of the moment.

Boldness and scope are preferable in interpreting the research on supervisory styles, however; indeed, they are truly necessary. For the target is not merely a specific managerial technique or structural arrangement. More essentially, the target is a pervasive and comprehensive way of thinking about organizational matters. This mini-analysis challenges the adequacy of any monolithic theory of organization.

It is as unwise to settle for too little, therefore, as it is unrealistic to wait patiently. There is much that can be done beyond an emphasis upon training and short of some testing millennium. One requirement seems clear. The evidence of the inappropriateness of an authoritarian style of supervision under wide conditions will only influence practice as structural innovations and managerial techniques complementing a supportive style are developed. For the authoritarian style of supervision is imbedded in, and reinforces, structure and techniques consistent with the traditional theory of organization and the guidelines of classical job design. A directive style of supervision is reasonable, if not necessary, for example, given that work designed according to the traditional notions is hyperspecialized. Each of these various pieces of work must be integrated, and that implies close and constant oversight and a limited span of control. One factor upsets these neat relations: multifaceted man. If most men in the American work environment had the "proper" personality characteristics, authoritarian supervision and all the rest would be both effective and logically consistent. As matters stand, authoritarian supervision usually must settle for logical consistency with the traditional theory.

Those bent on increasing effectiveness, therefore, must do more than attempt to change some one feature of the logical system. This analysis lives with the need to scrutinize the whole body of thought about organizing. The preceding analysis is cumulative in a vital sense, then. It stresses the usefulness of complementary structural arrangements and managerial techniques. For example, job enlargement implies that the individual worker will actively integrate many of the steps in a work cycle. This simplifies inspection, and decreases the supervisor's burdens in monitoring work. A broad span of control becomes more realistic. Relatedly, an authoritarian supervisory style is less necessary.

The interplay of theory, structure, and techniques requires a further extension of the argument. Overemphasis upon dependence in traditional thought not only reinforces structural arrangements such as a narrow span of control and managerial techniques such as an authoritarian style of supervision. That overemphasis also rests upon a theory of motivation. Managing dependence and permitting greater individual freedom, then, require demonstrations of the inadequacy of the underlying theory of motivation as well as proof of the awkward consequences to which structures and techniques generated by that theory have led.

MAN-CENTERED ORGANIZATION

Motivating by Growth versus Deficiency

Serious thinkers always have been concerned with ways of motivating man to his best efforts, of encouraging him to bring both buttocks to whatever occupies him. The relatively recent preoccupation with the detailed analysis of work could avoid this classical problem even less. Hence the burden of this chapter is unavoidable: the contrast of two extreme approaches to motivating, here called motivating by deficiency (or deprivation) and motivating by growth.

A story of paradise gained in logic and lost in practice underlies the following contrast. Solving the motivational problem was one of the major promises of pioneers in the study of work. This promise captivated generations of students. And no wonder. For—given a crucial assumption or two—the case in logic was persuasively affirmative. Practice was another matter, however.

Motivational problems could be solved once and for all, students such as Frederick W. Taylor argued straightforwardly. Work can be scientifically analyzed into its component operations; work standards can be based on standard times required for these component operations; and the appropriate financial incentives can be applied so as to assure optimum output. Workers would be motivated by Science, thereby, and to just the proper degree.

Matters turned out to be infinitely more complicated. "Standard times" for "standard motions" proved to be anything but standard. To go to the heart of things, these concepts were not up to the task of providing an absolute definition of a "fair day's work." For this must be defined in terms of complex values that are influenced in intimate ways by prevailing social and economic conditions. No "scientific analysis" can determine what these beliefs and attitudes should be. Indeed, even Taylor could not avoid the point graciously. He stumbled over this question: How tired should one be after having put in a fair day's work? Taylor's standards helped him little in formulating a convincing answer, even in the simple case of materials handling. Illustratively, Taylor's "science of shoveling" rested on this advice to laborers:[30]

At the end of the day I do not want you exhausted or anything like that, but properly tired. *You know what a good day's work is.* In other words, I do not want any loafing business or any overwork business. If you find yourself overworked and getting too tired, slow down.

Taylor's advice, as Lahy noted, was of "a simplicity approaching poverty." [31] This estimate seems generous, in fact. However, the difficulty does not lie in Taylor's sophistication. The question he raised is not amenable to the kind of analysis he employed.

Since traditional methods of analyzing work did not automatically produce highly motivated employees as a by-product, the spur to worker motivation had to be supplied from other sources. Any brief summary of these sources of motivation must distort reality to some degree. But essential understanding may be gained with little effort. Three sources of motivation have been available in the history of organizations. These sources may be identified as deficiency motivation, paternalistic motivation, and growth motivation. They correspond to successive historical emphases in the search for sources of motivation. There are no clear and definite cutting points for these emphases, and all find some support today. As the trend lines in Figure 14 reflect, however, reliance on the three sources of motivation has changed sharply over time. The trend lines are nothing more than gross characterizations that aid the following analysis.

Without this analysis pretending to a kind of organizational Genesis, it can be seen that man historically made ample use of "deficiency motivation," "motivation by deprivation," or "negative motivation." The building of the pyramids was accomplished largely via the bite of whiplash on bare flesh. Man's freedom increased enormously over the centuries—and the extreme forms of deficiency motivation declined appreciably—but the narrow span of control and the authoritarian style of supervision reflect how "deficiency motivation" has significantly influenced the design of structure and the choice of managerial techniques to this day. The limits of deficiency motivation have long been recognized, however. Consequently, deficiency motivation has seldom existed in unadulterated form. But its influence is clear enough throughout the history of organized activity. In this country, the approach was dominant and relatively unchallenged well into the twentieth century. Its hegemony coincided with that of the Individualistic Ethic.

"Paternalistic motivation" came into vogue as a subtle complement of deficiency motivation. As closely as such matters can be reckoned, it

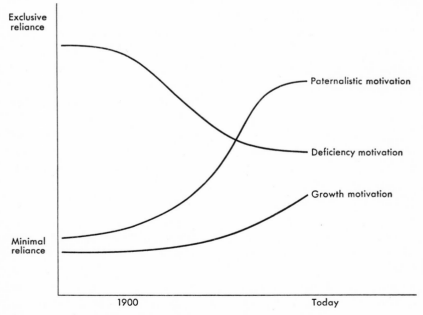

Figure 14. Rough Trends in the Reliance on Three Sources of Motivation.

came into prominence in the 1910s and 1920s as one of the progeny of the Social Ethic. The emphasis upon paternalistic motivation left a spoor of athletic programs, pension plans, and employee cafeterias that are not easily associated with the Individualistic Ethic or with deficiency motivation. But an essential similarity underlies these externals. Both types of motivation were designed to induce the worker to accept whatever demands work made upon him. The difference was one of tactics only: deficiency motivation leaned toward threat or punishment; paternalistic motivation relied on rewards outside of work.

A sizable period of recent history can be characterized this simply because management's approach was basically simplistic. As one summary described the common strategy of paternalistic motivation:[32]

> The rewards in this approach tended to be outside lines of work (as recreation programs), to have no clear relation to performance (as most retirement programs), and to be administered by individuals who did not supervise the performance of the individuals receiving benefits (see the phenomenon of the "Personnel Department" intended to fill "social needs" while the rest of the organization concentrates on "technical needs").

Specifically, "nondirective counseling" at Hawthorne sought to explain away problems induced at work rather than to change work. Revealingly, the counselors were appendages added on to the technical organization as free-floating advisers without other administrative responsibilities. Indeed the entire "human relations" movement shied away from considering changes in the organization of work. The sociologist Peter Blau, for one, was disgusted. The emphasis *was* all on human relations, but on human relations as free-floating and independent of the group, the technical, and the formal organization contexts in which they occur.[33] And this left too much to be desired.

Paternalistic motivation reflects the tight grip that simple ideas can have on the mind of man. The approach was more convenient than convincing. Its major implicit selling point was its congeniality to traditional thought about organizing while it seemed to challenge just that thought. One could change one's tune without the bother of changing one's mind. This is a potent combination.

The assumptions supporting paternalistic motivation are basically three. It assumed that reward within work was not possible. Work could be organized effectively in one way only, and this one way was more or less starkly at odds with human satisfaction. A second assumption, therefore, was natural enough. Paternalistic motivation also assumed that performance within work could be motivated by rewards outside of work. Finally, and this was doubly comforting to traditional thought, managements (or unions) assumed that they knew more about the form in which employees wished their rewards than did employees. Such stuff, apparently, inspired that regulation by organizations of marital life and housekeeping which was historically a prominent part of paternalistic motivation.

These assumptions proved overdrawn. Their limitations are illumined by the work of Frederick Herzberg and associates.[34] Paternalistic motivation is preoccupied with what may be called "hygiene factors," that is, matters of physical working conditions, benefits, job security, and a hail-fellow-well-met supervisory style. In Herzberg's observation, hygiene factors operated mostly to *prevent the deterioration* of motivation to dangerously low levels. Much less did they motivate increased effort. We are all familiar with the employee who sticks to a job because the benefits are so attractive that he cannot afford to leave. Some such effect seems to operate quite generally. Job factors, in contrast, were more

	Job factors	Hygiene factors	Effect on level of motivation
(1)	+	+	Heightens
(2)	+	−	May heighten
(3)	−	+	Prevents deterioration
(4)	−	−	Reduces

Where + designates a set of factors that satisfies employees' needs

       − designates a set of factors that does not satisfy employees' needs

Figure 15. Job Factors and Hygiene Factors as They Affect Levels of Motivation. Following Frederick Herzberg, Bernard Mausner, and Barbara Bloch Snyderman, *The Motivation to Work* (New York: John Wiley & Sons, Inc., 1959), pp. 113–119.

potent. When both job factors and hygiene factors satisfied the needs of employees, motivation was high. Even satisfactory or superior job factors by themselves might challenge an employee to high motivation despite unsatisfactory hygiene factors. Figure 15 sketches these patterns.

Stimulating work often made up for a multitude of organizational sins. It was a positive motivator. Even very attractive benefits outside of work, in contrast, could do no more in general than hold the line: they could be "satisfiers" but not "motivators."

The pattern isolated by Herzberg may not be universal, but it seems a common one. Consider but one striking example of the subtle interaction of hygiene and job factors. In an experimental study of five simple operations conducted three decades ago, three wage systems had significantly different effects on productivity.[35] The highest output was achieved under the piece-rate system, which permitted the greatest income; a bonus system, which permitted medium income, induced moderate output; and the lowest output occurred under the time rate, where pay was independent of output. The differences were substantial. The bonus system yielded output approximately 50 per cent above the time rate; and piece rates improved on production under time rates by some 100 per cent.

The differential impacts of the three wage systems sit well enough with long-current ideas about the preeminence of hygiene factors, but the data hide relations more interesting than they reveal on the surface. The piece-rate system increased output as much as 300 per cent on some operations and affected output hardly at all on other operations. This is a striking bit of information. Figure 16 summarizes the relevant data.

What accounted for the striking differences? They are beyond the traditional notions about motivating work, for output increased only on those operations which operators preferred. Increased earning potential had little influence on productivity on operations which the operators disliked. The point may be put directly. Significant improvement in hygiene factors was not sufficient to heighten motivation, except in those cases where job factors were favorable.

Such considerations have forced many observers to stress the limits of the paternalistic approach to motivation. As two students expressed their feelings on this issue: "We are beginning to see that something

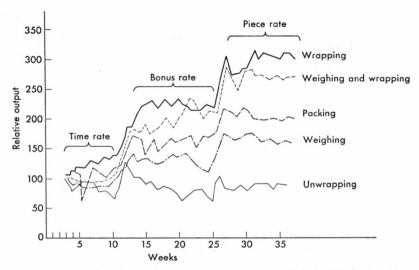

Figure 16. Influence of Three Wage Systems on Output on Each of Five Simple Operations. Based upon S. Wyatt, *Incentives In Repetitive Work*, Industrial Health Research Board Report no. 69 (Her Majesty's Stationery Office, 1934).

more is necessary than the grafting on of external rewards (as through programs in Departments of Personnel) to an individual organization that was built without respect to motivational considerations. . . ." [36] That "something more" is the fundamental redesign of structural arrangements and the development of new managerial techniques.

"Growth motivation" attempts to provide just this something more. It has the happy faculty of doing the apparently contradictory. It encourages an emphasis upon both job factors and hygiene factors, which neither deficiency motivation nor paternalistic motivation do; and at the same time growth motivation explains why these two approaches to motivation could work tolerably well earlier in our economic development and less so under contemporary conditions. Growth motivation permits greater understanding, but not at the expense of arguing that earlier approaches are all wrong. They are, however, wrong enough.

The most convenient approach to growth motivation is that of the psychologist Abraham Maslow.[37] He proposes a hierarchy of needs which individuals must strive to satisfy or feel frustration because of their failure to do so. This striving motivates behavior. A relatively satisfied need will be a relatively ineffective motivator of behavior; and a relatively unsatisfied need can be a very effective motivator of behavior, provided that its satisfaction is not deemed improbable or impossible. Such a hierarchy of needs, proceeding from the "highest" to the "lowest," is proposed:

1. Self-actualization needs
2. Status, or prestige, needs
3. Self-esteem
4. Belongingness, or love, needs
5. Safety needs
6. Physiological needs

Only self-actualization should be unfamiliar. It may be defined as a tendency to fulfill one's potential capacities and talents, one's calling or vocation, and one's own nature.

The usefulness for organizational analysis of a hierarchy of needs may be sketched briefly. Such favorable hygiene factors as high rates of pay would suffice to meet needs 5 and 6, and perhaps contribute in part to meeting other needs. However, only favorable job factors could substantially meet the "higher" needs. A traditionally organized assembly-line job may carry an attractive wage, for example, but it probably will not fill belongingness needs, given the nature of the work. And the minor differences in skill between jobs might threaten an individual's self-esteem by depriving him of status, and might also reduce work's efficacy in meeting his needs for self-actualization by reducing opportunities for training.

The notion of a hierarchy of needs also is consistent with other facets of this analysis. Deficiency motivation, for example, would provide the greatest spur to effort when physiological and safety needs are relatively unsatisfied or are threatened. The threat of dismissal may be awesome when business is slow, when unemployment is high, and when there is no unemployment compensation. The past few decades have approached opposed conditions. Deficiency motivation must be relatively inefficient under present conditions. It appeals to needs that are being, or can be, relatively satisfied. These needs are thus poor motivators.

The relevance of the hierarchy of needs also may be demonstrated in terms of specific structures and techniques. Only when employment security is low, for example, will activation of the lower needs by structural arrangements or managerial techniques be associated with high productivity and low turnover and absenteeism. The traditional theory of organization would do an effective job of motivating under this condition. When higher needs must be activated as motivators, the work environment must increasingly facilitate growth motivation, and an authoritarian (or "production-centered") style of supervision loses much of its potency. An "accommodative" style—in which the supervisor respects group and individual desires of his subordinates, but nothing more—becomes more appropriate. A group-centered style of leadership—which implies a condition of mutual influence between superior and subordinate, as opposed to mere accommodation—would prove even more facilitative of the "higher" needs of most employees.[38]

The efficacy of growth motivation rests on two basic factors. First, massive socioeconomic forces have operated to change once-potent motivators of behavior into the relatively ineffective ones. Organization planners, consequently, must broaden their concept of motivational sources; they must increasingly allow growth at work. Paradoxically, the more effectively (for example) belongingness needs are utilized as motivators, the more those needs will be satisfied and the less effective they will be as motivators of behavior. Growth motivation is not merely convenient now, in sum. It will be increasingly inescapable.

There seems no imminent danger that man will exhaust available motivators of behavior, however. Not every worker will successively satisfy all five needs and despoil them. It has taken some 300 to 400 years to largely satisfy physiological needs for all (or virtually all) of the population of the industrialized countries. At least an extended period, then, will be required before similar service can be rendered to (for example) man's desire for self-actualization at work. Neither are the higher needs satiated as easily as the lower needs. One can only eat a small amount before that need is assuaged, but the boundaries of self-actualization are indefinitely expandable. Man can always become more perfect in his knowledge of himself and of his work; the walls of the stomach have more finite limits.

Second, there is ample evidence that the several needs are no phantoms, created because they serve this analysis. Most or all individuals have strong tendencies toward self-actualization. Support comes from a bewildering variety of sources. Psychotherapy, the treatment of brain-injured soldiers, child psychology, the study of creativeness: all these and many more bear ample testimony to the massive forces oriented toward growth or self-perfection.[39] Maslow illustrates the general point by noting that: "Observation of children shows more and more clearly that healthy children *enjoy* growing and moving forward, gaining new skills, capacities and powers." More traditional concepts of growth are radically opposed, as in the Freudian view that children make adjustments only with great trepidation and that they cling desperately to whatever organismic state they have attained.

If such forces toward self-actualization do commonly exist, there are enormous penalties for their neglect in organizations. Evidence supporting the point can only be hinted at. But notice that—among pups and human babies and various animals alike—the satiation and partial satiation of such needs as sucking had these significant consequences, in Maslow's words:[40]

In all cases, it was discovered that a need that was fully gratified ran its typical course and then, depending on its nature, either disappeared altogether, e.g., sucking, or else maintained a certain low optimum level for the rest of the life span. . . . Those animals in which the need was frustrated developed various semi-pathological phenomena, of which the most relevant for us were persistence of the need past its normal time of disappearance, and secondly, greatly increased activity of the need.

This describes a self-heightening process, if anything does. For those who like more spectacular examples, I am informed that monkeys deprived of cuddling during their early feeding have proved incapable as adults of successful coitus. This implies an arrested development due to deprivation of a need. There are awesome forces at stake in meeting man's needs at work, then, to extend the example.

There are significant implications for organization practice in all this. "Growth motivation" provides some relatively clear directions for the development of appropriate structure and managerial techniques. An authoritarian style of supervision, for example, is generally inappropriate for encouraging self-actualization. More broadly, Argyris has developed a useful list of the major opportunities that structure and techniques must provide in order to facilitate self-actualization at work. The employee must be given the opportunity to:[41]

1. Experience the totality of the organization
2. Be self-responsible, self-directed and self-motivated
3. Aspire toward excellence in problem-solving
4. Strive to decrease compulsive and defensive behavior, while increasing the degree to which he can control his own environment
5. Employ his diverse abilities, especially cognitive and interpersonal abilities
6. Increase his time perspective

Increasing just such opportunities has preoccupied this study. This and the two preceding chapters approached growth motivation from the standpoints of the individual's capacities and the job's demands. They also describe ways of facilitating growth motivation by increasing the probability that work is psychologically acceptable and by expanding man's opportunities to develop his faculties at work. The present chapter enlarges this focus to include a number of immediate, job-related factors that influence the degree to which the individual can be self-determinative at his work. Specifically, all of the elements discussed above—job enlargement for supervisors and operators, training, a supportive style of supervision, and a wide span of control—detail specific structural arrangements and managerial techniques that can facilitate self-actualization. Two following chapters will enlarge the field of view to include the possibilities for growth motivation implicit in the employee's control over the immediate work environment and in structural arrangements that increase the freedom of employees at both high and low levels in organizations. In sum, the entire analysis details the specifics of an alternative to dependence of the employee upon management as the basic goal of organizing.

MAN-CENTERED ORGANIZATION

Lincoln Electric and Growth Motivation

The preceding looks backward and forward may seem to overemphasize the conscious consideration of substantive changes in structure and techniques. Two points demonstrate that the insistence is worthwhile. First, laying the traditional theory of organization to rest requires the specification of superior structural arrangements and managerial techniques. The traditional theory of organization is no friend of growth motivation. This puts the matter mildly, in fact. Second, the approach to work through growth motivation can yield rewards for the organization and the individual.

That the strident insistence on structure and techniques is its own reward may be established briefly by considering the experience of the Lincoln Electric Company. James F. Lincoln, president of the firm, observed that enormous savings can be achieved in any enterprise, given the genuine cooperation of all concerned. He cites the early record of Ford to support the point. "Henry Ford reduced the price of the Model T Ford car," Lincoln noted, "from $900.00 in 1914 to $290.00 in later years. The car was the same during all of that time. Raw material costs were progressively higher. Wages were nearly three times as great per hour as in 1913, yet the reduction shown above was made with great gain in profit." [42] Building upon such experience, Lincoln Electric has developed a program that seems one useful approach to growth motivation. Lincoln outlines four general major elements of this program. They are:

1. Challenge the worker with jobs beyond his present ability.
2. Make the employee realize that his only limits are self-imposed.
3. Encourage the worker to develop his latent capabilities, especially by demonstrating that advancement in the organization is from within and depends on ability alone.
4. Develop managerial capabilities by putting "the development pressure on yourself."

These job-related prescriptions conflict sharply with the guidelines of job design and the traditional theory of organization. Hygiene factors, however, are not neglected. Each employee is rated three times yearly, for example, and these ratings determine his share of a yearly bonus.

Despite substantial questions that have never been researched, the consequences of Lincoln's programs cannot be dismissed. Thus Lincoln himself puts greatest emphasis upon the increased skill and motivation of the employees developed under the program of "incentive management," which seems close to the sense of "growth motivation." Relatedly, overhead costs drop sharply. The need for inspectors also is reduced as the employee is motivated to do his work properly. Moreover, there is a sharp reduction in the number of "usual foremen," whose role Lincoln describes as consistent with an authoritarian style of supervision and a narrow span of control. The usual foreman has the function of curbing adverse reactions to work: ". . . to see that the man does not leave the job or break up the tools so that he can loaf or so he can show how important he is."

Lincoln concludes that a *tenfold* increase in output is within reach under incentive management. This seems no idle boast. Given the 100 per cent increase in price indexes in Lincoln's product line, its record is outstanding. More or less typically, the price of Lincoln's 300-ampere motor-driven welder was reduced from $770 in 1933 to $430 in 1949, a reduction of some 44 per cent that can be traced in significant part to reduced labor and overhead costs. Dividends and "seed money" for future growth do not seem to have been sacrificed, even though Lincoln's bonus program is such as to encourage a flood of applicants for employment. Each worker has the same wage rates as others in the same labor market performing comparable operations. In addition, each employee receives his share of the amount set aside for bonuses. This bonus fund has varied, in the aggregate, over the period 1933 to 1949 from a yearly low of some 20 per cent of all wages and salaries to a high of 128 per cent. In more concrete terms, the average total bonus for each factory worker over those sixteen years exceeded $40,000.

The combination of satisfactory job factors and satisfactory hygiene factors can yield rewards for the organization and for the individual. The latter emphasis hardly requires stress, so much has it been stage center in management thought. Hence the insistence here on satisfactory job factors—specific structural arrangements and managerial techniques—appropriate for growth motivation.

Footnotes: CHAPTER 6

1. National Industrial Conference Board, *Measuring Labor's Productivity*. Studies in Business Policy, no. 15 (New York: 1946).

2. Cited in Morris S. Viteles, *Motivation and Morale in Industry* (New York: W. W. Norton & Company, Inc., 1953), pp. 4–5.
3. Quoted in Georges Friedmann, *The Anatomy of Work* (New York: The Free Press of Glencoe, 1961), p. 34.
4. Quoted in Viteles, *op. cit.,* p. 58.
5. Alexander R. Heron, *Why Men Work* (Stanford, Calif.: Stanford University Press, 1948), p. 103.
6. Adriano Tilgher, *Work: What It Has Meant to Men through the Ages* (New York: Harcourt, Brace and World, Inc., 1930), p. 141.
7. Maurice D. Kilbridge, "Turnover, Absence, and Transfer Rates as Indicators of Employee Dissatisfaction with Repetitive Work," *Industrial and Labor Relations Review,* vol. 15 (October, 1961), pp. 22–24.
8. Charles R. Walker and Robert H. Guest, *The Man on the Assembly Line* (Cambridge, Mass.: Harvard University Press, 1952), p. 55.
9. *Ibid.,* pp. 120–121.
10. Clinton S. Golden and Harold J. Ruttenberg, *The Dynamics of Industrial Democracy* (New York: Harper & Row, Publishers, Incorporated, 1942).
11. Stanley B. Mathewson, *Restriction of Output among Unorganized Workers* (New York: The Viking Press, Inc., 1931), p. 146.
12. Donald Roy, "Quota Restrictions and Goldbricking in a Machine Shop," *American Journal of Sociology,* vol. 57 (March, 1952), pp. 427–442.
13. Saul W. Gellerman, *People, Problems and Profits* (New York: McGraw-Hill Book Company, 1960), p. 158.
14. Melville Dalton, Orvis Collins, and Donald Roy, "Restriction of Output and Social Cleavage in Industry," *Applied Anthropology,* vol. 5 (Summer, 1946), pp. 1–14.
15. Chris Argyris, *Personality and Organization* (New York: Harper & Brothers, Publishers, Incorporated, 1957), p. 50.
16. See William M. Fox, *The Management Process* (Homewood, Ill.: Richard D. Irwin, Inc., 1963), pp. 96–97. For examples of critical efforts, see Waino W. Suojanen, "The Span of Control: Fact or Fable?" *Advanced Management,* vol. 20 (November, 1955), pp. 5–13; and Gerald C. Fisch, "Stretching the Span of Management," *Harvard Business Review,* vol. 41 (September–October, 1963), pp. 74–85.
17. Chris Argyris, *Executive Leadership* (New York: Harper & Row, Publishers, Incorporated, 1953), pp. 46–48.
18. Donald C. Pelz, "Interaction and Attitudes between Scientists and

Auxiliary Staff," *Administrative Science Quarterly,* vol. 4 (December, 1959), pp. 321–336, and vol. 4 (March, 1960), pp. 410–425.

19. Rensis Likert, *New Patterns of Management* (New York: McGraw-Hill Book Company, 1961), pp. 56–57.

20. James G. March, "Influence Measurement in Experimental and Semi-Experimental Groups," *Sociometry,* vol. 19 (March, 1956), pp. 260–271.

21. William F. Whyte, *Man and Organization* (Homewood, Ill.: Richard D. Irwin, Inc., 1959), p. 13.

22. Theodore V. Houser, *Big Business and Human Values* (New York: McGraw-Hill Book Company, 1959), p. 24.

23. *Ibid.,* pp. 21–22.

24. Harry Levinson, Charlton R. Price, Kenneth J. Munden, Harry J. Mandl, and Charles M. Solley, *Men, Management, and Mental Health* (Cambridge, Mass.: Harvard University Press, 1962), p. 51.

25. Likert, *op. cit.,* pp. 56–57.

26. Edwin A. Fleishman, "Patterns of Leadership Behavior Related to Group Grievances and Turnover," *Personnel Psychology,* vol. 15 (Spring, 1962), pp. 43–56.

27. Daniel Katz, Nathan Maccoby, and Nancy C. Morse, *Productivity, Supervision and Morale* (Ann Arbor, Mich.: Survey Research Center, University of Michigan, 1951), p. 36.

28. Mason Haire, *Psychology of Management* (New York: McGraw-Hill Book Company, 1956), pp. 53–76.

29. Martin Patchen, "Supervisory Methods and Group Performance Norms," *Administrative Science Quarterly,* vol. 7 (December, 1962), pp. 275–294, presents a study that suggests such an interpretation. See also John R. P. French, Jr., E. Kay, and H. H. Meyer, "A Study of Threat and Participation in an Industrial Performance Appraisal Program," *Behavioral Research Service Report* (Schenectady, N.Y.: General Electric Co., 1962), pp. 118–119; and Victor H. Vroom, *Some Personality Determinants of the Effects of Participation* (Englewood Cliffs, N.J.: Prentice-Hall, Inc., 1960).

30. Quoted in Georges Friedmann, *Industrial Society: The Emergence of the Human Problems of Automation* (New York: The Free Press of Glencoe, 1955), p. 60.

31. *Ibid.,* p. 60.

32. Robert T. Golembiewski, "Is Personnel Management Bankrupt?" *The Personnel Administrator,* vol. 8 (March–April, 1963), p. 18.

33. Peter M. Blau, "Formal Organization: Dimensions of Analysis," *American Journal of Sociology,* vol. 58 (July, 1957), p. 58.
34. Frederick Herzberg, Bernard Mausner, and Barbara Bloch Snyderman, *The Motivation to Work* (New York: John Wiley & Sons, Inc., 1959). Supporting evidence is provided by Milton M. Schwartz, Edmund Jenusaitis, and Harry Stark, "Motivational Factors Among Supervisors in the Utility Industry," *Personnel Psychology,* vol. 16 (Spring, 1963), pp. 45–53; and Frank Friedlander and Eugene Walton, "Positive and Negative Motivations Toward Work," *Administrative Science Quarterly,* vol. 9 (September, 1964), pp. 194–207.
35. S. Wyatt, *Incentives in Repetitive Work,* Industrial Health Research Board Report no. 69 (London: Her Majesty's Stationery Office, 1934).
36. Daniel Katz and Robert L. Kahn, "Human Organization and Worker Motivation," in L. Reed Tripp (ed.), *Industrial Productivity* (Madison, Wis.: Industrial Relations Research Association, 1951), p. 147.
37. Abraham H. Maslow, *Motivation and Personality* (New York: Harper & Row, Publishers, Incorporated, 1954).
38. James V. Clark, "Motivation in Work Groups: A Tentative View," *Human Organization,* vol. 19 (Winter, 1960–1961), pp. 199–208.
39. Abraham H. Maslow, "Deficiency Motivation and Growth Motivation," in Marshall R. Jones (ed.), *Nebraska Symposium on Motivation, 1955* (Lincoln, Nebr.: University of Nebraska Press, 1955).
40. Maslow, *Motivation and Personality,* pp. 112–113.
41. Chris Argyris, "The Integration of the Individual and the Organization," in George B. Strother (ed.), *Social Science Approaches to Business Behavior* (Homewood, Ill.: Dorsey-Irwin, 1962), p. 76.
42. James F. Lincoln, *Incentive Management* (Cleveland, Ohio: Lincoln Electric Co., 1951), pp. 110–111, 114–115, 126–127.

7

A "Sense of Partnership in, and Responsibility for," I: Influence over the Macro-environment

Institutions devoted to producing goods and services—no less than the world's political institutions, and perhaps more so—must respond to and guide those awesome forces associated with the ongoing revolution of rising expectations. Failure to respond and to guide imply their own comeuppance. For change there will be whether by peaceful means or violent, and the failure by men of good will to guide change only inspires the malevolent to indulge themselves more freely.

The essential point may be put simply. Unquestionably, most of us want more of the "good things" of life—both material possessions and the freedom to enjoy them—and we want these good things in unprecedented volume and we want them soon. The only questions are whether we are willing to pay for them and whether institutionalized ways to pay for them are available.

The appropriate strategy for managing this revolution of rising expectations within productive organizations seems clear enough. The times call for, and the technology increasingly permits, a closer approach to the fourth component of the Judaeo-Christian Ethic: that the employee should exercise greater control over the broad environment within which he works. The English commentator Austen Albu came to such a conclusion as he reflected on the failure of British nationalization to solve the problems of large-scale organization. Apathy and lack of cooperation were not eliminated by nationalization, he observed, and it was at least possible that matters had worsened. Neither employee nor manager acted with a new and zealous self-interest because he "owned" the factories or the mines. The slogans of "industrial democracy" and "worker's control," Albu argued, simply could not overcome the massive reality that "the problems of human relations which the nationalized industries face are due to the size and complexity of their organizational structures and are faced equally by all organizations of similar size." Whatever the ownership pattern, then, the challenge of contemporary organizational life is similar: if only the employees could have a "sense of partnership in, and responsibility for, the industry in which they work." [1]

Albu's basic strategy of approaching the fourth value of the J-C Ethic implies two tactics for satisfying man's deep and persistent needs at work. Following Georges Friedmann,[2] solutions on the *technical plane* must be developed. Previous chapters suggest a number of appropriate structural arrangements and managerial techniques. Such tactics do but part of the required job, however. Man's needs also must be met on a *social plane* by institutional ways that give the employee some share in managing and directing the enterprise. This and the following chapter stress such institutional developments.

THE REVOLUTION OF RISING EXPECTATIONS

My Friend, the Manager

Anything as formidable as the "revolution of rising expectations" encourages an approach tailored to massive proportions. Let us scale down matters to more human dimensions, to the level of one manager and his plant. They played only a very small part in the adjustment of the roles of labor and management after World War II, which readjustment in turn is one facet of the contemporary revolution of rising expectations. This focus is arbitrary in many senses, then. But that manager and his plant played characteristic parts, and parts I knew well. Moreover, even if no innovative solutions that set a standard for the economy were developed in this plant, its problems after all were solved in some fashion and the solution implied its own important lesson. In any case, that manager, my friend, was a man of many moods and is worthy of passing remembrance.

He was a patriarch of a man, that manager. And he stood erect with violence all about him, at once not comprehending why it happened to him and yet knowing that he was acting out the last scenes of the drama that is life-death. For just as surely as his vitality was being drained forevermore by a malignancy within, so also did he know that his kind of manager would first be desiccated and then blown away by the winds of change. He had so little time; and he could do as little about the one as he could about the other. What he could do, he did. He died as the manager and the man he had lived, with dignity.

That man died as a manager first, and this because of the actions of his employee-friends. He had been good to them, in his own way. It was a community he had created for his people, after all, not merely a factory. And for many years the way of the manager was that of his employees. But there were demands. That manager never let it be forgotten that this efficient plant and its many well-paying jobs were once his solitary dreams as he trundled a pushcart of fruit through his adopted city. Thus it was that he, personally, gave each employee his weekly pay envelope, and often more besides for a birth or death or a boy in the seminary. The young bucks home from the Great War bore such symbolic rituals only for a while and then rose to demand something different. That something was embodied in a labor union. After some blood was shed, a labor union was what they got. The manager saw their demand only as a betrayal. "Didn't I try to do everything for them?" he once asked in despair. He had tried, and his efforts were their own undoing.

Fate left little time for understanding to grow. With little left for him as the kind of manager he was, he died as a man soon thereafter. He was buried by his employee-friends, for they loved him still, if in their own way.

Modern organizational history is saturated with evidence to a similar point, of a revolution of rising expectations expressed as demands by members for greater control over the organizations and institutions affecting them. For example, in some General Motors plants recreation programs outranked most of the major sources of job satisfaction, but these plants usually were those in which the employees themselves organized and ran the programs. Where management exercised more direct control, signs of dissatisfaction with the programs were common, and this in spite of the fact that the company-run programs tended to be more ambitious and costly.[3] More generally, employees often peg their organizational commitment to the level of their control over the work environment. For example, absenteeism rates have been associated with the attitudes of the employees about their degree of freedom to discuss problems, the degree of responsibility they have, and the degree to which work requires skills that the employees consider important.[4] The lower the degree of control by the employee over such aspects of his work, the higher his rate of absenteeism.

The temptation to leap to extreme interpretations must be resisted, but an analytical paralysis is equally inappropriate. It seems safe enough to assume that both workers and supervisory personnel "may have a strong desire, particularly in a nation with deeply-ingrained democratic traditions, to participate in the determination of matters affecting them."[5] And if it is impossible to specify precise limits (in Daniel Katz's terms), workers tend to "do better when some degree of decision-making about their jobs is possible than when all decisions are made for them."[6] Moreover, the desire of employees to participate in the meaningful control of their environment cannot be disregarded without paying a price. Employees may be motivated or goaded by a supervisor who is constantly "on them," but this condition is difficult to attain and maintain. In addition, if individuals or groups can be made self-motivating within broad policy statements, many nasty supervisory problems can be avoided while high levels of performance and satisfaction can be reached.

Closer analysis must be given the question of whether the revolution of rising expectations in organizations can be met in such ways that the deeper needs of employees are satisfied, that the fourth value of the Judaeo-Christian Ethic is approached, and that productive efficiency is enhanced. Two working propositions reduce the associated problems to manageable proportions. First, the problems of work must be met primarily at the workplace, at least in the foreseeable future. A richer leisure life may make the burdens of work more endurable, but eliminating causes is morally and practically preferable to doctoring symptoms. Moreover, too many things remain undone to allow an uncongenial workplace to encourage a headlong rush into an orgy of leisure. Second, only a small minority of individuals will reject out of hand a sense of partnership and responsibility in management, and only a few tasks are not amenable to organizational arrangements and managerial techniques congenial to participation.[7] The proposition seems appropriate, on the evidence.

THE MORE-LESS HYPOTHESIS

Contra Those Famous Professors of That Dismal Science

The revolution of rising expectations implies particular difficulties because of the general acceptance of what may be called the More-Less Hypothesis. For whatever employees gain through their demands for a greater voice in the managing and directing of an enterprise, according to this hypothesis, that something must show up as a loss for management. Sharp conflict seems unavoidable.

There are many cases in which the More-Less Hypothesis actually holds, and certainly we often assume that it does hold. Thus the more air I breathe in some enclosed space, the less oxygen other individuals in that space will have. More elaborate (and more questionable) examples abound. The Malthusian variation on the theme, for example, argued that: (1) the supply of food was increasingly inadequate to meet the needs of the world's multiplying hordes; moreover, (2) there was no possibility of increasing the stock of food available to the average man, short of major wars or plagues; because (3) population was increasing far faster than the food supply and, indeed, technological developments leading to short-run increases in the food supply would only trigger a procreative binge that would soon make matters worse than before. Malthus relied on several variations of the More-Less

Hypothesis, then, including the paradoxical one that the more technological development in agriculture, the less the average store of food. The several variations come to a common point, however, and that point is not an optimistic one. Malthus was not alone in his dark predictions. Indeed, with Ricardo—whose "iron law of wages" similarly reflected the More-Less Hypothesis—the ideas of Malthus were the crucial ideological supports of the Individualistic Ethic. So uncompromising and so widely accepted were their "laws," in fact, that Ricardo and Malthus were referred to as "those famous professors of the dismal science" of economics.

General acceptance aside, however, the More-Less Hypothesis holds only under conditions that are hardly universal. On a superficial level, the more good will I have for others, the more good will are they likely to have for me. More generally, at least these three conditions must obtain in cases in which the more I have of x, the less must everyone else have on the average: (1) the demand for x must already equal or exceed the supply; (2) the supply of x cannot be increased significantly, at least in the short run; and/or (3) if the supply of x can be increased significantly, the individuals demanding x also increase in such a way that no one has more of x than before, if everyone does not have less.

With little regard for these conditions, the More-Less Hypothesis has been the guiding principle of the traditional theory of organization. Figure 17a helps make the point. It sketches the orthodox organization of a simple set of operations that yield some Product P_1. Figure 17a centralizes the control of the work environment in M_{ABC}. Hence little of significance will be delegated to any supervisor. Only M_{ABC} monitors enough operations to make meaningful decisions about the total flow of work $A + B + C$. Consistently, only a few supervisors report directly to M_{ABC}. The implicit rationale underlying Figure 17a, then, seems clear: any increase in the power of M_{ABC} implies a decrease in the power of the supervisors, and vice versa.

The More-Less Hypothesis provides awkward guidance for the traditional theory of organization. The point may be made via the concept of "power," defined simply as the ability to control the work environment. Getting recommendations for promotion accepted, for example, indicates that a supervisor has relatively high power. Power thus conceptually complements "authority," which refers to the degree to which the formal organization legitimates a supervisor's control of the job environment. Typically, all supervisors at the same level monitoring similar operations have similar authority; and typically, these supervisors will differ in their power.

The guidance of the traditional theory of organization by the More-Less Hypothesis implies some significant, unanticipated consequences.[8] Illustratively, M_{ABC} often will find it difficult (if not impossible) to assign praise or blame for performance to some one of the units be-

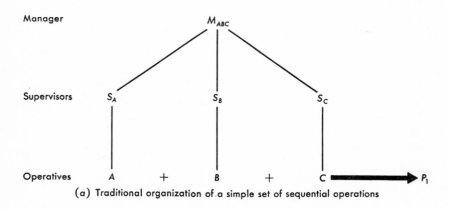

(a) Traditional organization of a simple set of sequential operations

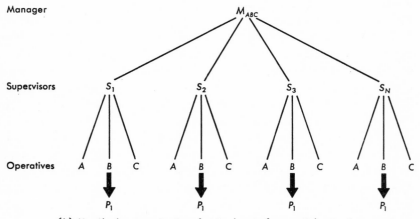

(b) Unorthodox organization of a simple set of sequential operations

Figure 17. Two Approaches to Organizing a Simple Set of Sequential Operations.

neath him. Even elaborate inspection systems may not eliminate the opportunities for "buck-passing" built into the structure, for no one short of M_{ABC} has clear responsibility for P_1 as a totality. And although the manager may be held responsible for problems in the several units, this merely avoids the problem of assigning responsibility at the work level, if it does not encourage operatives to make merry as supervisory heads roll. This fact implies significant motivational problems. Thus M_{ABC} is likely to resort to a directive style of supervision, and he is likely to induce crises to stimulate performance. These reasonable adaptations to the liabilities of the traditional structure are likely to prove self-defeating, however, at least over the longer run.

Figure 17b differs radically from Figure 17a in husbanding power. Figure 17b rests upon the More-More Hypothesis. Clearly, the structure permits very substantial delegation to the individual supervisors, each of whom controls all of the operations in the sequential flow of work $A + B + C$, and each of whom is in a position to make meaningful decisions affecting the total flow of work. That is, the structure permits supervisors to develop and exercise greater power.

But does not "substantial delegation" imply the decreased power of M_{ABC}? An affirmative answer is necessary only if the supply of power is somehow constant, and this need not be the case. Consider the outline of a case-in-opposition. As the power of the several supervisors increases, the more are they able to control and motivate their employees. The employees in the unorthodox structure probably will gain power, in turn, for their supervisors are likely to allow more leeway at work than the supervisors in a Figure 17a structure. Notice also that the measurement of the comparative performance of the individual units in the unorthodox structure is a very simple matter.

The Figure 17b structure has interesting advantages, then. One can expect more productivity, higher employee satisfaction, and reduced labor turnover. In other words, increased supervisory power will tend to be associated with increased power of M_{ABC} under the conditions described, as well as with an increase in the power of employees and supervisors. No doubt of it, M_{ABC} relinquishes some of the outward signs of "control," narrowly defined as detailed and continuous oversight of performance. But M_{ABC} does gain more of the substance of "control," broadly defined as the achievement of objectives at lower economic and human costs.

The paradox, then, is that what seem the most straightforward ways of increasing one's power often are the most direct ways of reducing it. In effect, a Figure 17b structure permits all organization members to act to mutually increase their combined control over the work environment. Hence the assertion that a variation of the More-More Hypothesis underlies Figure 17b.

These complex relations are more than reasonable; they are observed regularly in organizations. Power is related to effective supervisory performance, whether that power is exercised "upward" or "downward." Consider power exercised upward, that is, influence with superiors. Pelz studied some fifty measures of supervisory practices and attitudes. He observed no marked correlations with employee morale and attitudes. When the influence of a supervisor with his superior was specified, however, rather sharp differences were observed in effectiveness. High supervisory power was associated with effective performance;[9] the ineffective supervisors had low power.

Similarly, power exercised downward—that is, as control of the job site—is associated with effective performance. A comparison between the top third and the bottom third of one firm's departments ranked in terms of productivity illustrates the general tendency.[10] Personnel in the top departments uniformly attributed greater influence over "what goes on in your department" to all four of these sources than did the bottom departments: higher management, plant management, department manager, and the workers themselves. Moreover, individuals in the top departments also desired that greater influence actually be exercised by all four sources than did the bottom departments.

Such findings defy the More-Less Hypothesis, but so much the worse for that hypothesis. The results are curious only if one assumes that there is only so much power to go around and therefore that what subordinates gain must be lost by superiors. The assumption does not seem apt. Indeed, the high-power supervisor is more likely to allow his subordinates freedom at work than the supervisor with low power. The high-power supervisor thus reinforces his own power and pleases his subordinates,[11] as in the departments referred to above.

The relation of supervisory power and effectiveness seems to be basically one-way. A low-power supervisor might lose out to his subordinates in the struggle for power. But these subordinates are not likely to desire that he should exercise greater power. Indeed they are likely to employ their power to embarrass him, as by restricting output. Consequently, the direction of power sharing is important. If it does not begin with the supervisor, that is, it may end up doing him in. Structural arrangements must respect this datum.

THE MORE-MORE HYPOTHESIS

Some Program Guides

Although the More-More Hypothesis need not rest on airy speculation, whether it can be acted upon in organizations in programmatic form remains to be established. This is the burden of the examination of several programs that are conducive to effective performance while they also permit varying degrees of approach to this fourth value of the Judaeo-Christian tradition: that the individual should exercise some degree of control over the broad organization of which he is a part. The present concern will be tripartite. Initial attention will be given a program for acting on the More-More Hypothesis which has an *ad hoc* bias, includes only a few levels of organization, and has been used most commonly at lower levels of organization. A following emphasis will raise its sights to a more comprehensive program particularly appropriate for the several lower levels of smaller organizations. The final focus will be a program designed for upper levels of organization and for the full range of management problems.

A. AN AD HOC, LEVEL-RESTRICTED PROGRAM:

GROUP DECISION-MAKING

The fourth value of the Judaeo-Christian Ethic extends individual self-determination to aspects of the broad environment within which the task is performed. Again, techniques approaching this value tend to yield high output and high satisfaction. The present and the following chapter thus complement and extend the demonstrations in Chapters 5 and 6 of the favorable consequences of building increased opportunities for freedom into the task.

Group decision-making concerning changes in jobs or output levels —certainly among the more important aspects of the environment within which specific tasks are performed—demonstrates the efficacy of employee control over the broader organizational environment. Although the specific illustration deals with a limited issue at the lowest level of organization, the technique can be used at all organization levels for a broad range of purposes.

Group decision-making is a simple, if revolutionary, technique. A typical application involves the setting by management of general goals to meet increasingly sharp competition. Work units in the concern, cognizant of these general goals, determine and enforce a level of output. Traditional organization theory countenances no such folderol. An order would suffice, in its terms.

Group decision-making generally leads to increased output, although precisely what makes for success (or failure) is not known. This may seem surprising, but the explanation is plausible. Group decision-making implies a low degree of threat, as opposed to exhortation by management. Consequently, less resistance results (for example, to high levels of output). Moreover, the group is free to develop and enforce a norm. The norm often serves as a potent guide for the behavior of members, in turn, even when the supervisor is away. The group can make strong medicine, and often far stronger medicine than management can brew under present economic and cultural conditions.

Despite the fuzziness surrounding the concept, group decision-making increases the probability of involvement in decisions by those who must carry them out. One experiment strikingly makes the point. Three degrees of participation in a minor change in a job were studied: *total participation,* or group decision-making by a formal work unit concerning the specific change in the level of output; *representative participation,* in which members of a work unit chose representatives to participate in the decision-making; and *no participation,* in which the workers were simply told that changes in the work and increased output were necessary and that they therefore would be made.

The degree of participation made a substantial difference. Originally, the work units had comparable output levels which clustered around

60 units per hour. *Total participation* led to the highest output after the change, substantially above the levels reached before the change. *No participation* resulted in the lowest output. Indeed, the *no-partici-pation* unit fell far below its previous output and did not recover dur-

TABLE 8   DEGREES OF PARTICIPATION IN DECISIONS ON INTRODUCING MINOR CHANGES AND THEIR EFFECTS ON OUTPUT

Condition	Production (in units per hour) at Five-day Intervals after Change in Job					
	5	10	15	20	25	30
Total participation	64	63	75	71	71	72
Representative participation	50	53	60	68	64	66
No participation	45	53	55	51	49	55

Approximated from a graph in Lester Coch and John R. P. French, Jr., "Overcoming Resistance to Change," in Dorwin Cartwright and Alvin Zander (eds.), *Group Dynamics: Research and Theory* (New York: Harper & Row, Publishers, Incorporated, 1953), p. 268.

ing a thirty-two-day period of observation. The data in Table 8 summarize these results.

Differences in participation imply human as well as economic advantages. No-participation conditions are likely to encourage high levels of "quits" as employees leave an unsatisfying situation. Or employees may respond aggressively to such conditions, as by filing abnormally high numbers of grievances, by expressing hostility toward management, or by conscious efforts to restrict production. And the catalog could be continued. Failure to approach the fourth value of the Judaeo-Christian Ethic, then, can have substantial human costs that do not always show up immediately as increased economic costs.

Such human costs are difficult to estimate, but a comprehensive program of group discussion and decision-making utilized in a change in methods in several plants during 1954 to 1956 permits a guess of their magnitude. In general, the participation program proved a tonic. Not only did output increase somewhat in three of four cases, but the changes were accomplished with far less of the emotional costs historically associated with similar changes in this firm. Thus absenteeism decreased, and turnover rates continued to decline throughout the period of the change. Table 9 shows the average turnover rates by plants

TABLE 9   RATES OF TURNOVER IN THREE PLANTS OVER TIME

Year	Plant 1	Plant 2	Plant 3
1952	*	*	.703
1953	*	*	.623
1954	.618	.398	.320
1955	.545	.291	.282
1956	.380	.243	.248

* Data not available.
NOTE: The changes were begun late in 1954 and were completed in the first part of 1956.
From John R. P. French, Jr., Ian C. Ross, et al., "Employee Participation in a Program of Industrial Change," *Personnel,* vol. 35 (November–December, 1958), p. 24.

over time. Both absenteeism and turnover are commonly regarded as measures of frustration and dissatisfaction, of course.

Data like those illustrated often have been their own worst enemy. They have been used to oversell "participation," and interpretations sometimes have been more convenient than justifiable. In contrast, any results are not inevitabilities but more or less marked tendencies which will be more or less dominant as conditions vary. Illustratively, group decision-making yields most positive results when the individuals involved are low on authoritarianism and dependence.[12] Broad cultural patterns may be of great import, then, as with German workers who apparently prefer forceful and unequivocal orders to sharing in the making of decisions.[13] Similarly, Norwegian workers found participation less attractive than might be expected because of questions about its cultural "legitimacy." [14]

Second, there is participation and there is participation, and different techniques can be expected to have different effects. The *opportunity to discuss* the need for an increase in output, for example, may be distinguished from the *actual choice* by a work unit of a new standard which is self-enforced. Participation of the former kind may serve to reduce anxiety and resistance to change, but it could also have just

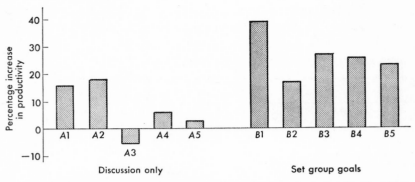

Figure 18. Two Types of "Participation" and Their Consequences in Ten Matched Units of Office Workers. From Lois C. Lawrence and Patricia Cain Smith, "Group Decision and Employee Participation," *Journal of Applied Psychology*, vol. 39, October, 1955, p. 335.

the opposite consequences, as when employees recognize that the opportunity to discuss only permits assenting to a decision that is already made. Available evidence gives but little encouragement to the manipulator who sees in participation only a slick technique with no strings attached. Five matched units of office workers were exposed to each type, for example, and Figure 18 shows that participation depends far more upon substance than upon form. The More-More Hypothesis, in short, should guide the use of participative techniques: management must give more to get more.

B. COMPREHENSIVE, FACTORY-LEVEL PROGRAM:

THE SCANLON PLAN

Curiously, the principle of group decision-making has had few full-fledged applications. Various bastardized "participation plans" do exist. Often they attempt to get without giving and must take their place in the storehouse of gimmicks that might (or might not) work in the short run and are likely to fail in the longer run. The Scanlon Plan, in contrast, attempts to exploit the possibilities of participation *and* distribute the benefits among all. It does not pussyfoot.[15]

The characteristics of programs based upon the Scanlon Plan may be outlined briefly. Basically, the Plan's purpose is to heighten coop-

eration between labor and management, to sustain it by mutual participation in decision-making, and to nourish it by mutual sharing of the
fruits of that cooperation. The underlying assumption may be phrased
in such terms: there is a wealth of imagination and inventiveness in
most organizations that remains untapped (if not turned against the
organization) when the individual has inadequate incentive to make
suggestions and appropriate adaptations on his own. The Scanlon Plan
strives toward greater collaboration, and with these high expectations:[16]

> The challenging opportunities that are inherent in every industrial or-
> ganization for people to assume responsibility, achieve status, acquire new
> skills, learn, develop, [and] exercise creativity become apparent once this
> area of collaboration is carved out. The idea that workers are paid to do
> what they are told and management is paid to tell them not only prevents
> effective collaboration but automatically creates the feeling of psychologi-
> cal failure. It leads either to indifferent passivity or to active hostility.
> Genuine participation in problem solving removes the causes of these com-
> mon reactions.

Perhaps more sharply, the Scanlon Plan rests upon a novel interpretation and implementation of this maxim: A good day's work for a
good day's pay. The Plan recognizes that a good day's work from each
man is not the same as a good day's work from all men.[17] In sum, the
Plan assumes that the activities of individuals are highly interdependent
at work and that, therefore, a good day's work from all men requires
more than monetary rewards to each man based upon his performance
of his limited activity. A good day's work from all men requires creating the conditions under which cooperation can flourish, conditions
which permit a deeper and mutual involvement of the individuals whose
efforts are parts of a common flow of work. In terms of our earlier
analysis, then, the Scanlon Plan tends toward motivators that tap the
"higher needs" of man, particularly his social needs.

The mechanics of the Scanlon Plan are uncomplicated practical
translations of the More-More Hypothesis. The heart of the Plan is
one or more production committees, composed of equal numbers of
management personnel and hourly employees who are elected periodically. Such committees consider management problems of appropriate
(usually departmental) scope, evaluate suggestions from all sources,
and perform an important function in communicating decisions and

in providing broad representation in decision-making. A higher-level screening committee—with a similar composition—reviews suggestions of a very broad scope or those which require substantial cash outlays.

The comprehensive participation required by the Plan is motivated by a bonus arrangement. The goal is the development of a labor-management team with this common interest: reducing the costs of productivity. The bonus arrangement plays a crucial role. "Real participation consists in finding a means to reward labor for any increase in productivity," Russell Davenport notes, "and then in building around this formula a working relationship between management and labor that enables them to become a team." [18] Specifically, the bonus is based upon some measure of "normal labor cost," with all (or a large proportion) of any savings over time going to each employee in the Plan as a calculated percentage of his base rate. "Normal labor cost" is variously defined in practice, and useful definitions often require some ingenuity. Moreover, some variations require periodic renegotiation.

The Scanlon Plan is not a profit-sharing plan, then. Rather, it is a cost-savings plan. It ties rewards directly to behavior that reduces labor cost. In contrast, profitability may be the result of many factors over which employees have little or no control.

The available evidence, none of it very complete, suggests that such fuller-scale participative programs as the Scanlon Plan have much to offer both employees and management. Even the breathless evaluation of a Stuart Chase seems relatively appropriate for describing this experience. Chase lauded the Plan's "joint committees which can take output right through the roof by releasing energy and intelligence in the rank and file which hitherto had been bottled up." [19]

Several of the more specific senses in which even Chase's rapturous conclusion seems relatively apt may be considered briefly. The economic returns of the Scanlon Plan provide a convenient focus for this exposition. These returns often have been considerable. Thus employee bonuses 54 per cent above a high basic wage have been reported. Comparative data on increased labor productivity are no less compelling. Table 10 presents some more or less representative data from ten plants operating under the Plan, for example. These data demand little modification of Chase's ebullience. Notice that the two-year increases range from 10.3 per cent upward.

TABLE 10   PRODUCTIVITY RECORDS OF TEN FIRMS UNDER THE SCANLON PLAN

Company	Percentage Increases in Productivity		
	First-year Relative Efficiency	Second-year Relative Efficiency	Two-year Average Relative Efficiency (unweighted)
	(1)	(2)	(3)
A	14.9	10.9	12.9
B	21.9	12.7	17.3
C	16.7	13.2	15.0
D	36.7	29.3	33.0
E	28.9	49.4	39.2
F	32.9	42.9	37.9
G	38.7	25.1	31.9
H	14.1	16.5	15.3
I	12.9	23.2	18.1
J	6.8	13.7	10.3
Average (unweighted)	22.5	23.7	23.1

From Elbridge S. Puckett, "Productivity Achievements: A Measure of Success," in Frederick G. Lesieur (ed.), *The Scanlon Plan* (published jointly by The Technology Press of the Massachusetts Institute of Technology, Cambridge, Mass., and John Wiley & Sons, Inc., New York, 1958), p. 113.

Such striking increases in performance suggest some powerful biasing factors that made the firms in question somehow unusually suitable for the Scanlon Plan. In some senses, in fact, the firms were alike. For example, the data are from plants of from 30 to 1,200 employees. Small size, then, may be a factor in the successful Scanlon Plan applications summarized by Table 10. Successful and unsuccessful firms also tend to be alike in another particular. Thus Helfgott observed that efficiency increased in four of six Scanlon plants he studied. In both plants in which the Plan failed, management did not believe that the employees' suggestions could be worthwhile.[20] No wonder the Plan failed in those two cases. Where this belief is current, the Scanlon Plan will work largely in a manipulative sense, if at all. Notice, however, that such a belief may be accurately based in a technology that is so complex as to be beyond the capacities of the average employee. The Scanlon Plan would be less useful under this condition.

In most significant senses, however, the firms operating successful Scanlon Plans do not fit a unique mold which assures significant improvements in performance. The labor content of the ten plants considered in Table 10, for example, ranged from 10 per cent to a high of 60 per cent. Since "labor content" may be defined in terms of the total payroll as a percentage of the total value of production, the Plan obviously does not depend upon high labor costs in order to yield favorable returns. Moreover, of the four firms having average improvements over 30 per cent, only one had experienced serious financial problems; the others had better-than-average profit histories for their industries. "Cheap" improvements do not explain the data in Table 10, in short.

If the Scanlon Plan does not seem to depend on some narrow range of similar facilitating factors, applications of the Plan tend to a typical pattern. A description of labor relations at the LaPointe Machine Tool Co. before its adoption of the Plan helps identify some of the main components of this pattern. Labor relations at LaPointe were more or less typical: not really "bad" but not really "good"; better than in some plants yet worse than in others. The piecework incentive system generated this pattern in significant ways. Thus the rates on some jobs were so "easy" that the men earned large bonuses even while restricting output so as to protect the favorable rates; other rates were so "tight" that only very skilled hands could earn a bonus. In addition, "indirect workers" were not under the incentive rate, and they resented it. The consequences were generally unhappy. As Davenport concluded: "Grievances abounded—the union was processing fifteen or twenty a month. There were numerous production delays, spoilage was too high, and deliveries were bad." [21]

After the adoption of the Scanlon Plan at LaPointe, conditions changed for the better in important particulars. In general, the Plan tended to equate the interests of manager and managed. They could pull in the same directions, that is, while serving both themselves and the organization. Conditions had been less sanguine.

The experience at LaPointe also reflects many specific changes that may be attributed to the Plan. First, difficulties with the piecework incentive system were sharply reduced, thereby simplifying the many administrative problems associated with the prevailing wage-and-salary program, while preserving the motivation permitted by an incentive system. A typical reaction to the problems of traditional incentive systems, in contrast, is to resort to straight hourly rates and to bear the costs of a uniform work pace that tends to be biased toward the more ineffective employees.[22]

The congenial effects of the Scanlon Plan on wage-and-salary administration are so complex that they can only be savored here. Since the bonus under the Plan depends on how well everyone performs, for example, favoritism in assigning jobs becomes a less potent source of friction. Under the Plan, one can do whatever jobs are assigned to him—whether "easy" or "hard"—with the knowledge that any improvement of labor costs will bring its own rewards. Different skills command different base rates of pay, but all employees share the same bonus percentage. Previously, whether an employee was assigned a hard or an easy job made a great difference. Wages and effort would depend directly on the specific assortment of jobs given to (let us say) several employees performing the same operation. The Plan at once removes supervisors from the temptation of "playing favorites" while it protects them from charges of doing so. Under the Plan, moreover, both "direct" and "indirect" workers share in the production bonus. This implies a train of favorable consequences. Thus mechanics, who are indirect workers, have a direct interest under the Plan in performing their services with dispatch and efficiency. Previously, at least the possibility existed that indirect labor might raise this awkward question: Why should I work more efficiently just to increase the bonus of some production employee, and particularly so when a little attention on his part to regular maintenance would prevent many breakdowns? In addition, the Scanlon Plan reduces the probability that the production worker will try "to get away with murder" in sneaking shoddy work through inspection and quality control. Each production worker had a direct interest only in the quantity of his own output under the piecework incentive system. Thus it mattered little to him directly if returns by purchasers were high. Indeed, he might prosper only at the expense of the company and his fellow employees. The Scanlon Plan encourages greater attention to quality because charges for repairs increase "normal costs," and everyone suffers thereby. Finally, the individual incentive system discouraged the sharing by employees of tricks of the trade. Under the Scanlon Plan, however, each employee has an interest in the training of his colleagues. This interest has paid off extravagantly in some cases,[23] and it is consistent with the second and third values of the Judaeo-Christian Ethic.

Second, significant economic returns under the Scanlon Plan derive from unleashing the creativity and experience of the body of employees in making suggestions about how time and effort can be saved. Wide participation in company matters through the various committees and the greater availability of information about the company's position play major roles in the favorable experiences with the Plan, although employees tend to work more steadily and may work harder.[24] Information sharing, for example, will tend to reduce debilitating extremism by both labor and management. Much strife in human affairs derives from the unavailability of such channels for mutual moderation in solving mutual problems.

Whatever the motivating factors, applications of the Scanlon Plan induce considerable inventiveness. Thus in one relatively small plant the screening committee alone received 513 suggestions within twenty-four months, of which 380 were accepted and 65 were rejected.[25] This record is extraordinary when compared to the "suggestion-box" system under which the individual suggestion maker gets some small percentage of the savings for perhaps a year. These arrangements imply a high probability that suggestions will go unmade, that improvements will be used informally to make life easier for the employees, or that suggestions will be made by social isolates whose very participation is likely to encourage pointedly negative evaluations of the suggestion-box system.

Third, the important role required of the labor union in applications of the Scanlon Plan no doubt also helps account for its substantial economic returns. Thus the Plan implies "collective bargaining of a high order," not only in settling specific details of normal labor cost, but also in making the adaptations that may be required by changing conditions. The evidence is not conclusive. But effective applications of the Plan normally have been supported by a vigorous labor union;[26] and a number of failures of the Plan may be explained partially in terms of the lack of union support or of the weakness and ineffectiveness of an existing labor union.[27] The underlying reasons seem plain enough. In the absence of a strong union, employees may view any management program with some suspicion as just another way of getting more work for less money. Moreover, any participative program designed to eliminate labor unions would operate under a great liability.

Fourth, although no precise estimates are possible, favorable economic returns derive in part from the improved emotional tone induced by the Plan. As Davenport explained: ". . . the workers, like management, have derived many intangible benefits that cannot be measured in dollars and cents. They seem to enjoy working together and sharing the good and bad times. As one of them said, 'Formerly everyone was on his own. Now we all work for each other.' "[28]

Many factors contribute to such changes in feeling tone. For example, supervision need be less authoritarian. Moreover, the integration of the several activities should pose fewer problems, for each employee has an interest, not only in how well he performs his particular activity, but also in how smoothly the various operations blend. No longer can he adopt this dodge without personal cost: I only do x; how y and z are done is none of my business. Relatedly, labor costs provide a goal toward whose achievement each employee can meaningfully contribute. The behaviors encouraged by the Plan thus tend to move away from motivation-by-deprivation, dependence, and directive supervision. McGregor generalized the point in these terms:[29]

The management task in Scanlon-Plan companies becomes one of genuine leadership. The manager who is primarily a power seeker and a protector of management's right to be arbitrary finds little satisfaction in such a situation. The pattern of managerial behavior which tends to emerge does not mean abdication; it does not imply that "everyone decides everything." . . . it encourages responsible behavior and tough-minded self-control rather than reliance on external authority.

Argyris spotlighted the bias of the Plan toward growth motivation in these terms: "In all cases reported in the literature, the [Scanlon] plan results in the employees' using many more of their important abilities, in being less dependent, passive, and subordinate toward management, in having increased control over their own immediate work environment."[30]

This catalog of attractive consequences requires a counterweight.

Most pointedly, why have applications of the Scanlon Plan not swept through American industry? No simple explanation of the steady-but-unspectacular increase in adoptions of the Scanlon Plan seems appropriate. But at least two factors inhibit the spread of the Plan and its associated philosophy. First, the Scanlon Plan implies a revolution in managerial thought, and revolutions do not come easily. Certainly the Plan ill suits those relations implied by wide "management prerogatives." The Plan does not require that management abdicate control to the several committees, to be sure, and management retains the right to veto any suggestion. However, management must respond to initiative from below while it relinquishes domination. Such a position may be uncomfortable.

Second, the Plan best suits smaller plants or firms. That is, the Plan is a kind of group piecework system. Where it is adopted without basic changes in the organization of work, therefore, labor-saving efforts in one department are less directly related to the productivity bonus shared by all *as size increases.* Members of a department in a large plant would be more likely to ask: Why should we do much of the work and share the bonus with others? That is, the Scanlon Plan runs afoul of the departmentation by individual functions or processes prescribed by the traditional theory of organization. Beyond all but the most modest-sized plants, the need to integrate the several bits and pieces of work sharply raises the probability of interdepartmental conflict that can negate the interest in cooperatively saving on labor costs.

The point can be supported only indirectly, although it seems reasonable. Some evidence does exist.[31] Moreover, the Plan has been adopted chiefly in small plants, usually of a thousand employees or less.[32] These data must be taken seriously, since both suggest the inability of the Scanlon Plan to cope with problems in large organizations.

C. A COMPREHENSIVE, CORPORATE-LEVEL PROGRAM:

MULTIPLE MANAGEMENT

The More-More Hypothesis also motivates programs that are comprehensive in the areas they open to employee influence over the broad organization and are applicable at the plant and the corporate level. Group decision-making and the Scanlon Plan, respectively, provide only discrete areas for employee influence or do not extend beyond the level of the individual plant. "Multiple Management" is chosen for specific attention, although variations of a similar kind have been developed.[33]

Multiple Management is a technique that proudly shows its philosophical skirts. Charles P. McCormick developed Multiple Management early in his career as head of a firm manufacturing and selling teas and spices, the program being a natural outgrowth of McCormick's acceptance of these principles:[34]

1. Business is primarily a matter of people.
2. Employees are human beings first, citizens of our nation second, and factors in production third.
3. The United States is the bulwark of individual freedom and economic stability in the world today.
4. The welfare of the people cannot be legislated satisfactorily by any government.
5. The ability of American business managers acting jointly with American workers to preserve the "dignity of man" and "freedom of choice" for the individual is the only positive approach toward obtaining and preserving democracy throughout the world.
6. Finally, the destiny of man lies in being of service to others. No government or philosophy has ever lastingly endured unless it was based on a "religious" or "service" motive for bettering mankind.

The procedures developed to serve these principles are straightforward, and were motivated particularly by a problem facing McCormick as he took on the firm's presidency. His predecessor—a relative—had been a one-man show, and the company's management and board of directors reflected it. With the aim of generating new ideas and providing a pool of trained, experienced executives, McCormick instituted a junior board of directors. The junior board's original membership was appointed, including assistant department heads, accountants, and junior executives. Subsequently, the junior board became self-directing within very wide boundaries and within a self-developed constitution. Thus the junior board evaluates all old members and elects some new ones as part of its normal operations; and the board can make suggestions about all aspects of company operations and policy. Members are paid fees for their work on the junior board. The major restraints on the junior board are basically two. First, all recommendations must be unanimous, the purpose being to make each board member feel personally responsible for every suggestion. Second, all recommendations must be approved by the President or the senior board of directors before being acted upon.

McCormick's satisfaction with the junior board soon led to the development of other boards for several other levels of the company and for certain important activities. They included: a factory board, a sales board, and an institutional sales board. These boards operate under ground rules similar to those sketched above.

No definitive studies exist, but Multiple Management seems to have its manifold attractions. Thus we are told that in its first five years the junior board made a prodigious 2,109 unanimous suggestions, of which only six were rejected. The ratio has apparently remained more or less constant. We are also told that the factory board at McCormick made as favorable a showing: output was reported up some 30 per cent in five years, given little change in the work force and almost no change in the firm's machinery. Moreover, the various boards also seem to have had the intended effects of discovering and training a pool of executives. Or, at the very least, relevant experience has been favorable enough to encourage McCormick to choose members of the senior board only from the junior board. Moreover, labor turnover is reported to average a strikingly low 5 per cent per year at McCormick. How much of this can be attributed to Multiple Management, and how much to a handsome wage program or to favorable working conditions, is not known. No doubt all such factors make their contributions. Finally, several hundred firms have adopted Multiple Management programs, and only a relative handful of companies have abandoned them.[35]

One final impact of Multiple Management deserves more extended treatment. Such programs apparently have been successful in reducing the interdepartmental conflicts that are so common in today's organizations. The traditional monofunctional or monoprocessual pattern of departmentation has been preserved, at least in the McCormick firm. But membership on the several boards, as it were, makes the best of this structural pattern by providing an institutionalized way of encouraging favorable horizontal contacts between members of the several departments represented. This tends to break down the particularistic departmental identifications that can create major obstacles to integrating the several activities into a smooth flow of work. And this constitutes a major point of advantage of the Multiple Management approach. Since the board system brings together officials from many departments, McCormick explained, board business is an excellent training ground for taking into account the needs and objectives of other departments.

Coordinating a company's several functionally organized activities is a major goal of Multiple Management.[36] Indeed, "organic wholeness" is an organizational lodestar at McCormick. Workers may be shifted from department to department to meet fluctuations in workload; departmental transfers are common; and production teams rotate jobs hourly or daily. The effects seem satisfactory. McCormick reports that: ". . . such arrangements help eliminate work fatigue brought on by monotony. Further, they produce a wealth of ingenious suggestions for improvements in various departments. We carry out this philosophy on all levels. . . ." [37]

The picture is not unrelievedly bright. As with the Scanlon Plan, Multiple Management is likely to prove less useful in large organizations. Without significant changes in organization structure, the several boards may inhibit interdepartmental separatism less effectively. For Multiple Management superimposes relations having a horizontal bias on the vertically oriented relations encouraged by the traditional theory of organization. In large, multiplant organizations, therefore, the superimposition may fall prey to the very departmental separatism it successfully handles in smaller organizations.

ACTING ON THE MORE-MORE HYPOTHESIS

Some Compelling Factors

The preceding three sections permit straightforward summary. Whatever its scope, the possibility of the employee influencing his broad work environment tends to pay off in increased output and heightened satisfaction. That is, approaching the fourth value of the Judaeo-Christian Ethic that should govern man-to-man relations has practical as well as moral support. Indeed, management has but limited choice in the matter. It can attempt to mesh the norms of the informal group with the goals of the formal organization or it can thrust its head into the proverbial sand by neglecting the need for participation.

Although the unreasonable choice often has been made, the question of the employee's control over the work environment will be raised even more insistently by automation. Under the older technology, workers often handle parts or feed machines whose pace they control.[38] The technology consequently permits some minor but cherished opportunities to break the monotony and to exercise some control over their work. Automated machinery eliminates these opportunities. It also requires close and constant attention, demands increased functional interdependence among employees, and enormously increases the difficulties of interaction.[39]

Less trivially, one changeover to automated operation eliminated some 50 per cent of the previous jobs and changed another 30 per cent substantially. Some 90 per cent of the workers were directly affected.[40] Popular demand for some kind of control over the work environment is probable under such conditions. Providing the employee with opportunities *at work* to influence his organizational environment, then, will become more difficult in many senses and more necessary in all important senses.

A BIRTHRIGHT FOR A MESS OF POTTAGE?

Practical Limitations and Manipulative Potentials of Participation

That participation has lurched through cycles of extremes is no surprise. Human affairs are not notable for their moderation. Participation exists in a polarized field of argument, and treatments are clustered around ecstatic (but improvident) acceptance and utter (but careless) rejection.

The extremes of acceptance and rejection deserve illustration. One commentator phrased his support dramatically: "Two thousand years ago we put *participation* in the religion which has come to dominate the Western world. Two hundred years ago, we put this essential element in our political and social structure. We are just beginning to realize that we ought to put participation in business as well." [41] Others see only the devil incarnate in participative techniques. Rather than a final answer to the problems of freedom in an industrial society, they see participative techniques as "at best paternalistic." Lewis Corey saw them as worse. He described one application as "vicious" and "despotic." Dividing the workers into small teams, Corey argued, served to "fragmentize the labor force and make managerial control of it easier." Management gave up none of its control. The motivation was "to get the workers to accept what management wants them to accept but to make them feel they made or helped make the decision." [42]

The critics make some important points. There are a number of significant senses in which the organization member should not sell his birthright of self-determination in exchange for the boon of participation. For participation can be an empty delusion as well as a means of exercising some control over the organization. Three factors which encourage the former outcome will be sketched here. The following section will outline some structural arrangements that can encourage the latter outcome.

The several illustrated techniques for achieving participation moderate some problems associated with the traditional theory, first, but they remedy rather than cure. How much they can contribute remains an open question. Where the organization of work is more or less patterned after man and his needs—for example, in those specifics sketched in Chapters 4 to 6—participative techniques should encourage positive and lasting results. Where structural arrangements and managerial techniques are less congenial to man, participative programs may wear off quickly, if indeed they do not compound the very difficulties they are designed to avoid.

No direct proof of this position exists, but numerous data fit the picture well enough. For example, a long experiment with different degrees of participation by clerks performing repetitive and low-level operations yielded mixed results. As expected, high-participation work units did become more satisfied with their work life than did similar units exposed to increased hierarchical controls. However, the low-participation units had higher output.[43] One interpretation of these results holds that, since no changes in the organization of work were made, the high-participation condition merely made it easier for clerks to protect themselves from deprivations forced upon them by the organization of work. Hence their lower productivity, and perhaps also their higher satisfaction. The low-participation units may simply have found it more difficult to restrict their output, and their satisfaction therefore fell.

Second, "participation" facilitates manipulation by management for a variety of reasons. Distinguishing techniques that permit participation from those that merely engineer consent thus is both necessary in theory and difficult in practice. Indeed the same technique can be put to both uses. There is all the difference in the world when this occurs, however. Thus participation may be defined as eliciting that "mental and emotional involvement of a person in a group situation which encourages him to contribute to group goals and share responsibility in them." [44] Participation then is a two-way relation in which employees contribute their inspiration and involvement to decision-making. Consent is far more passive. It is basically a one-way relation in which employees contribute only their assent to a decision already made.

Why participative techniques often abort in the engineering of consent has no simple explanation, but one element in any explanation is that by and large executive authority in America has escaped the demands for "workers' control" that have been made in most industrialized nations, and with great effect in most of them. This country has seen its critics of the separation of ownership and control, but they seldom go beyond more or less ambitious doses of government regulation. And the role of American labor unions has been one of bargaining within existing organizational arrangements rather than of changing them radically. Whatever the reasons, in any case, the major consequence was plain enough to three acute commentators on the "American business creed." They pointed out that the "authoritarian structure of the enterprise" has attracted little discussion, with the overwhelming opinion being that the strictly managerial activities of the owner and/or executive should not be diluted by the claims of the workers or other interested parties. These commentators concluded: "The actual operation of business has been to a striking degree 'monarchical,' that is, with a single head directing normal operations. The powers of executives to determine the formal organization and to select personnel have been very extensive; they have been jealously defended. . . ." [45]

A conclusion comes freely. The relative monopoly accorded the American executive in organizing work provides little motivation to go very far beyond the engineering of consent with participative programs.

But the striking (and sometimes exaggerated) results attributed to participative techniques provide motivation aplenty to go some distance with them. Consequently, participative programs are trafficked in but with a hesitance to accept the psychologist Daniel Katz's conclusion that if small work units are to be given responsibility for maintaining production levels, they ought also to help determine the levels of production. Anything less, Katz observed, would condemn the use of group dynamics as "a manipulative device for getting more out of the workers without giving them more." [46]

Third, the overenthusiastic acceptance of participative techniques also may work against management's interest. There are many variations on this theme. Thus not all jobs nor all conditions need large doses of participative techniques, and vigorous management action to universalize the gospel may prove its own undoing. Moreover, the employee can manipulate management through such techniques, particularly under the "happiness" approach to matters organizational. Thus work has become an extended coffee break by mutual consent of employees and manager for fear of disturbing "group equilibrium"; or a worker is dismissed from his local for not restricting output as per agreement arrived at in group decision-making sessions inaugurated by management. There also are more important and more subtle ways in which exaggerated participative applications may prove a disservice to management. William H. Whyte pounces hard on one such anti-management consequence of participation as an unqualified gospel. "Now no one need be ashamed of going along with the herd," he phrased one objection to participative techniques; "indeed, with the aid of the new jargon he can be articulately proud of the fact. He is not just conforming, he is using 'group skills.' He is maintaining 'equilibrium.' He is 'participating.' " [47]

SAFEGUARDS AGAINST "GROUPTHINK" AND OTHER ORGANIZATIONAL ILLS

Specific Structural Arrangements

Preventing the abort of the revolution of rising expectations expressed in employee demands for greater control over the broader work environment, then, faces three main challenges. First, participative techniques cannot be expected to magically surmount massive problems deriving from other sources. Specifically, participative programs must be imbedded in a system of compatible structure and techniques, not superimposed on some more or less hostile system. Second, participative techniques must be delivered from careless misuse as well as from malevolent manipulation, and this poses a delicate practical problem. The general requirements are quite plain, however. Participative techniques must really give as well as get. They must do more than "create a sense of participation," and they must reward and reinforce the substantial participation of the employee. Third, participative techniques must be protected from their own extreme tendencies. Practically, this requires developing structural arrangements and managerial techniques which sharply reduce the chances that participation will lead to a kind of homogenized going-nowhereness and which increase the freedom of organization members at work.

These challenges must be accepted. On the one hand, the dangers *in extremis* of the Social Ethic are patent. "Fitting into a group" as *the* guide for organizational life leaves no room for moral questions. The "standards for conduct" are defined by group processes; man is important only in his roles as a member of groups; and "groupthink" processes leave members satisfied that they have made a decision while they can place responsibility for it on the "group spirit." One analyst succinctly put the dangers of the Social Ethic: "Many people have come to worship THE GROUP." [48] Similar notices often become the battle cry of those seeking a return to the Individualistic Ethic. On the other hand, the neglect of group relations surrenders too much. Schneider, for example, lists the following advantages of membership in informal groups: [49]

1. Relief from monotony, boredom, and fatigue, which advantage is most applicable to production and clerical employees doing routine business
2. Opportunities to gain status, an advantage which is applicable to employees at all levels of organization
3. Opportunities for emotional responses and self-expression, an advantage applicable at all levels
4. Opportunities for increased security, support, and reinforcement of the individual, an advantage applicable at all levels

These advantages are forfeit if group relations are neglected in developing structural arrangements and managerial techniques.

The Judaeo-Christian Ethic permits accepting the three challenges to the use of participative programs. It facilitates making good use of group relations while it admits structure and techniques capable of making the best of participative programs, or at least of inhibiting the worst. This claim will be supported by an illustration dealing with an assembly operation and lower-level supervisory relations. The illustration is a hybrid, but it permits useful description and analysis of related structural arrangements and managerial techniques that have been observed under various conditions: in lower-level operations that were worker paced, as well as those that were conveyor paced;[50] and in operations at middle and upper levels of organizations, as in "project management." [51] The illustration here has the advantage of simplicity, while it permits a range of analysis[52] beyond the reach of even more complex examples. In addition, the illustration challenges the usual opinion that managerial decision-making must become unrelievedly more unilateral in lower-level factory operations. Common opinion allows greater deviation from the traditional model at higher levels, of course. This opinion concedes a crucial point too easily. As Seymour Melman noted:[53]

Is it possible to have high productivity with freedom? In detail: can we operate large and intricate industrial plants at high and rapidly advancing levels of productivity, and also enjoy wide personal and political freedom? If one holds fast to the idea that managerial rule is essential for operating industrial plants, then the answer to this question must be given as: no! [We challenge] the validity of these views.

The present alternative to the massive concession implicit in common opinion outlines ways to safeguard participative programs from a bad end, whether it comes by way of an incompatible environment, conscious manipulation, or such extreme extensions of participation as "groupthink."

Demonstrating how participative techniques may be disciplined involves a comparison of alternative ways of organizing a three-step set of assembly operations and three sustaining activities. Figure 19 depicts the orthodox structure. Its emphasis is patently upon individual opera-

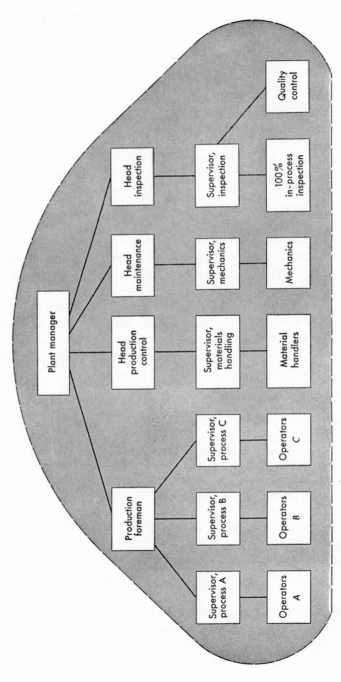

Figure 19. Orthodox Organization of an Assembly Operation. Based upon Eliot D. Chapple and Leonard R. Sayles, *The Measure of Management* (New York: The Macmillan Company, 1962), esp. pp. 20ff.

tions and subfunctions around which basic units of organization are formed. The flow of work, however, is not so tidy. As in Figure 20, the flow of work ties these assembly operations and subfunctions together in a long chain of interdependence which is a stranger to the formal structure. The quality-control stations aside, all the other activities must be delicately adapted to the same pace of work. If necessary repairs are not made at *A* with dispatch, for example, a shock wave of effects will sweep throughout the entire system. The problem may simply be the differential timing of reactions, as when operators at *B* must slacken their pace of work because of a breakdown at *A* which, in turn, requires a similar adaptation at *C*. Adjustments back to some steady state also must snake their way through the entire flow of work. The consequences can be difficult under the best of circumstances. In practice, however, factors like antagonism between personnel at the several stations serve to exaggerate such effects.

The single-mindedness of the formal structure depicted in Figure 19 is at once its strength and its weakness. Thus the formal structure at-

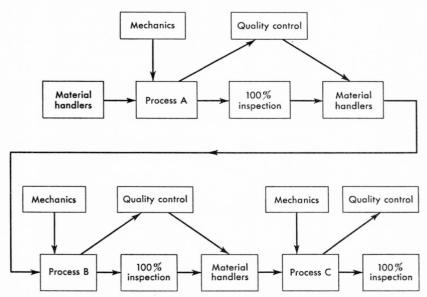

Figure 20. The Flow of Work in an Assembly Operation. Based upon Eliot D. Chapple and Leonard R. Sayles, *The Measure of Management* (New York: The Macmillan Company, 1962), p. 28.

tempts to meet the mechanical requirements of productive efficiency alone. No specific attention is given to two other sets of requirements that may affect coordinated human activity: the requirements of individual satisfaction; and the requirements of organizational change and adaptation.[54] At times this neglect may be of little practical consequence. Since the three sets of requirements are interconnected in complex ways, however, the single-minded serving of one set often is its own undoing. As the work flow requires something more than mechanical adjustments, that is, the weaknesses of the formal structure depicted in Figure 19 become increasingly serious.

The specific senses in which the formal structure in Figure 19 neglects the requirements of individual satisfaction and of organizational change may be outlined briefly, and the resulting costs may be itemized. First, the structure poses its integrative problems in awkward terms. Thus the flow of work requires the delicate integration of the several activities; but each activity tends to foster particularistic identifications and interests in the unit organized around it. These particularistic identifications and interests can and do clash, as each organization unit stresses taking care of itself and its own. The flow of work is the usual loser. Scuffles over shares of the budget, controversies over the allocation of the costs of an error, and the like: these are the issues that set activity against activity while the flow of work requires their smooth integration.

Second, a structure like that in Figure 19 commonly is reinforced by a wage-and-salary program that rewards individuals only for their performance of the several bits and pieces required for a flow of work. Different basic wage rates may be assigned to each of the three assembly operations A, B, and C; moreover, the several items produced also may have different incentive rates. The logic is obvious: process A may require more skill than Process B; and Part 1 may require more time for the completion of Process A than does Part 2. The consequences of this logic also often are obvious, and in a troublesome way. In one case, for example, there were sixty-eight different job rates! Derivative difficulties are numerous. Complex administrative and control problems must be faced; the individual incentive rates may involve arbitrary elements; and operators may seethe at real or alleged favoritism in the awarding of "easy" jobs to some operators. Typically, also, only production workers are under the incentive program. As at LaPointe, one may expect derivative friction between production workers and those performing the other activities that must be integrated into the flow of work.

Third, the individual employee commonly is offered no positive incentive to recognize the values of cooperation and flexibility. Indeed, both the formal structure and its associated individualistic wage program deny the significant interdependence of the several activities. Rather they stress the importance of individual functions or processes, and the employee tends to respond accordingly. Both the employee and the flow of work pay the price in various senses. A brief listing must suffice: the individual has no incentive to learn about or adapt to the broad range of activities of the organization; he will be less receptive to the needs for change and adaptation; and the individual must focus on his own specific and relatively meaningless activity, for which he pays the associated psychological costs.

Fourth, the Figure 19 structure often raises problems of assigning responsibility. For example, low output at C carries no simple interpretation. The fault may lie in untimely materials handling, or inept repairs by the mechanics, or what have you. Such nuances tend to be lost in the fixation on end-result measures of performance, however. The modern idiom well puts the implied lesson: "Do unto others, and cut out."

Problems of assigning responsibility cause considerable mischief in organizations. They place onerous demands upon management, and they imply unattractive consequences for the rank and file. Illustratively, management will incline toward close supervision and toward the use of contrived pressure to resolve and avoid the difficulties put in the way of the integration of operations by the traditional theory of organization. Numerous inspections also are required. The probable consequence is a massive defensiveness by the rank and file and by lower-level supervisors against a punitive management and its supporting activities such as inspection.

The four major products of the traditional theory's preoccupation with the mechanical requirements of productive efficiency are likely to drive practitioners to one of two conclusions: to avoid the use of techniques consistent with the More-More Hypothesis, so opposed are the interests of employees and managers in the traditional structure; or to use participative programs manipulatively only to sugarcoat traditional structural arrangements and managerial techniques. Consider group decision-making. It often has its attractions, managerially viewed. However, the technique also could serve to increase the capacities of a work unit to resist management, and particularly so in the formal structure sketched in Figure 20. Thus any one work unit might effectively restrict output in an entire flow of work in such a structure and might even shut down a long flow of work. No one unit in such a structure, oppositely, can increase total output. Thus it is painfully inadequate to note that group decision-making "works" in eight or nine of ten cases. That tenth case may undo all that was accomplished. Managers may be justifiably leery about permitting "real participation" within the traditional structure.

A structure suitable for acting upon the More-More Hypothesis permits more optimism. Figure 21 illustrates an unorthodox structural arrangement that can substantially decrease the chances of participative techniques coming to a self-defeating end. Basically, all operations in some flow of work are represented on each of the several basic units of organization. Each basic unit requires the integration of several organizational activities, then, as opposed to the supervision of a single process or subfunction.

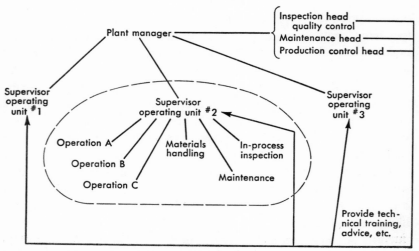

Figure 21. Unorthodox Organization of an Assembly Operation.

The very cartography in Figure 21 sharply contrasts with the traditional structure. In sum, the former structure is wholistic and integrative. Note only that the supervisors of each of the operating units directly control *all* of the activities required for a flow of work, and these supervisors therefore can make reasonable decisions about the entire flow of work. Materials handling, inspection, and maintenance heads now advise and aid the plant manager; they are no longer the direct administrative superiors of large, organizationally separate units, each of which contributes to the same flow of work. The quality-control inspection is lodged at the plant manager's level for two reasons. It is not in the same production sequence as the other activities. Moreover, quality control helps the plant manager assess the efficiency of the several operating units. The traditional structure in Figure 20, in contrast, is particularistic and fragmentative. It builds its basic units of organization around *each* of the several activities required for some total flow of work.

That developing basic units of organization around flows of work is not the same as organizing around each of its parts still requires proof. Much experience with Figure 21 structures at both high and low levels of organization permits this confident conclusion: the whole is definitely not equal to the sum of its parts in this case. The review here of this experience will be a hybrid. The several enumerated advantages of the structure did not characterize some single case. Rather, they have occurred in various complex combinations in a wide range of cases.

Following Figure 21, first, permits having one's organizational cake and eating it as well in the matter of the size of organizations. The structure permits developing a community of interest within each of the basic units of organization, and this without sacrificing the benefits of size and without creating greater problems of managerial control. The traditional structure is far less useful in this regard. Developing a community of interest in its basic units of organization encourages the myopia of specialists who see only their own process or function. Such problems of identification intensify greatly beyond some relatively small size and have significant consequences. For example, absenteeism and dissatisfaction tend to increase as the number of individuals necessary to perform some meaningful, related set of operations increases.[55]

The point here is that such a "related set of operations"—James Worthy[56] calls them a "managerial unit"—can be as small as a single operational unit in Figure 21 or as large as the total structure depicted in Figure 19. The crucial issue is the level in the hierarchy of the supervisor who controls enough elements of the total sequence of operations to make reasonable decisions concerning the total sequence. The higher his level, by a very large factor, the greater the size of the administrative unit. The broken ellipses in Figures 19 and 21 circumscribe two such managerial units of radically different size generated by the same set of operations.

The size of the total organization, then, is not the crucial factor. Reducing the size of the managerial units can tame many of the effects of size of the total enterprise. For example, the orthodox structure cannot help losing even as it wins in the matter of facilitating identification. That is, as individuals develop strong identifications with some organization unit performing a single process or function, so also are created some of the more difficult problems of integrating the several activities in a large organization. "They only think of their own department" is among the more common complaints heard in today's organizations. Such localized identification is natural enough, and members of the individual units can be pardoned for protecting themselves from responsibility for the total flow of work. But the flow of work often suffers. Figure 21, oppositely, attempts to make the natural less troublesome by organizing around relatively autonomous flows of work. Any psychological identification the individual develops with his primary unit of organization, then, can facilitate an entire flow of work.

Size at once is and is not a problem in a Figure 21 structure, in sum. Size is a problem in a relatively trivial sense. The individual operating units must be large enough to do the required job yet small enough to permit the individual to relate meaningfully to them as he contributes to a complete flow of work. How small is "small"? That will depend on the type of work. R. H. Landes covered the point in a discussion of group incentives for production workers.[57] His firm centers group incentives around a single product, such as a telephone transmitter and receiver, in whose manufacture some 450 employees share a natural community of interest. This was a large unit in Landes's experience, where work units of several dozen employees are the most likely organizational centers for group incentive programs. Where the logic of

Figure 21 has been followed, however, even larger managerial units have been developed.

Size is troublesome in the traditional theory of organization in many other senses. Consider that traditional structures grow "tall" very quickly, particularly because of the limited span of control. Unorthodox structures can be very "flat."

The differences can be extreme. Thus a British firm closely approaching the Figure 21 structure has one supervisor for every 250 production employees. An otherwise-similar American plant was more faithful to the traditional theory, and has some ten production workers for each supervisory foreman.[58] If the span of control were restricted uniformly to ten at all levels in the American firm, then, 111 supervisory employees would be required for each 1,000 production workers. That is, a hundred supervisors would directly monitor the production workers, ten individuals would manage the supervisors, and one general manager would oversee them all. The organization would have four levels. Only four supervisors reporting to a general manager would be required for a similar number of production workers in the British plant, in contrast, where the several units of organization each encompassed a flow of work. Such an organization has but three levels. Moreover, the Figure 21 structure includes substantial slack for growth without adding levels. One need but add the appropriate number of basic operating units, and the total size of the enterprise can be increased significantly with few changes in overhead supervisory patterns. Many more production workers in several managerial units might be added in the unorthodox structure without overburdening the general manager, who still would have only a relative handful of supervisors reporting directly to him. A similar increase in production workers in the traditional structure would require an additional level of supervision, at least.

Such differences in the "height" of organizations are far from trivial. At the very least, lines of communication become attenuated; relations become more formalized; and the elaboration of these long action chains encourages organizational rigidities and excessive preoccupation with procedural formalities. Subsequent analysis will add to this catalog of costs that may be eased by following the unorthodox structure, at least in a wide range of industries and technologies.

The "communities of interest" around which the unorthodox structure organizes its basic units, second, imply a great reliance on self-control and self-discipline. Hence the greatly reduced supervisory force in the British plant referred to above, as well as in similar cases.[59] At the very least, the present point does not offend reason. Since each operational unit contains all of the activities necessary for some complete flow of work, malingering or buck passing have a sharply reduced attraction. For they will be directly reflected in the record of one's own unit. The point will be clear to most individuals without instruction. Moreover, other members of a unit are very likely to introduce their less-sensitive co-workers to the common interest. The traditional structure at least opens the possibility that successful skulduggery will be counted against someone else's organization unit. The great potential for self-discipline in the unorthodox structure can be very significant, then.

Third, self-discipline in the unorthodox structure can be reinforced conveniently. In contrast, wage-and-salary administration often is troublesome in organizations patterned after the traditional structure, which favors individual incentive systems. Some of these troublesome aspects were reviewed in the survey of the effects of the Scanlon Plan. The unorthodox structure has the happy faculty of providing economic incentives that help integrate a total flow of work.

Many variations on the theme of reinforcing organizational self-discipline are possible, and they apply to many different industries, many technologies, and a wide range of skills. In a complex assembly operation, for example, sixty-eight piece rates under an individual incentive system were eliminated and eight broad job classes were set up. Each employee still performed only one of the several activities required and was paid a corresponding base rate. But each employee also was paid a production bonus depending on the efficiency of everyone in that employee's flow of work.[60] Each flow of work thus was a managerial unit *and* the basic unit of organization. There were several hundred employees in each unit. At the other extreme, an organization unit performing all of the operations in coal-getting negotiated with management an all-in, per-ton price for coal extracted, and decided to share the proceeds equally among all unit members. The miners moved from task to task as the situation required, with no supervision as conventionally understood; they were true multispecialists, each performing as necessary all of the required activities. This uncomplicated system replaced the troublesome and cumbersome wage-and-salary system required when individual organization units each performed but a single operation in the total sequence of coal mining. The managerial unit in this case was quite small, including some seven individuals. Moreover, output at least equalled that of conventionally organized units. Indeed, it improved substantially, although a number of complex factors preclude a strict comparison. Employee satisfaction also improved, and certainly the emotional tone was more acceptable to both labor and management.[61]

Where the unorthodox model is approached, whatever the size of the total enterprise, incentives may be clearly and directly associated with effective total performance. This is a significant point.

So great is the hold on men's minds of the traditional theory of organization, however, that the point above is neglected. Thus "group bonus" arrangements may be characterized fairly as: providing numerous advantages; and guiding few wage-and-salary programs. Consider this brief itemization of the advantages of the bonus arrangement encouraged by the unorthodox theory:[62]

Under individual incentives, full and accurate records of each individual's work must be maintained continuously. When group incentives are used, counting and crediting of work is done after the completion of all operations. Similarly, inspection is done after the completion of the product, except for the occasional process inspection at the various stages of manufacture. Obviously there is some saving in counting, crediting, and inspection by the utilization of group incentive, and the economies continue on into the job of payroll accounting.

With it all, wage-and-salary administration specialists usually regard such group arrangements as "second best" or as "temporary expedients" that should be replaced by individual incentive systems wherever and whenever possible.[63] In some part, people being people, the common opinion no doubt derives from the desire of professionals to protect their expertise as it has developed over the years. The professionals thus have a vested interest in preserving the existing complexity, where it has survived. There also are more impersonal explanations of this strong support by professionals in wage-and-salary administration for individual incentive programs. Consider that many group bonus arrangements—like the Scanlon Plan—are conceived as company-wide systems. They are thus particularly prone to difficulties in larger organizations. Hence some of the caution of the professionals may derive from sad experience with the traditional theory of organization and from the failure to innovate structural arrangements more appropriate to group bonus systems.

Fourth, useful changes in the style of supervision also might be expected when the unorthodox model is followed. These changes will have important consequences for many levels of organization. In general, these changes derive from the more facile and less arbitrary measurement of performance possible under the unorthodox structure; and, in general, these changes imply significant advantages. The contrast of structures may be put simply. Given its control of an entire flow of work, any operating unit in an unorthodox structure can raise output independently. In an orthodox structure, a single organization unit can exert strong pressures only to restrict output, and (as in the case of the treaters in the rubber industry) can even stop output entirely. The smaller risk of the unorthodox model permits a less-authoritarian style of supervision.

If we add some flesh to this simplified analysis, the disadvantages of the traditional model become more marked. Consider that in the orthodox structure, work standards must be developed and monitored closely by some overhead unit lest worse come to worst. But even the most ingenious and well-administered programs have some high probability that standards are arbitrary, unevenly applied, and difficult to change. The comparative performance of organizational units on similar flows of work provides standards that are at once inherently meaningful, are generated by the employees themselves in the very act of working, and can be changed as soon as any unit develops more effective techniques or relationships. Specifically, this means that supervisors in an unorthodox structure are more preoccupied with monitoring things. Pressure is natural in that it is built into work. In contrast, supervisors in the traditional structure monitor people. "Artificial pressure" exerted by one person against another is necessary to overcome the obstacles to work and to its measurement implied by the emphasis upon particular functions and processes.

Two derivative changes in supervision may be expected as organizations move toward the unorthodox model. Quantitatively, fewer employees per production worker will be concerned with creating and sustaining "artificial pressure." Fragmentary data provide some support. In one firm patterned after the unorthodox model, for example, there were 15.7 administrative, technical, and clerical employees per 100 production workers. A similar plant patterned after the orthodox model had thirty-six such employees as a minimum estimate and fifty-eight as a maximum. These data do not directly prove the present point, but they are suggestive and understandable. As Melman described one organization patterned after the unorthodox model: "There were no supervisory foremen in plants of this firm, in the accepted sense of the term. This meant that in order to obtain satisfactory conditions of plant operation it was necessary for the management to police directly the performance of the production workers." [64] Qualitatively, the supervisor often will be placed in a rewarding role. An earlier chapter implies the importance of this change in a variety of senses. Here note only that in one study the supervisor-as-coercer often was the villain in stories that members of organizations wrote about specific instances in which their performance and satisfaction were low. "High" instances, in contrast, often showed the supervisor-as-rewarder playing an important role, particularly in recognizing effective performance.[65]

The unorthodox structure often will yield savings in man-hours by avoiding certain inflationary tendencies in the traditional model. The basic rub is that peak loads commonly are reached at different times at the several work stations in any flow of work. The traditional model for organizing, however, does not encourage flexibility in reassigning personnel to work stations where they are temporarily needed. Since each supervisor in the traditional structure is primarily concerned with his monoprocessual contribution, he will tend to fight for sufficient personnel to meet the maximum demand on his work station, while other supervisors do likewise. Moreover, each supervisor will resist the borrowing of this personnel lest he lose them or get caught short himself.

The unorthodox structure permits, encourages, and requires more flexibility in this regard. Since the responsibilities of any organization unit are defined in terms of some broad flow of work, colleagues in such a unit are predisposed to react quickly and positively to temporary overloads at some specific work station within their own flow of work. After all, their fat is in the fire too. The point does not apply so directly to individuals in different organization units in an orthodox structure. In the long run, even there the success of any single unit does depend upon the success of all units and of the firm. But a short-run myopia tends to preoccupy most of us.

Cost advantages of such flexibility cannot be calculated easily. They often are considerable, however, as in the case of a small department in which fifteen employees were required to meet peak loads. Changes toward the unorthodox model were made, and employee income was increased some 50 per cent because seven persons proved enough to carry the load except in emergencies when additional help could be reassigned temporarily. Rensis Likert concluded favorably that: "The work is being done well, peak loads are handled, those doing it have more favorable attitudes, and there is less absence and turnover than under the [old] system." [66]

The unorthodox structure charted in Figure 21, sixth and finally, also is congenial to a number of useful organizational arrangements and managerial techniques. For example, the structure enlarges the job of the supervisor, and this has a variety of generally positive effects. The power of the supervisor tends to be increased thereby, for he has direct control over the several operations required for a total flow of work. And high supervisory power tends to be associated with high output and high satisfaction. Relatedly, the unorthodox structural arrangement facilitates training and job rotation. The advantage of the unorthodox structure is elemental: each supervisor can assign his own employees to different tasks that are under his own control and for which he is responsible.

The traditional theory muddies these waters considerably. Job rotation requires the collaboration of several supervisors monitoring different tasks, each of whom is asked to expose his best men to the allures of other departments where they are under another supervisor's control, while no one operating supervisor has a direct organizational interest in the success of the program. No wonder that job rotation and training programs have their many difficulties.

The unorthodox structure also permits the use of certain interesting techniques that can serve the diverse interests and needs of organization members. Recall the work on personality testing, and particularly on assignments of individuals to work teams in terms of their "compatibility." The traditional theory of organization—reflected in much glib talk about personality testing and in some testing programs—encourages emphasis upon *a* personality type. Crudely, since the several basic units of organization are interrelated in an extended sequential chain, the premium is upon the recruitment of individuals who "get along with others" and who tend to conform to the same profile of personality characteristics. The usual critical argument is that abject conformity results, if it is not raised to the level of an organizational virtue.

The unorthodox structure avoids such jibes. For assignments to each of the operating units can be made so that (for example) one unit might have all highly authoritarian members, another might have all lows, and their supervisors could employ appropriate and different styles of supervision. Neither do such differences in group composition disrupt the flow of work, as they well might in an orthodox structure. The Figure 21 structure is built around operating units that are relatively or completely autonomous. This drastically reduces the importance of personality differences between members of the several operating units. Indeed, since the performance of several units producing similar flows of work is meaningfully comparable, personality differences between the units may heighten performance.

This list of advantages of the unorthodox model might be continued, but the outlines should be clear. Indeed, there seems increasingly less need to plead the case for unorthodox structural arrangements and their associated managerial techniques. Successful daily experience at work encourages the spread of the gospel from one side. Moreover, the new technology forces adaptations of the traditional structure from the other side, as in modern rolling-mill operations and continuous-process refineries. The problem, then, is becoming less and less one of having our notions about organizing catch up with our moral judgments and increasingly one of having these notions about organizing catch up with the technology.

The general implications of the movement toward the unorthodox structure also are capable of concise summary. Let us rely on Friedmann, who reviewed a wide range of experience with operating units such as those sketched in Figure 21. He concluded:[67]

> The spontaneous reaction of certain technicians against the traditional organization of labour and the experiments they have tried, which are a kind of heresy from the orthodox point of view, have mostly led to the restoration of a margin of freedom to the team. It is through the increase of teamwork that these new practices have been able to slip between the meshes of a system rigidly organized by planning departments. It seems as if modern industry were discovering—or rather rediscovering, following Aristotle and certain other writers—the truth that man is by nature a social animal, made to live and work in a community. It follows that he is most likely to make full use of his capacities, and to obtain the best results from them, if he works in a group.

This chapter will rest content with having developed the inner logic of these "spontaneous reactions," with having established that the "heresy" they imply makes some very good sense in terms of the More-More Hypothesis, and with having given some little impetus to the "restoration of a margin of freedom" to organization members by approaching the unorthodox structure.

The point may be put otherwise. Participative techniques need not be either rejected or used manipulatively. Proper structural arrangements permit giving more control to the employee and receiving more controlled behavior in return. Consequently, the organization analyst need not cut himself off from the behavioral sciences, and he can respect the fourth value of the Judaeo-Christian Ethic without sacrificing economy and efficiency. Greater control by the individual over the broad organization, that is, can be disciplined by structural arrangements that safeguard the interests of employee, manager, and owner.

Footnotes: CHAPTER 7

1. Quoted in Daniel Bell, *Work and Its Discontents: The Cult of Efficiency in America* (Boston: Beacon Press, 1956), pp. 39, 41.
2. Georges Friedmann, *Industrial Society* (New York: The Free Press of Glencoe, 1955), p. 14.
3. Marquis W. Childs and Douglass Cater, *Ethics in a Business Society*

(New York: Mentor Books, New American Library of World Literature, Inc., 1954), p. 164.

4. Helen Metzner and Floyd Mann, "Employee Attitudes and Absences," *Personnel Psychology*, vol. 6 (Winter, 1953), pp. 467–485.

5. Robert Tannenbaum and Fred Massaryk, "Participation by Subordinates in the Managerial Decision-making Process," *Canadian Journal of Economics and Political Science*, vol. 16 (1950), p. 410.

6. Daniel Katz, "Morale and Motivation in Industry," in Wayne Dennis (ed.), *Current Trends in Industrial Psychology* (Pittsburgh, Pa.: University of Pittsburgh Press, 1949).

7. George Strauss, "Some Notes on Power-equalization," in Harold J. Leavitt (ed.), *The Social Science of Organizations* (Englewood Cliffs, N.J.: Prentice-Hall, Inc., 1963), pp. 39–84, disagrees.

8. For a fuller development, see Robert T. Golembiewski, "Civil Service and Managing Work," *American Political Science Review*, vol. 56 (December, 1962), pp. 964–969.

9. Donald C. Pelz, "Interaction and Attitudes between Scientists and Auxiliary Staff," *Administrative Science Quarterly*, vol. 4 (December, 1959), pp. 321–336, and vol. 4 (March, 1960), pp. 410–425.

10. Rensis Likert, *New Patterns of Management* (New York: McGraw-Hill Book Company, 1961), pp. 56–57.

11. James G. March, "Influence Measurement in Experimental and Semi-experimental Groups," *Sociometry*, vol. 19 (March, 1956), pp. 260–271.

12. Victor V. Vroom, *Some Personality Determinants of the Effects of Participation* (Englewood Cliffs, N.J.: Prentice-Hall, Inc., 1960).

13. Robert S. Weiss, "A Structure-Function Approach to Organization," *Journal of Social Issues*, vol. 12 (January, 1956), p. 66n.

14. John R. P. French, Joachim Israel, and Dagfinn Ås, "An Experiment in Participation in a Norwegian Factory," *Human Relations*, vol. 13 (February, 1960), pp. 3–19.

15. The Rucker Group Incentive Plan is similar to the Scanlon Plan. See Carl Heyel (ed.), *The Encyclopedia of Management* (New York: Reinhold Publishing Corporation, 1963), pp. 845–849.

16. Douglass McGregor, "The Scanlon Plan through a Psychologist's Eyes," in Frederick G. Lesieur (ed.), *The Scanlon Plan* (The Technology Press of the Massachusetts Institute of Technology and John Wiley & Sons, Inc., New York, 1958), p. 92.

17. The point is neatly made by Harold J. Leavitt, *Managerial Psychology* (Chicago: The University of Chicago Press, 1958), pp. 179ff.

18. Russell W. Davenport, "A Case History of Union-Management Cooperation," in Paul Pigors, Charles S. Myers, and F. T. Malm (eds.), *Readings in Personnel Administration* (New York: McGraw-Hill Book Company, 1959), p. 542.
19. Stuart Chase, "Social Science: Friend of Management," *Personnel,* vol. 27 (January, 1951), p. 247.
20. Roy Helfgott, *Group Wage Incentives: Experience with the Scanlon Plan* (New York: Industrial Relations Counselors, February, 1962).
21. Davenport, op. cit., pp. 539–540.
22. Strauss, *op. cit.,* pp. 50–54.
23. Davenport, *op. cit.,* p. 549.
24. *Ibid.,* p. 546.
25. *Ibid.,* p. 546.
26. Joseph N. Scanlon, "Profit Sharing under Collective Bargaining: Three Cases," *Industrial and Labor Relations Review,* vol. 2 (October, 1948), pp. 58–75.
27. Thomas Q. Gilson and Myron Lefcowitz, "A Plant-wide Productivity Bonus in a Small Factory," *Industrial and Labor Relations Review,* vol. 10 (January, 1957), pp. 284–296.
28. Davenport, *op. cit.,* p. 549.
29. McGregor, *op. cit.,* pp. 92–93.
30. Chris Argyris, *Personality and Organization* (New York: Harper & Row, Publishers, Incorporated, 1957), p. 182.
31. George Strauss and Leonard R. Sayles, "The Scanlon Plan: Some Organizational Problems," *Human Organization,* vol. 16 (Fall, 1957), pp. 15–22.
32. George P. Shultz, "Variations in Environment and the Scanlon Plan," in Lesieur, *op. cit.,* p. 101.
33. See also, for example, William Given, *Bottom-up Management* (New York: Harper & Row, Publishers, Incorporated, 1949); and by the same author, *Reaching-out Management* (New York: Harper & Row, Publishers, Incorporated, 1953).
34. Charles P. McCormick, *Multiple Management* (New York: Harper & Row, Publishers, Incorporated, 1938), pp. 2–3.
35. *Ibid.,* p. 30, reports the early experience. For more recent experience, see Charles P. McCormick, "Multiple Management," in Heyel, *op. cit.,* pp. 570–572.
36. McCormick, *Multiple Management,* p. 21.
37. *Ibid.,* p. 22.

38. Howard B. Jacobson and Joseph S. Roucek (eds), *Automation and Society* (New York: Philosophical Library, Inc., 1959), Chap. 4.
39. Charles R. Walker, *Toward the Automated Factory* (New Haven, Conn.: Yale University Press, 1957), especially p. 41.
40. Walter Buckingham, *Automation* (New York: John Wiley & Sons, Inc., 1958), pp. 96–97.
41. Ralph M. Besse, "Business Statesmanship," *Personnel Administration,* vol. 2 (January–February, 1957), p. 12.
42. Lewis Corey, "Human Relations," *Labor and Nation* (1950), p. 50.
43. Nancy C. Morse and Everett Reimer, "The Experimental Change of a Major Organization Variable," *Journal of Abnormal and Social Psychology,* vol. 52 (January, 1956), pp. 120–129.
44. Keith Davis, *Human Relations at Work* (New York: McGraw-Hill Book Company, 1962), p. 427.
45. Francis X. Sutton, Seymour E. Harris, Carl Kaysen, and James Tobin, *The American Business Creed* (Cambridge, Mass.: Harvard University Press, 1956), pp. 97–98.
46. Daniel Katz, "Satisfactions and Deprivations," in Arthur Kornhauser, Robert Dubin, and Arthur M. Ross (eds.), *Industrial Conflict* (New York: McGraw-Hill Book Company, 1954), p. 104.
47. William H. Whyte, *Is Anybody Listening?* (New York: Simon and Schuster, Inc., 1952), pp. x–xi.
48. William F. Whyte, "Leadership and Group Participation," *New York State School of Industrial and Labor Relations Bulletin,* no. 24 (Cornell University, Ithaca, N.Y., 1953), p. 31.
49. Eugene V. Schneider, *Industrial Sociology* (New York: McGraw-Hill Book Company, 1957), pp. 193–203.
50. P. G. Herbst, *Autonomous Group Functioning* (London: Tavistock, 1962); and Seymour Melman, *Decision-making and Productivity* (New York: John Wiley & Sons, Inc., 1958).
51. Adolph Vlcek, Jr., "Functional-Operational Organization Structure," *Line-Staff Relationships in Production* (New York: American Management Association, 1957), pp. 39–53.
52. The example particularly facilitates analysis of wage-and-salary administration. Similar programs can be developed for high levels of organization, but the point cannot be demonstrated simply.
53. Melman, *op. cit.,* p. 4.
54. Gilbert K. Krulee, "The Scanlon Plan: Co-operation Through Participation," *Journal of Business,* vol. 28 (April, 1955), p. 102.

55. Howard Baumgartel, "Organization Size and Absenteeism," *Kansas Business Review,* vol. 10 (July, 1958), sec. 2, p. 3.
56. James C. Worthy, *Big Business and Free Men* (New York: Harper & Row, Publishers, Incorporated, 1959), pp. 92–93.
57. R. H. Landes, "Application of Group Incentives," *Planning and Administering Effective Incentives,* production series, no. 172 (New York: American Management Association, 1947), p. 17.
58. Melman, *op. cit.,* pp. 175–176.
59. E. L. Trist and H. Murray, "Some Social and Psychological Consequences of the Longwall Method of Coal-getting," *Human Relations,* vol. 4 (February, 1951), pp. 3–38; and A. K. Rice, "Productivity in an Indian Weaving Shed," *Human Relations,* vol. 6 (November, 1953), pp. 297–329.
60. Melman, *op. cit.,* p. 37.
61. Herbst, *op. cit.,* especially pp. 64–81.
62. Landes, *op. cit.,* p. 16.
63. J. V. Miccio, "Objectives and Fundamentals of Wage Incentive Plans," *National Association of Cost Accountants Bulletin,* vol. 30 (1948), p. 65.
64. Melman, *op. cit.,* p. 12. See also pp. 175–176.
65. Frederick Herzberg, Bernard Mausner, and Barbara Bloch Snyderman, *The Motivation to Work* (New York: John Wiley & Sons, Inc., 1959), pp. 134–135.
66. Likert, *op. cit.,* pp. 111–112.
67. Georges Friedmann, *The Anatomy of Work* (New York: The Free Press of Glencoe, 1961), p. 125.

8

A "Sense of Partnership in, and Responsibility for" II: Individual Responsibility and Organization Structure

The fifth value which should govern man-to-man relations in organizations—that the organization ought not be the sole and final arbiter of behavior—is in many senses the linchpin of the Judaeo-Christian Ethic. The value's centrality is transparent. For if the organization were the ultimate measure of man, the first four values could be attained in small measure only.

This injunction on the side of the angels may seem easy to accept, but that ease is chimerical. The importance of an external moral order in controlling organizations was reaffirmed in the trials of war criminals after World War II, to be sure. But these very trials also revealed the lengths to which human beings could go in accepting even bestial organization demands in return for whatever rewards membership brought them. And, even though on a level far removed, one can still hear the words of Federal District Court Judge Ganey describing the majority of defendants before him in an important price-fixing case as "torn between conscience and an approved corporate policy, with the rewarding objectives of promotion, comfortable security and large salaries—in short, the organization or company man, the conformist. . . ."

AWAY FROM ORGANIZATION AS *THE* MEASURE OF MAN

Preliminary Rationale and Specific Requirements

Such cases-in-opposition suggest that this chapter faces real and formidable problems, but they do not establish that the fifth value of the J-C Ethic must be disregarded or that it has mostly negative consequences for administration. Brief illustration here of the significant costs of subjecting the naked individual to the organization sketches the preliminary, nonmoral rationale for a moral sensitivity in organizations.

There are several obvious senses in which organization as *the* measure of man is practically awkward. Thus creativity would be more likely in organizations in which the "true believer" was rare. This might seem to apply with most force to upper levels of the organization. But fortunate is the organization which can tap the enormous pool of creativity among its lower-level operatives. In addition, the person who accepts the formal organization as the sole and final arbiter of his behavior is only a step away from the man who might find it difficult to supply the most minuscule adaptations required by his work until they were completely programmed for him. Too much obedience to the organization can reduce its chances for survival, in sum.

In these terms, Whyte's conclusion that the successful executive typically has a somewhat jaundiced view of "the organization" rings true. The successful executive seems to support the organization only as long as it generally supports his needs and values. Some questions suggest an explanation. Is it reasonable to expect any employee to sacrifice his personality without exacting a high payoff for so doing? And can you really trust someone who would do anything to keep his job, even if it meant sacrificing his needs and values?

The suggested costs of a disregard of the fifth value of the Judaeo-Christian Ethic merely tease. Pious injunctions require strong support from specific organizational arrangements in this case; and allusions to the costs of disregarding the fifth value do not provide the managerial techniques necessary to put moral preachment into practice.

The main thrust of these arrangements and techniques seems clear enough, fortunately. We may rely on Drucker in sketching them.[1] Basically, the required structural arrangements and managerial techniques must imply a high probability that managerial excellence will be rewarded. Within broad policy guidelines, the manager at various levels should be free to reveal his talents while he provides his own detailed plan of action. Advancement by ingratiating one's self with those in power or by scrupulous adherence to detailed instructions from superiors—whether motivated by ruthlessness or blinding ambition or mediocre talents—must be restricted. This basic requirement for acting upon the fifth value of the J-C Ethic generates others, in turn. Further, managerial excellence will be most clear where *the* crucial test requires the supervision of some related set of activities within some enterprise. Moreover, there should be a succession of such jobs, all of which require the individual to integrate increasingly complex and significant sets of activities relevant to the purposes of the enterprise while failure in none of which will jeopardize the existence of the enterprise. Finally, the individual should move into these managerial jobs at a relatively early age, to facilitate his removal upon failure as well as to permit his placement in some nonmanagerial capacity when the necessary adaptations can be made without undue costs to individual and to organization.

These four requirements come to a single point. Meeting them does not safeguard the individual from mortal sin, as it were, but it does remove him from many of the temptations to look upon the organization as the sole and final arbiter of behavior. For example, the emphasis upon actual managerial performance takes much of the wind out of the sails of the malevolent or maladroit individuals who design to prosper by the carrying of tales. Or looked at from another point of view, meeting these requirements limits the ability of superiors to demand successfully that subordinates behave as if the formal organization were the single and absolute measure of man. Performance records moderate such demands.

We need not begin anew in seeking specific structural arrangements and managerial techniques appropriate to the four requirements for approaching the fifth value of the Judaeo-Christian Ethic. The "increasingly complex and significant sets of activities" mentioned above may be defined as several levels of the managerial units illustrated in Figure 21. Oppositely, the traditional theory of organization does shoddy service in this particular. Its emphasis upon functions or processes implies a less straightforward managerial test, even for those relatively high in the hierarchy. Individuals in such a structure run a great risk of a departmental myopia, of becoming specialists in orientation as well as training.

AN ORGANIZATIONAL PRIMER

Delegation and Decentralization

Moving away from the notion that man is to be measured solely in terms of his formal organization requires a complex variation of the More-More Hypothesis. Indeed, this chapter is essentially concerned with extending structure and techniques consistent with the More-More Hypothesis to higher levels of organization. The preceding chapter concentrated upon the first and second levels of supervision, that is, upon the lower levels of organization.

Distinguishing "delegation" from "decentralization-centralization" will help raise our sights above the lower levels of organization. These concepts have been much bruited about. Their use here thus may be at odds with some part of the splendiferous literature. No matter. Everyone has his own knothole for looking at reality, and the following will be ours.

A skeletal conclusion—by way of introduction—will set us on our way. There can be no organization without delegation, but organizations may get along well enough without (for example) decentralization. The main terms may be defined briefly. "Delegation" refers straightforwardly only to "the conferring of a certain specific authority by a [superior]." [2] How much authority is conferred and what conditions hedge that grant: these determine the degree of "centralization-decentralization." When much is conferred and the grant is not restricted by detailed controls, then the delegation is decentralized. While delegation cannot be avoided, the specific pattern of delegation can run the full spectrum from rigid centralization to extreme decentralization.

The traditional theory of organization ill-advisedly rejects this full spectrum. Centralization is its goal. Here, as elsewhere, the stress will be upon the moral and practical inappropriateness of the traditional. For many organizations will profit from a considerable degree of decentralized delegation, and almost every large-scale organization requires it.

The present argument does not deal with extremes. Rather, it is restricted to that middle range of the centralization-decentralization continuum where "trade offs" of decentralized for centralized delegation on balance have attractive consequences. Despite its clear bias toward the decentralized pattern of delegation, the argument recognizes that some activities must remain centralized. Trade offs that approach either extreme closely are increasingly risky. The traditional theory of organization, of course, proposes just such a risky approach to centralization.

Within this substantial range of trade offs between centralized and decentralized delegation, our interest will be relative. That is, no absolute criterion for differentiating the two patterns will be used. "Centralization" and "decentralization" will have a relative meaning only. Indeed, one is on safest ground when speaking of this particular organization as being more centralized than that particular organization in these specific respects. The more convenient shorthand—that "organization Z is decentralized"—is also less meaningful. Thus the United States Steel Corporation has been described as "two-thirds centralized and one-third decentralized." [3] And since far smaller organizations have a devilish complexity in many particulars, even this restricted usage may be too broad.

Centralization-decentralization usefully may be considered the end points of a continuum of planned and reasonable patterns for delegating. Indeed, along with chaos—the absence of planned delegation or its perversion—centralization and decentralization comprise the three major alternatives for organizing work.

A simple diagram conveys the sense of these three alternatives. Illustratively, centralization can get in its own way easily enough, and particularly in a larger organization. Thus Drucker tells us about the railroad president who went so far as to centralize purchasing of all keys for substations. These included keys to rest rooms, which were kept locked until a passenger asked to use the facilities. Then they were opened with the only authorized key, which passengers were asked to return. The number of unreturned keys was high and—although cen-

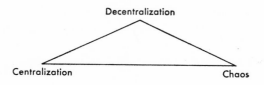

tralized purchasing therefore yielded some cash advantages—this was the rub. A request to headquarters for a new key might take several months since such orders were batched before they were sent to the manufacturer. More immediate action could be taken, however. Managers of the substations had no authority to buy a 20-cent key, but neither could they leave their passengers in extended distress. These same managers were authorized to make emergency repairs on their own initiative, into which category smashed rest-room doors conveniently fell. Emergency repairs on rest-room doors were frequent, we are told.[4] To a similar end, decentralization can riot in the absence of a subtlety in organizing that facilitates the measurement of performance. Decentralization also can be its own worst enemy in the absence of suitable overhead controls for enforcing corporate policies, for evaluating performance, and for rewarding or punishing.

That one must speak carefully of centralization-decentralization hardly means that one cannot speak meaningfully about its underlying structural arrangements and about its associated managerial techniques. Figures 24 and 25 begin this dialogue. The figures depict two simplified ways in which two national firms organized their service and repair activities. Three systems permit a judgment of the relative degree of centralization-decentralization of these activities: a reporting system; an action system; and a review system. These systems facilitate an answer to these three questions: What is the significance of the matters delegated? To what level of the organization is the delegation made? What kind of review is required? Henri Fayol provides the general rule of judgment: "Everything which goes to increase the importance of the subordinate's role is decentralization, everything which goes to reduce it is centralization." [5]

To respect the admonition to be careful, preliminarily note that the geographical dispersion of facilities is not necessarily related to the degree of centralization-decentralization. For physical facilities can be widely scattered while the pattern of delegation remains centralized; and a decentralized pattern is possible even when all facilities are at a single site. As a practical matter, however, the costs of centralization are likely to be less obvious in the latter case. Moreover, decentralization has been resorted to most often where centralized delegation became too unwieldy in larger firms with numerous scattered units.

Figures 22 and 23 sketch organizations that are relatively centralized and relatively decentralized, respectively. Thus Firm A requires that all individual breakdowns be reported to headquarters, that no request for repairs be acted upon at a level lower than that of the district head, and that the district head's office give prior approval to all repair requests. This puts a great strain on the upper levels of the organization. The underlying rationale is the effective channeling of resources by an official with a jurisdiction large enough to supervise services that could not be economically located in the local units. In general, these special services are required only for breakdowns of extended duration.

A different pattern of delegation obviously prevails in Firm B. Breakdowns of equipment are differentiated in terms of their expected duration. The higher levels of organization, then, tend to specialize in matters of increasing significance. For example, certain special maintenance

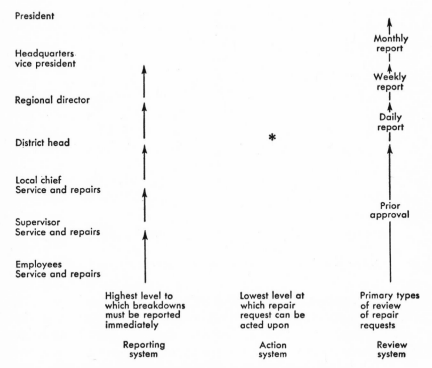

Figure 22. Firm A: A Relatively Centralized Service and Repair Organization.

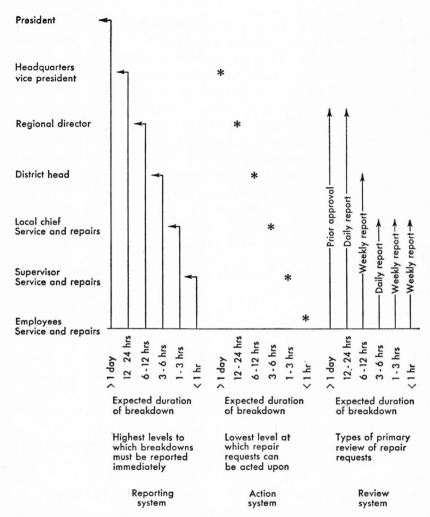

Figure 23. Firm B: A Relatively Decentralized Service and Repair Organization.

and service resources exist only at higher levels (as in Firm A), but these higher levels are involved only in those cases in which it appears that the breakdown is serious, as determined by the estimate of the duration of the breakdown. Top management, incidentally, keeps an interested eye on the accuracy of these estimates which are usually made at the lower levels of the organization.

In effect, organizational demands are more evenly distributed among the several levels in Firm B. Indeed, since a substantial proportion of breakdowns are estimated at less than six hours, and since the local chief or his subordinates have authority to act on all requests for repairs or service (see action system), upper levels are free to concentrate on the more serious cases and to evaluate lower-level performance in all cases. Relatedly, the review system is also keyed to the magnitude of the breakdown. In general, that is, the degree of decentralization increases as one moves through this list of types of review:[6]

1. Authority to act only after prior approval
2. Authority to act only after consulting with an appropriate staff official
3. Authority to act only after prior notice to higher levels of organization
4. Authority to act without prior notice or approval, with some form of reporting required
5. Authority to act with no prior notice, no approval, and no reporting required

Roughly, the primary review of the bulk of the service and maintenance in Firm B is delegated to the supervisors and chiefs, and the type of review is largely at the decentralized end of the continuum. The review system, however, becomes steadily more centralized as the expected duration of a breakdown increases.

The choice of some degree of centralization-decentralization implies many other choices. In fact, these two patterns of delegation involve contrasting philosophies of organization life. Thus one must do more than tinker with the bits and pieces of reporting systems. Rather, the role of management must be turned radically away from the traditional fascination with specific command-obey sequences. That role must move toward outlining and facilitating the job to be done, as by:[7]

1. Setting the goals for the enterprise and its major components
2. Defining the policy limits on behavior appropriate for achieving such goals

3. Checking progress toward such goals and isolating problems that inhibit progress
4. Offering advice and services
5. Relieving subordinate managers of activities which they cannot effectively perform

The job of approaching decentralization also implies changes as broad as the traditional theory of organization. That theory has a marked bias toward the centralized pattern. Consequently, decisions tend to be forced upward in the hierarchy. Functional or processual departmentation will be necessary at some level in all organizations, but the sooner it is resorted to, the greater the centralization of an organization. The traditional theory of organization is impatient in this matter: it provides that functional departmentation begin immediately below the level of the chief executive, as in departments of personnel, finance, production, marketing, and the like. The broad theory necessary to extend decentralization throughout an organization will concern us in due time.

The choice of some degree of centralization-decentralization also implies many specific decisions. First, different activities in organizations often will require different treatment. Decentralization requires basic policy judgments, that is, about which activities can be decentralized and which must be centralized so as to aid top management in controlling and evaluating the decentralized units. There is no appropriate hard-and-fast rule, and experience may require the modification over time of any policy judgments. Accounting and reporting procedures must be standardized throughout the enterprise so that the performance of the component units can be compared meaningfully, for example. However, many of the actual accounting operations may be decentralized later, with headquarters retaining only the general supervision of these activities. Or the initially centralized unit may remain so, as in the case of aspects of finance whose centralization permits economies and plays an important role in the overall control of the enterprise.[8]

Second, the logic of decentralization may not be a reasonable one to follow at all levels of all organizations. Some decentralized units include many plants and many thousands of employees, for example. Decentralization does not go very far down in this case, and there may be good reasons for it. Thus measures of performance traditionally associated with a decentralized pattern of delegation—e.g., return on investment—often are difficult to extend below very large units.[9] Similarly, some products may be highly complex and yet such that only a few small parts can be separated out both technically and economically. This may be the case with the Fisher Body Division of General Motors, for example. Hence Drucker's generalization that decentralization is universally applicable but not necessarily universally valid.[10]

Inventiveness often can surmount such obstacles, however. Consistent with the analysis of the unorthodox structure in Figure 21, for example, substantial delegation may be possible down to the level of the several managerial units at the lowest levels of an organization. Decentralization goes all the way where such an organizational arrangement is possible.

Third, the ways in which enterprises grow and the nature of their products will influence the degree of centralization-decentralization. As Alfred Chandler notes,[11] business concerns have tended to follow one of these strategies for growth: expanding sales of some existing product lines to the same types of customer; seeking new markets and new sources of supply; and opening new markets and developing new products for different types of customers. These several strategies have significant structural implications. The metals companies and those processing agricultural products generally followed the first strategy, according to Chandler. He noted that most firms in copper, zinc, iron, steel, tobacco, meat, sugar, liquor, and bananas have made much the same kind of product for much the same kind of buyer over the last half-century. "Thus their expansion brought few new types of administrative problems," Chandler observes. "In 1960 most enterprises in these industries continued to be run through the older, centralized, functionally departmentalized form." [12] Firms that have resorted to the second and third strategies to achieve growth, in contrast, have been forced into structural innovations biased toward decentralization. All but two of the twenty leading companies in the three industries obsessed with these strategies—electrical and electronics, power machinery (including autos), and chemical—adopted basically decentralized structures. The same pattern characterizes a host of industries: rubber and petroleum concerns, mail-order houses, chain stores, mass-marketing enterprises, and so on. These industries are ones in which firms tended to grow either by seeking new markets and new sources of supply or by developing new products for new markets.

The interpretation of this third condition is straightforward in one sense and tentative in another. That is, structural innovation was necessary in firms seeking new products and markets because their growth inescapably required the delicate fitting of both new and old activities to the varying demands of wider lines of goods and services. Such fitting raised integrative challenges beyond the competence of the traditional theory of organization, which is far more suited to the less complex integration of a few activities in the production of one or a few products. But more of this later. More tentatively, decentralization also may be appropriate in companies that have grown primarily by expansion of volume and were not forced into decentralization by massive integrative problems.

Much evidence supports the latter guess. Commonly, decentralization is a kind of organizational last resort, undertaken without joy and under extreme duress. This is true even of organizations which are decentralized at high levels but cling to centralization at lower levels. The U.S. Civil Service Commission is typical in this respect. "Essentially the delegation of authority [for a wide range of personnel activities] to the [various federal] agencies," one commission official commented on the recent moves toward decentralization, "was a matter of expediency." [13] Less circumspectly, decentralization was expedient because of the inability of any centralized agency to handle the huge volume of hires required by World War II. Indeed one wag noted uncharitably that the Civil Service Commission as centralized personnel agency was the single greatest early obstacle to the successful waging of the war. [14]

Why change toward decentralization has been relatively sticky is a complex question. Certainly the lack of experience with decentralization has been a factor. And centralization—whatever organizational creaks and groans derived from it—at least had well-known inadequacies. Further, Chandler notes that necessary reorganizations in many firms came (when they came at all) only after the death or retirement of some powerful executive or dominant group of executives. Moreover, as of 1955, many of the top fifty industrial firms that were most centralized were still dominated by men well beyond the normal retirement age. Although such firms tended to concentrate on a single line of products for a stable market, Chandler concluded that: "As these veterans leave the scene many of their firms undoubtedly will make significant changes in their management structures." [15]

DECENTRALIZATION

Meeting Organizational Problems Organizationally

Nature has its many curious parallels. Recall that changes in the propellers of World War II aircraft soon forced fundamental redesign of the entire vehicle. In much the same way, for many industries the pressure of growth via changing markets and products forced basic innovations in organization structure. Let us sketch the specific senses in which the problems facing contemporary organizations outstripped the capabilities of the traditional theory, with emphasis upon the common experiences of a number of firms. A thumbnail history of the experiences of one firm will illustrate the common experiences. Such a summary cannot do justice to even very large details, of course.

Decentralization came as a response to a number of specific challenges facing large organizations that also shared a general desire to retain the clear advantages of size. In this sense, the problems facing structural redesign seemed contradictory. "That problem is to combine the economical advantages of modern business with as little sacrifice as possible of that intimate control and development of managerial ability that is the character of the well managed small business," Donaldson Brown reflected on his experience at General Motors. [16] The general solution cut through this apparent contradiction by regrouping a big business into a number of smaller businesses. In some cases, indeed, these "small businesses" are legally independent entities. Johnson and Johnson has taken this approach. More generally, delegations of authority are made so that some unit of organization controls enough activities to make meaningful decisions about their integration. The specific variations are many. Thus General Motors has decentralized around products, such as Cadillac, Chevrolet, and so on; and the United States Post Office has decentralized on the basis of area. Whatever the basis of decentralization, headquarters provides advice and information, sets goals, and monitors performance.

More specifically, decentralization was the structural answer to many related difficulties induced in organizations of some size, and particularly those which developed new sources of supply, new markets, and new products. Let us focus preliminarily on one such multifaceted problem that encourages decentralization: the difficulty and importance of integrating the several functional departments, which both tend to escalate rapidly in larger organizations that follow the traditional theory. Consider the following much-simplified version of the problems facing Du Pont after World War I.[17] The traditional departmentation by major functions served the enterprise well enough when it handled only gunpowder and a few derivative products, and this even though the firm had grown to formidable proportions. Figure 24 sketches this basic structure.

Time left matters unchanged no more for Du Pont than for mortal man. Given the vastly enlarged physical plant and the sharply reduced demand after the Armistice, Du Pont decided upon a policy of diversification to use its existing plant and to develop new markets. This proved far easier to decide than to do. For the traditional structure stumbled badly over the task of integrating the several functional activities around which Du Pont was still organized, and integrating them in ways sensitive to the demands of the new products as well as the old.

Du Pont's structural failure requires exploration. In theory, each functional department provided its particular service for all products. In practice, matters were far more complicated. For example, the policy of diversification raised in acute forms the question of the preferences that each department would give to the various products in providing its service when conflicts about priorities arose, which they did often

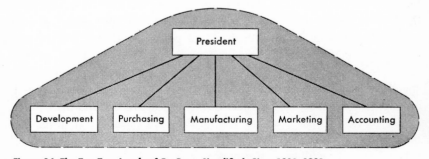

Figure 24. The Top Two Levels of Du Pont, Simplified, Circa 1919–1921.

and painfully. Moreover, the various departmental interests did not want for high-level representation of their particularistic points of view. The heads of many of the functional departments also were members of the finance and executive committees which provided overall direction for the firm. At best these department heads wore two hats. They individually represented the particularistic interests of their own department; and they collectively were to safeguard the wholistic interests of the corporation. These interests might coincide. But often what was best for manufacturing in the short run was most definitely not best for Du Pont in the long run.

The basic problem at Du Pont, then, may be conceptualized in terms of the pervasively different preferences that the several functional departments accorded to the traditional homogeneous product line that had made the company great and to the diversified product line prescribed by new policy. The traditional structure did not encourage bringing such preferences into harmonious phase. Officials in manufacturing, for example, assigned a relatively high preference to the gunpowder program. The technology was well known; operatives had been trained; and processes were finely tuned. The manufacture of the new products—paints and varnishes or Pyralin and Celluloid—in contrast, was full of treacherous unknowns. Consequently, the new product line could expect little more than tolerant treatment by manufacturing in the skirmishing for scarce resources. Manufacturing had the support of marketing, in addition. For one sold gunpowder in very large volumes to relatively few buyers, and with little need for delicate marketing activities such as advertising, market surveys, and the like. These historic experiences of marketing were such as to assign generally low preferences to the use of scarce resources for making a reality out of the new policy of diversification. The new diversification required sales in small volumes, with far greater emphasis upon the individual consumer, and with enormously more intricate problems of anticipating demand and of scheduling production. The contest was not all one-sided even within these departments, of course. Moreover, Development accorded a higher priority to the new diversified line. But this hardly counterbalanced the forces-in-opposition.

The new policy of diversification at Du Pont faced its difficulties. In large part, these difficulties were due to the unwieldiness at the corporate level of what James Worthy has called the "administrative unit," which can be "no smaller than that portion of the organization falling within the jurisdiction of an individual who controls enough elements of the total process to make effective decisions regarding the total process." [18] The high-level administrative unit in Figure 24 is enclosed by the broken elliptical area. This elephantine managerial unit posed the problems of change in awkward form. Briefly, successful diversification implied simultaneous, but differential, change in all of the functional departments of a vast enterprise. Change is difficult under any conditions, but sheer scale at Du Pont made it particularly treacherous. Matters were further complicated because no one department had a clear and direct interest in the profitability of the new products. That is, no one department had a positive incentive to undergo the pangs of change, at least in the short run.

The portrait of the clash of different preferences of the several functional departments might be elaborated interminably, both in detailing Du Pont's history and in summarizing the common experiences of numerous firms. But essential reality has been captured, and that must satisfy us. Certainly the consequences were typical enough. The Du Pont financial statement for the first half of 1921 was a shocker. Explosives returned a profit of nearly $2,500,000, but the total net loss for the firm was over 2.4 million dollars. The new product lines were the weak sisters: Dyestuffs had a deficit of over 1 million dollars; paints ran $717,356 into the red; cellulose products lost three-quarters of a million dollars; and the Fabrikoid deficit was $863,904.

Explaining this record poses some problems, but structural factors loom large. Thus the worsening post-war recession and the development costs of the new products explain part of the record. Even with this complexity, one Du Pont director attributed a very significant part of the dismal profit-and-loss picture to a "failure of our organization to adjust itself to present conditions." The centralized, functionally departmentalized structure must be replaced, he advised. "The trouble with the company is right here in Wilmington, and the failure is the failure of administration for which we, as Directors, are responsible." [19]

The directors of Du Pont accepted the challenge to innovate structure. Basically, as Figure 25 implies, two types of changes were made. A first change organized most of the major departments immediately

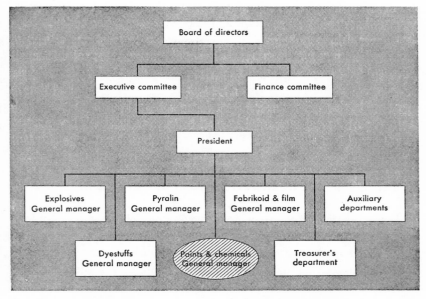

Figure 25. Organization of Top Levels of Du Pont, Simplified, Proposed August 31, 1921.

below the level of the president around each of the major product lines. Each department then became a high-level administrative unit in Worthy's sense: the big business of Du Pont was broken into a number of smaller (but still sizable) autonomous businesses, each headed by a general manager. The closed ellipse in the figure shows how sharply the size of the managerial unit was reduced, as compared to Figure 24. Consequently, a single general manager could do much of what only the president could have done under the centralized model. The general manager would integrate all the activities immediately required for (let us say) the manufacture and marketing of Pyralin. As a company report—which was later accepted in essence—explained:[20]

According to this plan, the head of each Industrial Department will have full authority and responsibility for the operation of his industry, subject only to the authority of the Executive Committee as a whole. He will have under him men who will exercise all the line functions necessary for a complete industry, including routine and special purchasing, manufacture, sales, minor construction, normal and logical chemical and engineer operative and experimental laboratory activities, work supplies, cost-keeping routine and analysis, products standards and complaints, orders, work planning, routine traffic, trade records and sales expense.

The structural innovation had its obvious advantages. Thus even very considerable changes could be made without involving the entire organization. Moreover, new product-oriented divisions could be added with relative ease. Each general manager was responsible for the profitability of his own enterprise, in addition, as measured by a calculated return on investment. And the manager controlled enough activities that he could not plead lack of control when he showed poorly in the meaningful comparison of performance permitted by the decentralized structure. Some support activities were to be provided centrally, to be sure, and they at once aided in the comparative measure of performance while they permitted the manager to tackle his job more single-mindedly. That is, the central services facilitated control by top management, as when the treasurer's department handled general company financing, custody of the funds and records, master accounting, and auditing. Or the central services could provide services deemed beyond the competence of the several industrial departments. The legal department was an auxiliary department that handled all legislative matters for the company, for example.

The reorganization also affected a second change. The executive committee surrendered all operating responsibilities and became primarily responsible for monitoring performance and for guiding the long-run development of the enterprise. A company report explained that this was the only way top executives could give all their "time and effort to the business of the Company as a whole." Without responsibility for a company division, the report continued, "they will be able to consider all questions or problems without bias or prejudice." [21] That is, Du Pont executives seem to have profited from their own experience.

This miniature administrative history illustrates two points. Organizing around relatively autonomous product units at once facilitated the integration of the several activities and also permitted the individual managers to blend those activities so as to meet the particular demands of the several products, existing and future. In addition, the measurement of the profitability of the separate industrial product divisions pinpointed responsibility and also permitted general supervision by the executive committee.

To note that decentralization facilitates the integration of the several activities necessary for some product and that it permits the nonarbitrary measurement of performance, however, conceals while it illumines. The focus is so broad that it glosses over much of significance. Several more specific points of the advantages of decentralization deserve notice, then. The analysis is framed conveniently by Drucker's list of the requirements of institutional order:[22]

1. The supply and development of capable managers
2. The orderly succession in top management without resort to wars of succession or to organizational geniuses
3. The formulation of a policy flexible enough to meet contingencies yet fixed enough to serve as useful guides
4. The development of impersonal, objective yardsticks of performance

Let us see how decentralization copes with these requirements of institutional order. First, decentralization encourages the development of effective managers. The key factor is that as far down the hierarchy as substantial delegation exists, supervisors cannot be narrow specialists. Oppositely, such individuals can—and do—hide their inadequacies in a functional structure, which imposes a more limited and different set of demands upon them. The research literature is not all that it should be, but relevant examples abound. Thus one company reorganized into autonomous product businesses and appointed eight division managers with the hopeful expectation that two "heirs apparent" would emerge from the experience as top-management material. The expectation was disappointed. One of the heirs-apparent was a competent production man in a functionally departmentalized structure, but he proved incapable of running a balanced business. The second—the assistant to the president in the old structure—continually "went upstairs" with problems rather than assume personal responsibility. The functional structure had not tested their managerial capabilities, in contrast to their specialist capabilities. As the president of the firm in question summarized the experience:[23]

We put in decentralization more because it was the fashion than because we really believed in it or understood it. It has developed our business almost twice as fast as we had dared hope; and the greatest growth of sales and profits has been in lines that had always been problem children before. Above all, it has saved us in the nick of time from making the fatal mistake of putting the wrong people in at the top. I'll never again make that decision on the basis of my judgment instead of by performance test in an independent responsibility. We put in eight division managers; only three performed as we had expected them to perform. Two—our winning entries—never got away from the post. And the three whom we thought the least of turned out to be world beaters.

Other evidence permits a different approach, but yields similar conclusions of the value of a decentralized structure in developing managers. The managers of medium-sized Sears stores, by company policy, are allowed to develop a suitable internal organization structure. Comparisons show that internally decentralized stores not only had better sales records than centralized ones, but they also developed many more managers who were considered promotable.[24]

Second, a decentralized pattern of delegation aids orderly succession in organizations. An adequate demonstration of the point is not possible here. Illustratively, however, consider that decentralization tests managerial worth in integrating some related set of activities, which is no small factor in easing the problems of succession. Moreover, decentralization requires the distribution of authority to a number of quasi-independent centers of initiative operating within a system of policy. This permits the comparative measure of performance and assures that some common goal is being pursued, if in different ways. There tends therefore to be neither a specific "organizational orthodoxy" nor a detailed "party line" in decentralized organizations, and this may include the lack of an enforced orthodoxy concerning decentralization. Recall that the Sears managers, working in a decentralized company, were free to choose (or reject) a centralized structure in their own stores. That similar problems can inspire such dissimilar solutions implies less disruption in succession. For the system is less rigid and permits the reality-testing of several methods of approach in the several decentralized units. In a centralized structure, in contrast, strong forces support *a* decision. It can be very right or very wrong, but in either case strong forces are mobilized to get the entire organization committed to that decision. Succession tends to be traumatic, as one consequence. The "ins" and the "outs" tend to have it out, if only because an organization-wide change in the prevailing orthodoxy is always possible whether centralization is retained or abandoned. In brief, the capture of *the one* center of formal influence in a centralized organization becomes very crucial.

Third, decentralization depends upon a policy that is flexible enough to meet the unexpected and yet is meaningful enough to provide fixed guides for behavior. Oppositely, centralization implies rigid policies that may prove capricious guides for behavior. The capriciousness will be most apparent where the many activities are performed on many products in markets that are complex and changing. These are just the conditions that are increasingly coming to challenge business and public administration.

Freedom to act in a decentralized structure is paid for by adherence to corporate policies; it is not somehow freely given. The balance between freedom and policy is a delicate one, but Marshall Dimock has put his analytical finger on the essence of a decentralized structure.[25] "The cohesive factor in the whole Bell System," he concluded, "appears to be more a matter of common targets and principles of management than a fear of exerting one's independence." This "more . . . than" point of equilibrium may be located more precisely somewhere between two sets of views, the first expressed by a corporate executive and the other by a field executive in the same firm. Headquarters "never issues orders," the corporate executive explained. "This makes for morale and progressiveness. A one-man show is a 'hen-and-chickens' type of organization. A.T. & T. tries to create independence and at the same time an institutional mind. The fundamental problem is that of encouraging individual initiative and responsibility within a corporate philosophy." An executive in the field had a different view of matters, but not radically so. "Each [decentralized] company is permitted to run largely as an independent business and to make its own decisions," he noted. A decentralized company within the firm can change its organization, it can create a new department, or it can merge other departments. Suggestions from headquarters do influence these decisions, the field official concluded, but a company need not "follow the suggestions of A.T. & T. unless it wants to. But for reasons of system cooperation, it usually winds up doing so." Indeed just this margin for choice may make corporate life more morally livable.

This margin for freedom is one of the attractions that is more or less unique to decentralization, and it seems well worth cultivating. For example, Drucker was struck by the dominant tone among executives in decentralized General Motors. It was "one of great individual liberty within which every man—at least among the three to five hundred first- and second-line executives—is allowed as much responsibility as he is willing to assume." [26] A centralized structure by contrast tends toward an insistence on conformity. The U.S. Forest Service of some years ago provides an unvarnished example of this insistence.[27] "For an officer in the field to question the policy outlined in the regulations on any point no matter how trivial," one close observer noted, "or to suggest that a change in regulation would be beneficial to the Service or conducive to better administration, was almost equivalent to religious heresy." Formal superiors in the service merely put the matter more briefly. "It is the duty of forest officers to obey instructions," went one variation, "and not to question them." Other extreme contrasts can be made easily. In decentralized General Electric the head of each of the one hundred-odd product divisions can expend up to $500,000 for capital projects on his own initiative.[28] Conformity to major policies is expected and enforced, of course. A centralized structure permits far less personal freedom from close and persistent oversight, at all levels. In one firm some $142,000 in executive time was spent yearly in the detailed checking of the work of a purchasing agent whose most flagrant error would cost the company only $100,000.[29]

Fourth, decentralization depends upon the development of impersonal, objective yardsticks of performance. These yardsticks may vary from return on investment in large units of organization to the comparison of a wide variety of performance data from decentralized operating units at the lowest levels. In the A.T. & T. system, for example, a central observing office may run daily tests on all phases of the telephone call sequence—including quality of the operator's voice, speed of answering, etc.—which are compared against statistical averages. Results for each central office are announced both to publicize the comparative level of performance and to direct attention to areas where more work is needed. Such measurement of comparative performance also has an interesting side effect. As Dimock noted: "Indeed, . . . this comparison of similar data from different operating companies . . .

is one of the more interesting features of administrative federalism as practiced by A.T. & T. because it supplies an element of competition from the outside." [30] Similar measures would be difficult to obtain and/or interpret in centralized enterprises, if only because functional and processual specialization often permits many levels of management to plead a lack of responsibility.

There literally may be no alternative but administrative chaos to the development of nonarbitrary measures of performance in many decentralized organizations. Thus a regional vice-president in Sears, Roebuck may have a hundred stores reporting directly to him, each an autonomous unit responsible for marketing and for profits. And each store manager may have thirty-odd section managers reporting directly to him, with each section manager in turn administering his own relatively autonomous unit organized around some product(s), e.g., men's outer garments. Hence there may be administrative units within administrative units. Since only two levels of organization may intervene between the highest and lowest management levels in Sears, close supervision is literally impossible.

The relation is not reversible. Decentralization can exist along with a narrow span of control. Indeed, one can argue with some justice that a narrow span of control in a decentralized structure can accomplish more for the freedom and growth of the employee, if supervision is supportive and service-oriented. But the point here still obtains. There is precious little room in the decentralized firm for "close supervision" or for "management by crisis."

The measurement of performance facilitated by decentralization permits the general abandonment of rules of the game that are competitive in the narrow, person-to-person sense. Decentralization does not forfeit the goad of competition, but reorients and defines it more broadly. As John Pfiffner and Frank Sherwood saw it, the social climate associated with decentralization played a crucial role. They noted that: "Such a social climate is difficult to describe because it is full of contradictions and enigmas. On the one hand it would seem to be welfare-centered, with a certain flavor of devotion to human uplift. On the other it retains the production drive and competitive atmosphere so characteristic of the industrial scene in the past." [31] Supervisors at all levels, then, need rely less on what may be called "inhibiting authority" whose purpose it is to keep people from going wrong. Rather the emphasis is upon "helping authority," that is, providing the resources that permit the subordinate to grow and to produce. Elements of both uplift and drive thus are combined.

Although other-than-anecdotal evidence is in short supply, moreover, such effects seem to spread far below the level of formal decentralization. One study reports findings that are consistent with changes in supervisory style at low levels as well as high in decentralized firms. Decentralized firms had lower rates of labor turnover, lower rates of absenteeism, and lower rates of frequency and severity of accidents.[32] Such indices measure aspects of what may be called "leaving the field" which is triggered by some felt deprivation. The more favorable showing by decentralized firms is consistent with the analysis in Chapter 5, which permits the guess that less leaving-the-field would be encouraged in decentralized organizations because (for example) of the supportive style of supervision consistent with this pattern of delegation.

ONE VARIETY OF THE SPECIES

Decentralization at Lower Levels

Any summary treatment of gargantuan organizations and of the requirements for institutional order can cause a kind of analytical giddiness: the air is so rarefied that few have really breathed it. And although a variety of authoritative reports does exist—such as those dealing with the American Brake Shoe Company, A.T. & T., Standard Oil of New Jersey, and the like—one still yearns for the comfort of relations that are built more to the scale of Aware Everyman and are therefore easier to understand.

Scholarship and practice conspire against us in this regard, but not with complete success. There have been a number of studies of what may be called (following William Given) "progressive decentralization" which spreads from one level to others down throughout the hierarchy.[33] And similar examples from department stores, food stores, government agencies, and other contexts are available.[34]

This variety of studies permits some assurance in sketching the human consequences of centralization-decentralization at lower levels. Consider a "before and after" sketch of life in a supermarket. Under a centralized pattern of delegation, the district manager (DM) was the operational head of a small number of stores. Each store also had three separate organizational units: grocery, meat, and produce. The heads of these sections were directly responsible to the DM, who was aided by two assistants (ADM) in the detailed supervision of the sale of perishables. The style of supervision of the DM and his assistants was consistent with the centralized model: it was highly directive and punitive, with the emphasis on observing and correcting errors. The following sequence is representative:[35]

ADM: I don't see why you've got some of your potatoes up there on the end rack. They shouldn't be there. They should all be in the stack of regular potatoes. You could put turnips up at that spot. You've got them down below now. Another thing I notice, you're practically out of the cider business out there. Haven't you got some cider you can put out there and sell?

These directions were received stolidly. A researcher recounts that when the assistant district manager finished reading from his list the produce manager immediately turned on his heel to execute the suggestions. The produce manager said nothing during the confrontation.

Some significant, unintended consequences are implied in such apparently simple command-obey sequences. First, the DM's role was conflicted. His job had attractive features, of course. District managers enjoyed the mobility and the freedom from direct supervision inherent in the job of overseeing several stores. Perhaps more basically, the DM found himself torn by two sets of pressures. The DM strongly tended to act as a middleman: passing on the specific instructions of headquarters to the people in the field and trying to enforce the specific kinds of performance that headquarters required. Therefore his role was punitive, but it lacked organizational power because the prime locus of decision-making was at headquarters. Conditions made the worst of this unbalanced role. Indeed, the DM often felt trapped between the general demands of headquarters and the particular problems of the individual stores. The resolution of this conflict implies significant human and organizational costs. Thus the typical DM resolved conflict in several ways. He worried and worked harder; he acted out his internal conflicts in his relations with his supervisors; and he condoned a certain slippage between what headquarters expected and what store employees provided. The last accommodation seemed particularly popular. For the typical DM identified more closely with *his* territory and *its* problems than with officials and *their* problems. Moreover, condoning a certain amount of slippage was relatively safe because of inconsistent follow-up by top management. This is a characteristic resolution of the forces-in-opposition generated by a centralized structure. Some DMs no doubt identified strongly with top management, but "splitting the difference" between the pressures of headquarters and the field in favor of the latter was the most common adaptation. This pattern had numerous motivators. In part, for example, a DM's conviction that he could not or would not do the things necessary for promotion could have encouraged such an identification. Many DMs were not promotable, in point of fact, and most no doubt realized it.

The common adaptation of the DM was a difficult one to sustain without emotional turmoil, however compelling the factors that supported it. Thus the typical DM's close identification with his store implied some anxiety and duplicity in dealings with top management. But the typical DM also was denied the full measure of social and psychological support from store employees, at the very least, because he was encouraged to employ close supervision and a directive style by the firm's centralized structure and by its traditions. The DM, then, acted to push away that which he held dear. The condition is unstable, with significant negative consequences for both the manager and those managed.

Second, the consequences of the centralized pattern spread beyond the district manager and his assistants. Consider only that the training opportunities open to subordinates were limited by the close supervision of the DM. "Training" of a sort was encouraged by the centralized structure, but it was training in dependence upon the superior rather than in the development of increased personal competence in grappling with the requirements of store management. This training in dependence had its bitter fruits: evidences of dissatisfaction were common and many employees protected themselves psychologically by decreasing their involvement in work. The reaction of one produce manager to a peremptory order from a young ADM to rearrange a display illustrates the point: "I don't see where it makes any difference but I don't question it. I used to question things like this but not any more.

I've learned that what they want is yes men, so I yes them. If I had learned that when I was younger, I would have been an assistant district manager myself by now and long before this fellow made it." In similar ways can the neglect of local conditions and individual autonomy be compounded by a centralized system. Dependence, dissatisfaction, and lack of involvement, that is, can eliminate whatever incentive to make local adaptations survives the withering blizzards of detailed formal orders.

Third, the centralized pattern helped divide the loyalties of supermarket employees. There were many evidences of a lack of interest in the store as a whole, for example, and this is not surprising. By organizational definition, that interest is the job of the DM and his assistants. What they could not get done by their own orders and follow-up—and much could not be done by them because of their relatively brief visits—often did not get done. The three heads of grocery, produce, and meat thus had a ready organizational reason for being preoccupied with their own specialities. Moreover, the style of supervision gave them a human reason for "letting the district manager do it."

The fragmentation of the store as a managerial unit may be illustrated briefly. For example, departmental identifications tended to be mutually exclusive. Hence one grocery clerk noted that he never took his coffee with members of the meat department in "*their* back room." "Hell no," he put it. "You start eating with them meat bastards and they'll start acting like you're obligated to them or something." The preoccupation with departmental activities also is reflected variously. For example, preserving customer relations was considered an evasion of primary responsibility. "Oh, God," one clerk exclaimed, "I must spend an hour a day with those customers. . . . They really give you a pain." Similarly, employees were not likely to volunteer when an overload occurred in areas of the store for which others had primary responsibility. Helping out at the cash register was roundly disliked, for example. "No, we'd never come up here if we had our own way," one grocery clerk observed. "You get behind, and you never catch up again. No, [checking] is work for them damn part-timers." A good day's work from each man, that is, differed markedly from a good day's work from all the men.

The consequences of such departmental fragmentation assume significant proportions. No wonder that the enterprise found itself without a pool of trained replacements with experience and orientation encompassing the store as a whole. Interdepartmental tensions imply a low probability that some individuals will be rotated through the several departments in some regular way. For the heads of the three departments would find it difficult to cooperate in such an effort, if only because they would prefer to keep their "best hands" busy doing the job of the one department for which each supervisor was responsible. Moreover, individual employees would be cautious about any program of rotation, for the organization's reward-and-punishment system heavily emphasized obedience to detailed orders in a specific activity. Finally, intense conflict between departments would inhibit employees from leaving their source of social and psychological support to enter the camp of the enemy.

As usual—to stress the broader consequences of centralization in this case—departmental fragmentation exacted a stiff toll. Basically, departmental differences reinforced by structural arrangements destroyed the sense of the store as a common enterprise in which all employees shared. Hence there was a neglect of customer relations and a vehement dislike of helping out in other departments, despite the patent importance of both to the store-as-an-entity. For these were trans-departmental matters and thus outside the scope of narrow departmental definitions of their "own concern." The outcome is common when the traditional theory of organization is respected. Since each store was something more than the sum of its component departments narrowly conceived, however, the store-as-an-enterprise suffered. Paradoxically, indeed, the more single-mindedly each department pursued its "own job," the worse the consequences for each store. Consequently, DMs often would be put in the position of reproaching departmental employees for doing a narrowly defined "good job." This sets the stage for very trying supervisory relations.

Decentralization proved the required tonic for the food chain's several organizational difficulties. That pattern of delegation helped improve the awkward role of the DM; decentralization required and facilitated the development of a corps of managers with a storewide point of view; and the new structure helped induce and sustain a sense of the entire store as an enterprise. The dynamics of these multiple consequences of structural change are usefully outlined.

Rapid growth of the food chain created irresistible pressures for change. There were too many stores for the existing pool of district managers and their capable assistants, and there were no reinforcements to fall back upon. The firm more or less backed into decentralization. A new position was developed, therefore—that of store manager, with general responsibility for managing a store and with the authority to do it—and the role of the DM was redefined as basically advisory and helpful rather than supervisory and punitive. All new store managers were put through a six-week training program during which they were relieved of all operating responsibilities. They were moved from assignment to assignment to learn more about the several activities they would have to integrate in their new jobs. The district managers also went through a period of training for their new duties.

There was much evidence that this training tended "to take." The transition was more or less difficult for various individuals, of course, but one sequence typifies the new pattern of decentralized delegation toward which both the old DM and the new store manager (SM) were working. In walking past the meat counter, one district manager agreed to a meat manager's request for some overtime work. The store manager had been accompanying the DM, and he noted when they were alone:

> *SM:* You shouldn't have done that, DM.
> *DM:* What do you mean?
> *SM:* Spoken to the meat manager like that. I'm the one who should have answered his question.
> *DM:* (pause) I think you're right. And thanks for reminding me.

Significantly, both individuals were long-term employees of the firm and thus probably were familiar with the starkly opposed behavior encouraged by the centralized pattern of delegation.

The training seems to have had its favorable effects. Relevantly, the new role of the DM enabled him to be more effective in judging the store manager's performance in terms of the criteria set by top management. For example, the new DM was no longer preoccupied with transmitting orders and (within limits) exacting obedience in a host of detailed matters. Rather we find the DM active in a family of novel behaviors: aiding and evaluating the store manager in his handling of personnel matters; encouraging and helping the store manager in the development of his personnel; and emphasizing favorable customer relations with the store as a whole. Previously the individual department managers were apparently evaluated in terms of their conformity to detailed instructions relevant to their own departments and in terms of their dependence upon the authoritarian DM. In addition, the new structure required far less imposition of goals from on high. And it seemingly elicited far more commitment to the goals of the formal organization. For example, the store manager played a very important (and perhaps crucial) role in the projections for the next quarter of both sales volume and payroll requirements. As one DM noted to a store manager at the conclusion of one such forecasting session:

> *DM:* Well, there they are. You set the goals, my boy. Don't complain to me if you don't make them.
> *SM:* Well, we set them, we'll try to make them. (DM left the room for a minute.)
> *Researcher:* Seriously, whose idea was it to raise the sales volume $1,000 in here?
> *SM:* It was mine.

Relatedly, although little direct evidence was gathered, the store manager did not seem to be paying for some degree of personal freedom at work by playing games with the DM. Many changes in work permitted the store manager to make a real commitment to the management of his store. Thus the power of the store manager over his environment, as previous analysis demonstrates, should help unfreeze and change some of the negative attitudes of employees developed under the centralized pattern of delegation. Consequently, conflicts between departments probably would abate. The rationale is straightforward. Under the decentralized structure, in a far more immediate sense than before, the performance of *their* store was at issue. In addition, the probable change in the style of supervision within each store would tend to curb destructive behavior. Finally, each store manager not only had responsibility for a specific store, but he also had considerable power to make adaptations in the details of operation to local situations, and he had a very definite voice in determining the broad goals for his particular store. The earlier analysis of supervisory power implies the usefulness for both manager and employee of this aspect of a decentralized pattern of delegation.

Acting upon the More-More Hypothesis in this case, then, does not seem to have been manipulative. The approach to the fifth value of the Judaeo-Christian Ethic—that the formal organization would not be the sole and final arbiter of behavior—was both real and effectual.

TOWARD DECENTRALIZATION

Some Costs

The advantages of decentralization do not come free of costs. Perhaps the biggest "cost" they imply is associated with the wide delegation by top management necessary for decentralization. Centralization of authority is reasonable under the traditional theory of organization, and perhaps necessary. The influence of this theory upon many managers has been marked. The decentralized delegation of authority comes with great difficulty for most of them. The More-Less Hypothesis has a firm hold on much management thought, no doubt of it.

Reservations about delegating bode ill for decentralization, for the pattern of delegation does not sit well with a general pessimism about man. Indeed, decentralization requires precisely the kind of manager who has the strength of character and ability to make his decisions and let others make theirs. The very act of decentralization—of setting an individual loose within general boundaries—is optimistic. Decentralization also implies that there is much to be gained in terms of increasing the chances for adaptation, training, and involvement at lower levels.[36] This is accomplished by cultivating the attitude that the formal organization above an officer's level is not the sole and final arbiter of behavior.

Moreover, freedom via decentralization has its costs. To choose what may be an extreme case, the freedom of the decentralized units may be expressed in terms of resistance to innovations developed by the auxiliary services reserved to top management. Villers, for example, recounts the curious history of a safety device for a punch press that also made possible very marked increases in output. The device was adopted by the various plants in a decentralized firm in time, but "time" in this case meant more than ten years.[37] Such cases try the souls of top-level management, testing both their patience and their maturity.

The change toward a decentralized pattern also implies some significant costs-of-transition. For example, overhead administrative costs and problems may be increased as measures of performance and appropriate procedures are developed. Over the longer run such costs probably diminish, but the mixed available evidence does not permit easy judgment.

Training is another cost-of-transition, and it must detain us longer. Consider only the "institutional identification" that is at once the basis and the product of decentralization. Briefly, the pattern of delegation cannot work effectively if all manner of actions are taken willy-nilly throughout the system and if individuals are not prepared for their new, enlarged jobs.

The training effort in a decentralized enterprise must be particularly intense and extended. Thus one wag remarked at this consequence of the selection and training program at Sears: "Sure, they can afford to decentralize; their men all think the same to begin with." [38] There are meaningful points to this barb. Certainly, careful attention must be paid to what Company X's officials are thinking alike about. Too much of the same kind of thinking about too many things could undercut the purpose of a decentralized pattern, if indeed the massive effort to indoctrinate employees does not prove its own undoing. Too little of the same kind of thinking about certain matters of institutional concern, however, is just as bad.

Related to the training problem, changeovers to decentralization imply some problems in reassigning personnel. In an extreme sense, some individuals may find a decentralized structure so threatening that they cannot perform effectively within it. Personality characteristics—some of which we can identify—seem acutely relevant to predicting such reactions.[39] Some research in Sears stores provides useful detail on the point. James Worthy characterized the managers predisposed to centralization sharply. They "seemed to expect the worst of their people and generally found their fears justified. They found that people had to be watched, that their work had to be checked closely—otherwise no telling what might happen." [40] Individuals with personality character-istics biased against decentralization must be provided for. Fortunately, whatever bias exists in social conditioning in this country tends to favor the requirements of the decentralized structure.

As implied at several points, decentralization also will require great skill in isolating administrative units or relatively autonomous flows of work. Even more difficult, if it is to work its way down through the hierarchy, decentralization requires the isolation of administrative units within administrative units at the several levels of complex organiza-tions. Such "wheels within wheels" pose a significant challenge to or-ganizational analysis, which is inured to simplistic thinking in terms of functions and processes. For example, Sears may seem to have faced no problem in settling on the store as an administrative unit—it being such a "natural" unit—and in delegating substantially to the store manager. There were, however, great barriers in the way of perceiving the advantages of such delegation and in the way of acting upon this perception. There were (and are) even greater difficulties in extending this perception below the level of the store, in isolating smaller admin-istrative units within the store. And this despite the fact that Sears stores have been traditionally organized in terms of product depart-ments, which also seem "natural" administrative units. Far greater prob-lems confront the enterprise whose technology is not so "obviously" adapted to the decentralized pattern of delegation. [41]

A final point deserves far greater attention than can be given here, so much is it in the managerial air. That is, decentralization will require some moderation in the use of the new computer technology. Modera-tion may be difficult to achieve, however, given the cost of the equip-ment. Indeed, the fantastic power of such electronic equipment in as-similating data has led some observers to conclude that an age of re-centralization is upon us. [42] And indeed such an age it may be, for one of the motivations of decentralization was the sheer difficulty of assem-bling the data required for centralized decision-making in larger enter-prises.

Perhaps a hesitancy to leap to a conclusion is appropriate, for it is not at all clear that the present ferment in thought and practice will yield a recentralization along traditional lines. [43] Alternatively, as Dimock notes, the new age may be only one of "wing clipping" in overall strategy areas such as long-term planning, product development, and research.[44] "Recentralization," that is, might mean only new definitions of selected relationships between headquarters and its operating units in areas that are quite appropriate for headquarters but which had been decentralized out of convenience or out of despair at the once-overwhelming burdens of data collection and collation. If "recentralization" means anything more, to that degree will some of the benefits of decentralization be forfeit.

TOWARD DECENTRALIZATION

Denouement

If with some reservations, decentralization permits an approach to the fifth value of the Judaeo-Christian Ethic which should guide man-to-man relations in organizations, and this while on balance enhancing effectiveness. This is the case despite the patent difficulties of saying "when" to attempts at decentralization, of training personnel, and of developing suitable controls.[45]

Indeed, this may put the matter too cautiously. If we restrict attention to the "big picture" of organizational success and growth, the experience of many of our larger enterprises at least supports the usefulness of decentralization. Experience testifies that this innovation was *the* structural key to meeting the demands of the strategy of diversification of products and markets into which both business and public enterprises have been increasingly forced. Research on the "little picture" of individual satisfaction and growth—while it could be far stronger—does nothing to contradict this picture of the value of the decentralized pattern of delegation.

In important senses, finally, decentralization is the creature and the creator of this entire analysis. Notice that one may "build up to" decentralization from the several managerial techniques and structural arrangements considered in earlier chapters. One may also "build down to" such techniques and arrangements from this chapter. The success of a decentralized pattern of delegation implies and encourages a generally supportive style of supervision; and such a style, in turn, derives from and contributes to appropriate structural arrangements at the highest levels of organization (organizing around products versus functions, for example) as well as at the lowest levels of organization (organizing around administrative units versus individual processes). The argument could be embellished upon in many similar ways, but this example will be allowed to stand here as a sparse illustration of the complex interplay between decentralization and the various managerial techniques and structural arrangements enumerated above as consistent with the Judaeo-Christian Ethic. The economy of illustration does not imply middling significance, however. Rather, subsequent analysis can more conveniently develop the cumulative and interacting features of the total analysis.

Indeed, this book can rest on this reference to its reversible nature. The present argument has no beginning or end. Rather it deals with structure and techniques which can be treated serially for analytical purposes but which must be interrelated in complex ways in practice.

Footnotes: CHAPTER 8

1. Peter F. Drucker, *The Practice of Management* (New York: Harper & Row, Publishers, Incorporated, 1954), pp. 204–205.
2. James D. Mooney and Alan C. Riley, *Onward Industry!* (New York: Harper & Brothers, Publishers, Incorporated, 1931), p. 35.
3. John Chamberlain, "Industrial Firms Explore Diverse Forms of Organization," *Wall Street Journal,* Dec. 17, 1956.
4. Related in Drucker, *The Practice of Management,* p. 125.
5. Henri Fayol, *General and Industrial Management,* trans. by Constance Storrs (London: Sir Isaac Pitman & Sons, Ltd., 1949), p. 33. For an attempt to meet the difficulties of more precise description, see Thomas L. Whisler, "Measuring Centralization of Control in Business Organizations," in William W. Cooper, Harold J. Leavitt, and Maynard W. Shelly II (eds.), *New Perspectives in Organization Research* (New York: John Wiley & Sons, Inc., 1964), pp. 314–333.
6. Keith Davis, *Human Relations at Work* (New York: McGraw-Hill Book Company, 1962), p. 185.
7. Peter F. Drucker, *Concept of the Corporation* (New York: The John Day Company, Inc., 1946), pp. 49ff.
8. Raymond Villers, *Dynamic Management in Industry* (Englewood Cliffs, N.J.: Prentice-Hall, Inc., 1960), pp. 135–136.
9. Raymond Villers, "Control and Freedom in a Decentralized Company,"

Harvard Business Review, vol. 32 (March–April, 1954), pp. 89–90.

10. Drucker, *Concept of the Corporation,* pp. 120–121.

11. Alfred D. Chandler, Jr., *Strategy and Structure* (Cambridge, Mass.: The M.I.T. Press, 1962), p. 42.

12. *Ibid.,* p. 42.

13. Quoted in Bernard H. Baum, *Decentralization of Authority in a Bureaucracy* (Englewood Cliffs, N.J.: Prentice-Hall, Inc., 1961), p. 79.

14. John Fisher, "Let's Go Back to the Spoils System," in Dwight Waldo, *Ideas and Issues in Public Administration* (New York: McGraw-Hill Book Company, 1953), pp. 200–201.

15. Alfred D. Chandler, Jr., "Management Decentralization: An Historical Analysis," *The Business History Review,* vol. 30 (June, 1956), pp. 172–173.

16. Donaldson Brown, "Centralized Control with Decentralized Responsibility," in American Management Association, *Annual Convention Series,* no. 57 (1927), p. 11.

17. The summary derives basically from Chandler, *Strategy and Structure,* especially pp. 52–113. A wide range of materials corroborate this summary. They include Ernest Dale, *The Great Organizers: Theory and Practice of Organization* (New York: McGraw-Hill Book Company, 1960); and William S. Dutton, *Du Pont—One Hundred and Forty Years* (New York: Charles Scribner's Sons, 1942).

18. James C. Worthy, *Big Business and Free Men* (New York: Harper & Row, Publishers, Incorporated, 1959), pp. 92–93.

19. Quoted in Chandler, *Strategy and Structure,* p. 105.

20. Quoted in *ibid.,* p. 107.

21. Quoted in *ibid.,* p. 111.

22. Drucker, *Concept of the Corporation,* p. 84.

23. Quoted in Drucker, *The Practice of Management,* pp. 210–211.

24. See William F. Whyte, *Man and Organization* (Homewood, Ill.: Richard D. Irwin, Inc., 1959), pp. 11–16.

25. Marshall E. Dimock, *Administrative Vitality* (New York: Harper & Row, Publishers, Incorporated, 1959), pp. 217 and 208–209.

26. Drucker, *Concept of the Corporation,* p. 63.

27. Quotations are from Herbert Kaufman, *The Forest Ranger* (Baltimore, Md.: The Johns Hopkins Press, 1960), p. 85.

28. Ralph J. Cordiner, *New Frontiers for Professional Managers* (New York: McGraw-Hill Book Company, 1956), pp. 40–79.

29. Lawrence A. Appley, *Management in Action* (New York: American Management Association, 1956), pp. 278–279.

30. Dimock, *op. cit.*, p. 210. Not all coercive and arbitrary features of performance measurement are avoided in decentralized structures, of course, but many are. For interesting support of both emphases of this conclusion, see, for example, the discussion of "transfer prices" in Andrew Whinston, "Price Guides in Decentralized Organizations," in Cooper, Leavitt, and Shelly (eds.), *op. cit.*, pp. 405–448.

31. John M. Pfiffner and Frank P. Sherwood, *Administrative Organization* (Englewood Cliffs, N.J.: Prentice-Hall, Inc., 1960), p. 201.

32. Ernest Dale, "Centralization vs. Decentralization," *Advanced Management*, vol. 20 (June, 1955), p. 16.

33. William G. Given, Jr., *Bottom-up Management* (New York: Harper & Row, Publishers, Incorporated, 1949), p. 7.

34. See Whyte, *op. cit.*, pp. 11–16; and Herbert E. Krugman, " 'Just Like Running Our Own Little Store'," *Personnel*, vol. 34 (July–August, 1957), especially pp. 46–47; Chandler, *Strategy and Structure;* Dimock, *op. cit.;* and Drucker, *Concept of the Corporation,* among others, for reports of the experiences of numerous business concerns with decentralization. Less attention has been accorded decentralization in the literature of public administration. Particularly useful sources include: Baum, *op. cit.;* Frank J. McKenna, "Decentralization of Federal Disbursing Functions," *Public Administration Review,* vol. 16 (Winter, 1956), pp. 37–39; and Clara Penniman, "Reorganization and the Internal Revenue Service," *Public Administration Review,* vol. 21 (Summer, 1961), pp. 121–130.

35. Paul R. Lawrence, *The Changing of Organizational Behavior Patterns* (Boston: Harvard University, Graduate School of Business Administration, Division of Research, 1958), p. 23. The seven quotations following, in order, are found in this source on pp. 21, 23, 36, 36, 36, 82, and 86–87.

36. Victor H. Vroom, "Ego-Involvement, Job Satisfaction, and Job Performance," *Personnel Psychology,* vol. 15 (1962), pp. 159–178.

37. Raymond Villers, *Dynamic Management in Industry,* pp. 132–133.

38. This is paraphrased from David G. Moore, "Managerial Strategies and Organization Dynamics in Sears Retailing," unpublished doctoral dissertation, University of Chicago, 1954).

39. William D. Litzinger, "Entrepreneurial Prototype in Bank Management," *Journal of the Academy of Management,* vol. 6 (March, 1963), pp. 36–45.

40. Whyte, *op. cit.,* p. 13.

41. Applications consistent with the present analysis have been reported,

for example, by A. K. Wickesberg and T. C. Cronin, "Management by Task Force," *Harvard Business Review*, vol. 39 (July–August, 1962), pp. 111–118.

42. Herbert A. Simon, *The New Science of Management Decision* (New York: Harper & Row, Publishers, Incorporated, 1960), pp. 43–47.

43. The general inappropriateness of centralized delegation seems a strong theme in studies of the specific effects of automation, at least at middle-management levels. Relevantly, see the argument developed by Donald R. Schaul, "What's Really Ahead for Middle Management," *Personnel,* vol. 41 (November–December, 1964), pp. 9–16. Automation also seems often to facilitate (if not require) substantial delegation to lower organizational levels, as was detailed in Charles R. Walker, *Toward the Automatic Factory* (New Haven, Conn.: Yale University Press, 1957), pp. 127–143. Opinion has not been unanimous, however. For the classic argument-in-opposition that the new "information technology" implies recentralization at all levels, see Harold J. Leavitt and Thomas L. Whisler, "Management in the 1980's," *Harvard Business Review,* vol. 36 (November–December, 1958), pp. 41–48.

44. Dimock, *op. cit.,* pp. 460–461.

45. For a careful weighing of the advantages and disadvantages of decentralized delegation, see Mayer S. Zald, "Decentralization—Myth vs. Reality," *Personnel,* vol. 41 (July–August, 1964), pp. 19–26.

Organization as a Moral Problem: An Alternative to Pessimism

One must resist becoming giddy under the influence of the considerable evidence that it is advisable in organizing to approach the Judaeo-Christian Ethic. The difficulty of approaching these values seems considerable. For example, one must have acute ideological foresight to envision the time when these values will be achieved in substantial measure. Even minor advances often will require major changes in attitudes and techniques, and no change comes easily. Also, fundamental changes in traditional organization theory must be made. The job will be difficult.

Whether these changes are made or not, however, one point stands: *organization is a moral problem*. The available research makes it easier to recognize the moral problem and to face it in practice. But a moral problem is a moral problem, whatever the research technology tells us.

Even such restricted grounds for optimism concerning man's ability to cope with his organizations contrast prominently with the usual pessimistic run of thought.[1] And this raises an issue of consequence. Specifically, why does this analysis come to such a different end than the pessimistic approach to matters organizational? The issue cannot be dismissed, although it can be discussed only briefly, here. This section will consider a major representative of the pessimistic tradition to suggest the reasons for the different outcome here. A following section will consider a specific aspect of the pessimistic tradition—the common adverse reaction to bigness—with a similar aim in mind.

MARX'S DARK PROPHECY

Some Dimensions and Difficulties

An overview of the Marxian analysis helps explain the differences between the product of the pessimistic tradition and the product of this analysis. Not all of the pessimistic tradition in organization analysis is Marxian, but Marx's influence has been wide. Moreover, his method of approach is like that of many commentators, and even many who come to conclusions diametrically opposed to his own. For illustrative purposes, then, the focus on Marx has much to recommend it. Essentially, the relevant parts of the Marxian approach to organization may be outlined in terms of the following major propositions:

1. Behavior and attitudes are determined by economic, or technological, factors.
2. Conflict between individuals in any society can be explained exclusively (largely) in terms of "class differences."
3. In a capitalist economy two different classes will develop, based upon the ownership ("bourgeois") or nonownership ("proletariat") of the nonhuman means of production.
4. As the capitalist economy grows and organizations increase in size
   a. The ownership of the means of production will pass into fewer and fewer hands.
   b. The nonowners will become performers of increasingly routinized activities with less and less control over their work, the consequence being that the proletarians bring to work neither the interests of the owner nor the enthusiasm of a laborer for a meaningful job.

5. Ownership of the means of production is synonymous with the management of the means of production.
6. As the economy grows and organizations increase in size, the problems of management remain relatively constant or actually decrease, so that managerial decisions become more concentrated in the hands of those fewer individuals who come to own the means of production.
7. As ownership and decision-making fall into the hands of an ever-smaller bourgeois class, the needs and interests of the proletarians receive less attention.
8. Conflict in organizations thus is increasingly probable and revolution draws ever nearer.
9. When the few remaining bourgeois are eliminated in the revolution and when the ownership of the means of production passes to the proletarians, by definition, class distinctions will no longer exist and conflict will cease.

Not all of these propositions need be accepted to argue this claim logically: that organization is *not* a moral problem. Accept Proposition 1, for example, and there is precious little practical reason to trouble over moral considerations. "Economic determinism" is the negation of moral considerations in our sense. Similarly, accept Proposition 6 and many of the conditions forecast by Marx seem truly inevitable.

These propositions are central to the Marxian analysis, and rigidly so. And therein lies a basic difference between this analysis and attempts in the pessimistic tradition such as that of Marx. The two approaches are at irreconcilable odds. The pessimistic tradition tends to start with a world view to whose form it is often anxious to bend reality. The present approach has its own world view, of course, the Judaeo-Christian Ethic. However, reality is not a derivative of this world view. Rather, reality is the tether which determines in what ways and to what degrees the world view can be approached under the conditions that actually exist.

The implied question, then, is the usefulness of Marx's propositions for describing reality. In one sense, anyhow, accepting all of the propositions of the Marxian argument has its advantages. For the revolution of the proletariat at least provides an apparent way out of the pessimistic recesses of the Marxian argument into a golden society in which conflict has no place because class distinctions no longer exist. Those within the pessimistic tradition who accept more peaceful approaches to social change are left without even the ersatz solace of a by-and-by resolution of the problems of the organizational society.

In most senses that count, accepting all of the propositions of the Marxian argument is ill-advised. For the propositions are of a high order of generality and at best are problematic descriptions of reality. Derivations from these propositions may be accepted only at one's peril, therefore. The sociologist William F. Whyte thus appropriately prefaced a detailed study of a Polish factory in these terms:[2]

> The Communist ideology assumes that in a Communist system there is no difference of interests between the workers and management which theoretically represents the workers. Therefore, there is no need to design organizations to represent the workers in their conflict of interest with management . . . the conflict of interest is there nevertheless.

Similar reservations could be developed about the other propositions listed above, but a more convenient approach will be taken. The following section bears directly on the validity of Propositions 4b, 5, 6, and 7. In addition, let us consider Proposition 6 here explicitly. In sum, experience flatly rejects the Marxian notion of reduced or constant managerial burdens as organizations grow. As Chandler's *Strategy and Structure* particularly demonstrates, for example, great increases in managerial sophistication are required as organizations grow beyond some large (but unspecified) size and particularly as they grow by diversifying products, services, and clientele. If organizations grow by simple additions of volume of limited goods or services destined for a homogeneous clientele, Marx's Proposition 6 is more plausible. However, expanding volume in this simple sense is only a limited strategy for growth. Moreover, that limited strategy poorly characterizes the growth of most large business and government organizations.

BIGNESS AS A DARK PROPHECY

Orthodoxy and Reality

The common adverse reaction to bigness also reflects the limitations of the pessimistic tradition. Bigness often is considered a virtual evil per se, at least in business if not in government. Large organizations thus are said to strip man of his individuality and to subject him to unmerciful forces beyond his control. "The bigger the organization," Kenneth Boulding phrases a contemporary expression of this point of view, "the smaller the proportion of its members who can really be at the top of the hierarchy and participate in the major decisions, and the larger the proportion who must carry out policies which are set higher up." [3] Individual freedom increasingly exists for Boulding, when it exists at all, only in the interstices between organizations. Of such tinder were sparked the early crusades of those like Supreme Court Justice Louis Brandeis who sought to break large organizations into smaller, competitive units.

A view such as Boulding's can motivate only deep pessimism about our organizational society. For we are told that one of every four American employees in business works for one of the 200 firms with the largest assets, that one of every two employees is "tied directly or indirectly" to these firms. Such firms are alleged to "strongly influence, at the very least" some three-quarters of American "business life." [4]

There is every reason to believe that the general adverse reaction to bigness is indiscriminate. At the very least, to score a debater's point, what "large size" means specifically is a very complicated issue, and these complications give much of the pessimistic literature but little pause. However, this analysis is after bigger game than debater's points. It does not argue that bigness has only attractive consequences. This position is too broad. But the analysis does hold that the virtues of bigness are very considerable. Moreover, if nothing else, there seem to be substantial limits on the degree to which work—especially in our "developed" economy and particularly in organizations of some size— can violate the values derived from the Judaeo-Christian tradition without paying a heavy price.

This position contradicts commonly held views. For example, the Marxian analysis assumes an inevitable conflict between the "forces of production" (roughly, the technology) and the "relations of production" (roughly, the values which give meaning to man's life). This conflict is said to grow increasingly sharp as organizations grow in size. The same point may be put in terms more familiar to this analysis, although the effort must be laborious. The traditional theory of organization implies a conflict between technological requirements and values as organization size increases. Thus the closer the approach to the traditional theory, the greater the violation of the Judaeo-Christian Ethic. Moreover, approaches to the traditional theory are held to be particularly necessary as organizations become larger and more complex.

The predicted conflict is not inevitable, however. The tension between the technically necessary and the morally desirable cannot be eliminated, but the number of cases in which the technical and the moral need be at odds can be reduced substantially in all organizations, and such reductions often will be most possible in organizations of considerable size. The point applies to decentralization, for example.

Indeed, the point can be put more forcefully. For the forces of production and the relations of production can—indeed, perhaps *must*—complement one another as organizations grow in size. Consider only two supporting notes. First, the mass-production model at the hearts of both the traditional theory of organization and the Marxian analysis is increasingly inapplicable in today's burgeoning organizations. Technicians have come to characterize the new economy, not unskilled operatives; complex production sequences and services increasingly displace routine manufacturing as employers of men; increasing reliance must be placed on lower-level personnel to provide the adaptations required by the complex technology, as is the case with maintenance crews in an automated operation or with radar observers in our early warning system; and the abilities to learn and to change become increasingly significant.

Second, the development of a particular force of production—the technology of behavioral science—also makes it possible (and reasonable) to approach the J-C Ethic more closely. This technology derives in large part from the growth of organizations of considerable size, which both require and sponsor such research. The new behavioral science technology forces this point: the more closely work approximates the set of J-C values outlined above, under imprecisely known but general conditions, the more effective performance will be.

That such factors have not greatly influenced the common adverse reaction to bigness suggests a detachment in the pessimistic literature from the sights and smells and sounds of life in organizations. This detachment neglects organizations as they are, as they are increasingly coming to be, and as they might be.

The neglect of organizations-as-they-are clearly underlies much of the reaction to bigness. Commonly, a large organization is viewed as a single entity that speaks with a booming monolithic voice and as a rigid hierarchical structure restricting the exercise of power to the number one position in the organization. The individual, therefore, must seek his freedom in those ever-narrowing openings in our life space that have not yet been preempted by massive collective enterprises. There is no alternative to fearing bigness per se, in this view.

Such a view of organizations is certainly a gross caricature of organizations as they exist, however understandable is the caricature in terms of so much of the literature and some of the practice of decades past. Even casual study of the inner workings of any organization will quickly dispel the monolithic view. Organizations are an incredible diversity of formal and behavioral entities whose goals and activities overlap only partially. Those 200 corporations with the largest assets about which we hear are an incredibly larger number of competing subinterests. Thus the monolithic conspiracies hinted at broadly in some of the racier interpretations in contemporary popular literature seem overdone, even if we neglect the important external influences over corporate action exercised by government agencies, labor unions, or firms in the same industries or in industries producing close substitutes. This is no happy argument for a kind of massive invisible hand of countervailing powers. Rather, it dampens the over-enthusiasm for a conspiratorial view of life in organizations.

More room exists for determined individual discretion in organization than some would have us believe, in sum. The common incidence of "rate setting" or output restriction is merely one of the myriad senses in which "the organization" does not triumph in the struggle to homogenize the subinterests of which it is composed. Moreover, contemporary large organizations no doubt demand greater responsible freedom of a greater proportion of people than ever before. Harlan Cleveland has couched the point in particularly convincing terms in arguing that it is only through the development of his administrative skills that man can preserve and extend his freedom. "The complexity of modern society and the omnipresence of large-scale organizations not only pro-vide an opportunity for the fullest development of the responsible self," Cleveland concluded, "they actually place a premium on the exercise of a greater measure of personal responsibility than ever before." [5]

Cleveland's underlying argument may be abstracted and illustrated. First, since big organizations make decisions which significantly affect many people, they are less and less "private." Virtually all large or-ganizations—businesses, labor unions, and government agencies alike —are affected with a public interest, with a consequent increase in "political" decision-making that involves the reconciliation of inter-ests and the building of consent. Relatedly, the higher in the hierarchy of a large organization one goes, major (and many apparently "minor") decisions are less likely to escape some kind of review by agents within the organization or outside of it. The monolithic view of organizations implies the opposite tendency, of course. Over a wide range, imputing moral superiority to small organizations also seems inappropriate. Paul Appleby provides a case in point that illustrates one of the virtues of size. "Size of population in a jurisdiction in some respects seems to be one factor *favoring* morality," he noted in connection with public offi-cials. "Multiplication of governmental activities, causing a kind of cos-mopolitanism in government itself, also seems to put officials in stronger moral positions, enabling them to withstand temptation and pressure on a number of fronts in the strength of their popular service on many fronts." [6]

Second, the nature of the existing technology in large organizations requires that many significant decisions be made far down the line. Thus crews in our Distant Early Warning Line or in our SAC bombers have an unprecedented responsibility for making vital decisions. Less dramatically, a similar point applies to the crews in a continuous re-finery or a modern steel-rolling mill. Cleveland generalizes that the tendency in big organizations "is actually a diffusion of decision-making and decision-influencing processes far beyond the wildest dreams of those worshipers at the shrine of Louis Brandeis, who wanted to keep power diffused by keeping the units of society small." [7]

Third, the resources of large organizations permit attention to a very broad range of phenomena beyond the reach of smaller organizations. No wonder that most of the structural arrangements and managerial techniques discussed above have either been developed in large organizations or are most commonly employed by them. In sum, the problems of the orthodox structure tend to be experienced more intensely in larger organizations, which also have the resources to begin to cope with such problems. Relevantly, a study of attitudes among managers in several countries concluded that: "With but few exceptions, managers in large companies favor democratic managerial practices more than do those in smaller companies. In particular, they approve of sharing information and objectives. By and large, then, it is in larger companies that democratic ideas are fostered." [8] In part, such findings may reflect the ability of managers in larger enterprises to "talk a good game" because of greater exposure to current behavioral research through executive development programs and other sources that are, in general, more available to them than to the managers of smaller firms. But these differences in attitudes no doubt are complemented by appropriate differences in managerial practices, and for many of the same reasons.

The neglect of organizations as they are increasingly coming to be also underlies the negative reaction to bigness. At one time organizational growth often did imply changes in the nature of work that were undesirable: greater routinization of operations, greater alienation of the employee from a meaningless task, and so on. The view that these are the concomitants of organizational growth is increasingly anachronistic, however.

One study conveniently illustrates the common fruits of the new bigness. The study compared three kinds of plants in Britain: automated plants, plants with assembly-line operations, and job-order plants. [9] Roughly, these three types represent three stages in the development of organizations over time, with the automated plants representing what organizations are increasingly coming to be. Uniformly, the most technologically developed plants were most like the least developed plants in a number of significant particulars. The explanation for the implied reversal of tendencies lies in several characteristics of automated plants and job-order shops as compared with assembly plants: performance was more easily measured; the physical factors affecting production were more controllable; greater delegation was possible; discipline was imposed more by the work than by superior-subordinate relations; and workers and management consequently were drawn closer together, much as in job-order systems. By way of contrast, we are told that: "In the middle ranges of technology, however, management proceeded by drives; targets were constanly being raised; all kinds of incentives had to be offered and great pressures were exerted on people." [10]

The present point merely requires stating, if some simplification must be risked. Technological developments that increased the size of organizations once often meant a movement from a job-lot pattern to the assembly line, with consequent problems that some consider inevitable in our organizational society. However, contemporary technological development avoids many of the human costs of organizing work encountered in the intermediate stage. The new technology is not an unmixed blessing, of course. There are other problems with automation which we will neglect here. Some other book, however, must concern itself with the broader moral issues raised by the retraining and relocation of individuals affected by changeovers to automation.

The adverse reaction to bigness also neglects organizations as they might be, and as a number of them are coming to be. Bluntly, one must be impressed by the fact that many of those most suspicious of business organizations of scale are advocates of great size in our agencies of government. At least some part of the explanation for this fact lies in the relatively greater inventiveness devoted to the development of institutional means to control the effects of size in politics and government. And these controls—however cumbersome and slow to set in motion and however far they lag behind new problems—have done their job tolerably well. Indeed, the pronounced tendency of the American voting public to elect a president from one party and a majority in one or both houses of Congress from the opposition party almost suggests a sophisticated commitment to the preservation of alternative open channels for influencing public policy. Moreover, on the Federal level, our commitments to a system of states provide still more diverse channels for helping protect local interests from the clutches of their central government corrupted by power. Our more general commitment to a "pluralist" society tends toward a similar end. Problems there are, but at least a firm base of institutions and traditions exists in the public area that one can build upon.

Nongovernment organizations appear less clearly within a system of controls. The marketplace is not obviously an operative check in to-day's economy; the so-called separation of ownership from control is pronounced enough so that "stockholder's control" exists increasingly only in the public relations man's storehouse of useful myths; and the marked tendency for firms to draw capital out of profits raises significant problems of economic control.[11]

Slowly but definitely many business organizations are evolving an economic version of the pluralist state. Many of the organizational arrangements and managerial techniques analyzed above must be counted among the early products of this evolution. Their aim is common: ". . . to diffuse authority outward and downward so that the decision-making process occurs at the point at which there is a convergence of action with required knowledge," [12] as Richard Eells and Clarence Walton observe. Applications of this new economic pluralism are uneven. Many firms are still highly centralized, for example. But their number dwindles steadily as firms experiment on a front ranging from preliminary adventures with some simple techniques to a "progressive decentralization" that affects all or many of the levels of a complex firm.

Whatever the degree of actual practice reflecting an organizational pluralism, there is a growing self-consciousness about the need to innovate systems of economic control and an increasing awareness that pluralism provides a useful guide for the development of appropriate ways and means.[13] Moreover, and perhaps most significant, the sense of time running out on this search seems to be growing. Ralph J. Cordiner, then chairman of the board of directors of General Electric, stressed all three points in a 1960 address. He first drew attention to the genius of our economic system, which "not only preserves, but utilizes human freedom as the key to social and economic progress." And he outlined those many factors in today's world that are pushing nations toward statism or totalitarianism. Cordiner—more than once the harbinger of new pathways in managerial thought—went on:[14]

One of the basic principles of the American [political and economic] system is the principle of decentralized power. This country has what is known as a "pluralistic society." There is not just one source of initiative and decision here as in the government-controlled societies. Rather, in the United States, there are many competing points of initiative, risk, and de-

cision—and that is the secret of this nation's drive and creativity. . . .
This decentralization of power is the strength of the free society, and it
must be preserved.

There seem ample reasons, then, to modify the common reaction to
bigness. The genie of large scale has been bent to our will in a number
of ways; the coming development of organizations suggests still other
senses in which bigness can be disciplined; and the growing appreciation of an organizational pluralism implies still more far-reaching senses
in which organizations of size can be increasingly put to man's service
rather than he to theirs. In any case, a fascination with organization-
as-a-monolith is clearly out of place.

HOPSCOTCHING THE MANAGERIAL GRID

The Several Ethics as Motivators

Marx and others preoccupied with bigness had a similar point, then,
but its force depended in substantial part on there being only a single
way to organize work. As variations in structural arrangements and
managerial techniques are admitted to the picture, however, much of
the edge is taken off the pessimistic approach to organizational phenomena.

There is a grave danger in monolithic thought about organizing, and
this study attempts both to warn against and to avoid that danger.
Indeed, the entire analysis may be viewed usefully as a kind of hopscotching of a managerial grid of alternative ways of organizing, with
the several ethics serving as motivating forces. Let us make plain the
nature of the exercise. Robert Blake and Jane S. Mouton provide us
with a kind of managerial checkerboard on which major strategies for
organizing can be located.[15] To sketch their argument, envision a 9 × 9
grid on which are detailed five major strategies for organizing work.
These strategies differ in their varying simultaneous emphases upon
concern for production and concern for people in these ways:

   1,1 Management, which is characterized by minimum concern for both
   people and production and under which minimum effort is required
   to retain organizational membership;

1,9 Management, which is preoccupied with concern for people and whose major products are a congenial, comfortable organizational atmosphere and a slow work pace;

5,5 Management, which attempts to trade off the demands of people and production thereby achieving acceptable employee morale and adequate performance;

9,1 Management, which focuses upon operational efficiency and attempts to organize human needs out of work; and

9,9 Management, which strives to achieve high production through maximum concern for people, as by stressing common organizational purposes that lead to relationships of trust and respect.

This analysis covers in various ways all of the five basic managerial strategies detailed by Blake and Mouton. The point may be established briefly. To begin, 1,1 Management can be taken to define the state of affairs before close attention was given to the analysis and planning of work. Though we dare not give dates, this strategy historically gave way to 9,1 Management. Thus the traditional theory of organization reflects a maximum concern for production. And many practitioners of 9,1 Management—such as Frederick W. Taylor—were preoccupied with organizing work so that human factors were eliminated or rigidly controlled. No doubt the Individualistic Ethic provided much moral support for this strategy.

The negative consequences of 9,1 Management eventually got the best of it, but many of its characteristics withstood early efforts at change. Sparked by some revolutionary research beginning in the 1920s and by the excesses committed in the name of individualism, the Social Ethic became the dominant guide for organizing work. The basic strategy was 5,5 Management. The traditional organization of work was retained from 9,1 Management, however, although much attention was devoted to developing ways and means of somehow dissipating or making less burdensome the consequences of this organization of work. Hence the emphasis upon "human relations" and upon such of its freakish progeny as the extreme beliefs that problems will be resolved if only people will "understand," if only they will "communicate," if only they will recognize the "human equation at work."

5,5 Management has its distinct limitations. The retention of the traditional theory for organizing work left untouched a hard core of disaffection that neither "understanding" nor "communicating" could resolve. Smoothing over deeply rooted disaffection evidenced a preoccupation with symptoms rather than causes, which has its limits as a long-run strategy. Relatedly, this smoothing over often was accomplished with such obvious good will that many employees—though still troubled—were set to pondering what ingrates they were to chafe within the "great big family" of Organization Z. Psychologically, it was easier to cope with unfulfilling work in an obviously big and bad organization. At least the issues were uncomplicated, and one could hate such an organization with certainty and perhaps with an admiration for management's tenacity and single-mindedness. In contrast, a management that oozes a kind of unspecific, warm feeling—if largely through contrived images or in ways not directly related to work—is well designed to raise self-doubts in an employee reacting against his work for reasons he may not distinguish but which cause him to react nonetheless. Moreover, not rarely, 5,5 Management has degenerated into 1,9 Management or (what is worse) into highly manipulative variations of the kind spotlighted in Whyte's *The Organization Man*.

We are living through a period of reaction against the simplicisms of 5,5 Management. This leaves an opening for 9,9 Management, which is the strategy consistent with the Judaeo-Christian Ethic. At once, this strategy attempts to reflect the concern for production characteristic of 9,1 Management as well as the concern for people characteristic of 5,5 and 1,9 Management. The vehicles for this rapprochement are the various organizational arrangements and managerial techniques detailed above. They reject the traditional theory of organization in its entirety. The rejection of the trappings of structure and techniques derived from the traditional theory distinguishes the J-C Ethic from the Social Ethic and the Individualistic Ethic.

The managerial grid of Blake and Mouton has a more specific relevance to this analysis than the framing of details of structural arrangements and managerial techniques considered here. Indeed, the two approaches converge to a similar set of conclusions from different directions. *Men, Management, and Morality* demonstrates the usefulness of structure and techniques that approach the several values of the Judaeo-Christian Ethic, which structure and techniques may be characterized as consistent with 9,9 Management. *The Managerial Grid* draws valuable attention to a number of alternative managerial styles and stresses the usefulness of 9,9 Management, which is consistent with the structural arrangements and managerial techniques detailed above. This convergence toward common conclusions reinforces the claim to validity of the two approaches. For each approach draws upon essentially different sources of support and has different emphases. The sources of support of this volume have been detailed; and *The Managerial Grid* not only evolves from a massive literature but also can boast of interesting demonstrations of its internal consistency[16] and of its effectiveness in serving as the model for on-going organizations.[17]

We must settle for less than the best of all possible worlds here, however, and beg off the task of establishing the specific points of correspondence of this analysis and *The Managerial Grid*. That would require another book. Let us settle for this more general conclusion, then. Our values can influence technology if we have the wit and the will. Hopscotching the managerial grid can be motivated by a change in our ethics as well as in our technology. We are not the impotent creatures of technological demands, although neither are we at liberty to disregard the constraints in our environment. Indeed, individual freedom may be defined as the product of continual and successful attempts to act upon and enlarge the area of discretion open to us.

Such are the objectives here, in any case: to enlarge the area of discretion open to us in organizing and to increase individual freedom. This analysis has done its job if it demonstrates that—within the existing and developing technology and within a wide range of organizations—one can make morally meaningful and practically feasible choices between sets of structural forms and managerial techniques that imply significantly different behavioral consequences.

TOWARD A MORALLY BASED THEORY OF ORGANIZATION

A Set of Unorthodox Guiding Propositions

The analysis must be brought full circle back to the propositions of the traditional theory of organization from which it sprung. Recall that four such propositions were emphasized, and that they argued that efficiency would be increased as work is organized so that:

1. Authority is a one-way relation, flowing in a single stream from organization superiors to subordinates.
2. Supervision is detailed and the span of control is narrow.
3. Only the physiological properties of individuals are respected and individuals are considered to be social isolates.
4. Routinized processes guide structural relations at low levels of organization while higher levels emphasize individual functions.

Detailed considerations demonstrate that these propositions are at once inconsistent with the Judaeo-Christian Ethic and also often pay for it via low productivity and employee dissatisfaction. Following the traditional theory of organization, in this sense, implies its own punishment for the moral violation of the J-C Ethic.

Bringing this analysis back to the propositions of the traditional theory of organization is no sign that we are back where we started. Structural arrangements and managerial techniques consistent with the Judaeo-Christian Ethic, to put the real point directly, must derive from a set of propositions that differ radically from the traditional set. These unorthodox propositions have been implied throughout this study, but they have nowhere been set down in an orderly way. Therefore, the propositions may be sketched usefully in the following terms. They prescribe that efficiency will be increased as work is organized so that:

1. Authority has multiple sources that are oriented in the same direction while they follow the flow of work, whether up, down, or across the organization.
2. Supervision is general and the span of control is wide.
3. The multiple social identifications and psychological properties of individuals are recognized and so provided for in organizing work that they help integrate an organization's several activities rather than fragment them.
4. Entire flows of work are the foci for organizing at low levels, and products guide organizing at upper levels.

The two sets of propositions are at loggerheads. Their contraposition derives from the philosophic world views they reflect and also extends to specific structural forms and managerial techniques inferred from the two sets of propositions. There are many ways of making the point. McGregor provides a particularly useful approach, at this stage of the analytical game. He incisively characterized and contrasted two opposed world views as Theory X and Theory Y.[18] His seminal treatment may be consulted for the full argument. Here, however, a bare sketch must suffice.

Theory X undergirds the traditional theory of organization with a tangled web of wishes about how life ought to be and assumptions about how it is. This supporting web is seldom articulated in any comprehensive way—which fact goes a long way toward explaining the persistence of the traditional theory—and indeed these wishes and assumptions must be inferred from complex cues. We can only suggest some central propositions of this supporting web of ideas and attitudes. For example, Theory X assumes that most people prefer and require supervision that is close and continuous. Relatedly, Theory X assumes that motivation can occur mostly or only as a response to a real or fancied threat of deprivation. The traditional theory of organization is a natural for these assumptions.

Theory Y gives comfort to organizationally relevant propositions that are more consistent with the Judaeo-Christian Ethic. Thus it assumes that most people ideally prefer to be and actually can be self-controlling in the attainment of organizational objectives, given the proper organization of work. Theory Y also assumes that motivation can and often does occur as a response to social or ego rewards, and particularly so under conditions of relatively full employment and general unemployment benefits. Such assumptions—and they seem generally realistic—underlie the structural arrangements and managerial techniques consistent with the Judaeo-Christian Ethic.

These sketches of Theory X and Theory Y help summarize the aims of this analysis and give perspective to the ways these aims were sought. Indeed, the sum of this book is that a change in our world view about organizing is appropriate, and this because of both practical advantages and moral reasons. The details on specific structural arrangements and managerial techniques that have been developed merely support the role of the Judaeo-Christian Ethic as an important part of that moral basis which must underlie this new world view. The approach here does not exhaust those necessary to induce this new world view,[19] but it should help. And certainly the effort seems worthwhile. For, in turn, a new world view will aid experience as well as build upon it and develop from it. A new world view can generate structure and techniques that are beyond our present practice.

And so it is done. Experience has been analyzed, and the effort permits a leap to propositions about organizing that are at a higher level of generality. Hopefully, these propositions will generate further experience that will permit more refined syntheses.

Footnotes: CHAPTER 9

1. There are favorable signs that a massive reorientation of thought is in process, however. See the direction of Chris Argyris, *Integrating the Individual and the Organization* (New York: John Wiley & Sons, Inc., 1964).
2. William F. Whyte in the Preface to Jiri Kolaja, *A Polish Factory* (Lexington, Ky.: University of Kentucky Press, 1960).
3. Kenneth Boulding, "The Jungle of Hugeness," quoted in Harlan Cleveland, "Dinosaurs and Personal Freedom," *Saturday Review,* Feb. 28, 1959, p. 14.
4. Herrymon Maurer, *Great Enterprise* (New York: The Macmillan Company, 1955).
5. Cleveland, *op. cit.,* p. 14.
6. Paul H. Appleby, *Morality and Administration* (Baton Rouge, La.: Louisiana State University Press, 1952), pp. 57–58.
7. Cleveland, *op. cit.,* p. 13.
8. Mason Haire, Edwin E. Ghiselli, and Lyman W. Porter, "An International Study of Management Attitudes and Democratic Leadership," Symposium A9, paper no. A9a, *CIOS,* vol. 8 (1963).
9. Joan Woodward, "The Effects of Technological Innovations on Management Administration," *International Conference on Economic and Social Aspects of Automation,* International Associates for Cybernetics, Namur, Belgium, 1958.
10. Walter Buckingham, *Automation* (New York: Harper & Row, Publishers, Incorporated, 1961), pp. 60–61.
11. Adolph Berle, Jr., *Power Without Property* (New York: Harcourt, Brace, & World, Inc., 1959).
12. Richard Eells and Clarence Walton, *Conceptual Foundations of Business* (Homewood, Ill.: Richard D. Irwin, Inc., 1961), p. 375.
13. Herbert Kaufman, "Organization Theory and Political Theory," *American Political Science Review,* vol. 58 (March, 1964), pp. 5–14.

14. Quoted in Eells and Walton, *op. cit.,* p. 376.
15. Robert R. Blake and Jane S. Mouton, *The Managerial Grid* (Houston: Gulf Publishing Company, 1964), especially p. 10.
16. *Ibid.,* especially pp. 225–246.
17. Louis B. Barnes and Larry E. Greiner, "Breakthrough in Organization Development," part II, *Harvard Business Review,* vol. 42 (November–December, 1964), pp. 139–165.
18. Douglas McGregor, *The Human Side of Enterprise* (New York: The McGraw-Hill Book Company, 1960), especially pp. 33–58. Efforts have been made to validate the usefulness of Theory Y as a guide for organizing. Positive results are reported, for example, by Arthur H. Kuriloff, "An Experiment in Management: Putting Theory Y to the Test," *Personnel,* vol. 40 (November–December, 1963), pp. 8–17.
19. See, particularly, Chris Argyris, *Integrating the Individual and the Organization*; E. Wight Bakke, *The Individual and the Organization* (New Haven, Conn.: Labor and Management Center, Yale University, 1951); Robert T. Golembiewski, *Behavior and Organization* (Chicago: Rand McNally & Company, 1962); Rensis Likert, *New Patterns of Management* (New York: McGraw-Hill Book Company, 1961); and James G. March and Herbert A. Simon, *Organizations* (New York: John Wiley & Sons, Inc., 1958).

NAME INDEX

SUBJECT INDEX